THE ETHICS & POETICS OF ALTERITY IN

*Asian American Poetry*

The Ethics & Poetics
of Alterity in *Asian
American
Poetry*

Xiaojing Zhou

UNIVERSITY OF IOWA PRESS  IOWA CITY

University of Iowa Press, Iowa City 52242

Copyright © 2006 by the University of Iowa Press

http://www.uiowa.edu/uiowapress

Printed in the United States of America

Design by Richard Hendel

A different version of chapter 1 appeared in *Textual Ethos Studies*
(New York and Amsterdam: Rodopi, 2005), edited by Anna
Fahraeus and AnnKatrin Jonsson. A different version of chapter 6
appeared in *College Literature* 31.1 (Winter 2004).

Printed on acid-free paper

Library of Congress Cataloging-in-Publication Data
Zhou, Xiaojing, 1952 – .
   The ethics and poetics of alterity in Asian American poetry / by
Xiaojing Zhou.
      p.    cm.
   Includes bibliographical references and index.
   ISBN 0-87745-982-7 (cloth)
   1. American poetry—Asian American authors—History and
criticism.   2. Difference (Psychology) in literature.   3. Asian
Americans—Intellectual life.   4. Asian Americans in literature.
5. Ethics in literature.   I. Title.
PS153.A84Z98 2006          2005053852
811.009'353—dc22

06   07   08   09   10   C   5   4   3   2   1

*To Michael and Nathan*

# *Contents*

# Acknowledgments

The author gratefully acknowledges permissions granted by the following authors and publishers.

Marilyn Chin, *Dwarf Bamboo* (Greenfield, NY: Greenfield Review Press, 1987), copyright © by Marilyn Chin, used by permission of Marilyn Chin. *The Phoenix Gone, The Terrace Empty* (Minneapolis: Milkweed Editions, 1994), copyright © by Marilyn Chin, used by permission of Milkweed Editions. "Blue on Yellow" from *Rhapsody in Plain Yellow* (New York: Norton, 2002), copyright © 2002 by Marilyn Chin, used by permission of Marilyn Chin and W. W. Norton and Company, Inc.

Kimiko Hahn, *Air Pocket* (Brooklyn: Hanging Loose Press, 1989), copyright 1989 by Kimiko Hahn, used by permission of Kimiko Hahn. *Earshot* (Brooklyn: Hanging Loose Press, 1992), copyright © by Kimiko Hahn, used by permission of Kimiko Hahn. *The Unbearable Heart* (New York: Kaya Production, 1995), copyright © by Kimiko Hahn, used by permission of Kimiko Hahn. *Mosquito and Ant: Poems* (New York: Norton, 1999), copyright © by Kimiko Hahn, used by permission of Kimiko Hahn and W. W. Norton and Company, Inc.

Myung Mi Kim, *Under Flag* (Berkeley: Kelsey Street Press, 1991), copyright © by Myung Mi Kim, used by permission of Myung Mi Kim and Kelsey Street Press. *The Bounty* (Minneapolis: Chax Press, 1996), copyright © by Myung Mi Kim, used by permission of Myung Mi Kim and Chax Press. *Dura* (Los Angeles: Sun and Moon Press, 1998), copyright © by Myung Mi Kim, used by permission of Myung Mi Kim. *Commons* (Berkeley: University of California Press, 2002), copyright by Myung Mi Kim, used by permission of Myung Mi Kim and the University of California Press.

Li-Young Lee, *Rose* (Brockport, NY: BOA Editions, 1986), copyright © by Li-Young Lee, used by permission of Li-Young Lee and BOA Editions. *The City in Which I Love You* (Brockport, NY: BOA Editions, 1990), copyright © by Li-Young Lee, used by permission of Li-Young Lee and BOA Editions.

Timothy Liu, *Say Goodnight* (Port Townsend: Copper Canyon Press, 1998), copyright © by Timothy Liu, used by permission of Timothy Liu and Copper Canyon Press. *Vox Angelica* (Cambridge, MA: Alice James Books, 1992), copyright © by Timothy Liu, used by permission of Timothy Liu. *Burnt Offerings* (Port Townsend: Copper Canyon Press, 1995), copyright © by Timothy Liu, used by permission of Timothy Liu and Copper Canyon Press. *Hard Evidence* (Port Townsend: Copper Canyon Press, 2001), copyright © by Timothy Liu, used by permission of Timothy Liu and Copper Canyon Press.

David Mura, *After We Lost Our Way* (New York: Dutton, 1989), copyright © by David Mura, used by permission of David Mura. *The Colors of Desire* (New York: Anchor, 1995), copyright © by David Mura, used by permission of David Mura.

John Yau, *Radiant Silhouette: New and Selected Work, 1974–1988* (Santa Rosa: Black Sparrow Press, 1989), copyright © by John Yau, used by permission of John Yau. *Edificio Sayonara* (Santa Rosa: Black Sparrow Press, 1992), copyright © by John Yau, used by permission of John Yau. *Forbidden Entries* (Santa Rosa: Black Sparrow Press, 1996), copyright © by John Yau, used by permission of John Yau. *Borrowed Love Poems* (New York: Penguin, 2002), copyright © by John Yau, used by permission of John Yau.

I am deeply grateful to Li-Young Lee, Marilyn Chin, David Mura, Kimiko Hahn, Timothy Liu, John Yau, and Myung Mi Kim for taking the time to discuss their writings with me and to respond to my reading of their poems. I wish to thank Esther Iwanaga for indexing this book against a pressing deadline at the peak of the academic year. A small grant from the Provost's Office of University of the Pacific helped in getting the book manuscript to the printer in time.

# Abbreviations

The following are abbreviations used for the
works of Emmanuel Levinas:

AT        *Alterity and Transcendence*

CPP       *Collected Philosophical Papers*

DF        *Difficult Freedom*

EE        *Existence and Existents*

EI        *Ethics and Infinity*

EN        *Entre Nous: On Thinking-of-the-Other*

IIRTB     *Is It Righteous to Be? Interviews with Emmanuel Levinas*

OB        *Otherwise Than Being: Or, Beyond Essence*

OS        *Outside the Subject*

PN        *Proper Names*

TI        *Totality and Infinity: An Essay on Exteriority*

TO        *Time and the Other*

# THE ETHICS & POETICS OF ALTERITY IN

# Asian American Poetry

# Introduction

In his memoir, *The Winged Seed: A Remembrance* (1995), Li-Young Lee recalls painful experiences of learning to speak English at primary school. "More than once I was told I sounded ugly. My mouth was a shame to me, an indecent trench" (76). He often felt panic and anxiety when being asked a question in class, afraid that his classmates would be baffled and annoyed, or would wince and ask, as they often did: "*What did you say?* or, turning to someone else in complete exasperation, *What did he say?*" (77). Lee understands that these reactions to his accent are not as innocent as they might seem. "I noticed early on that all accents were not heard alike by the dominant population of American English speakers. . . . While some sounds were tolerated, some even granting the speaker a certain status in the instances of, say, French or British, other inflections condemned one to immediate alien" (76). Lee's experience of racial discrimination in the 1970s evokes the history of Chinese immigrants' exclusion from naturalization for U.S. citizenship on the grounds of their supposed inability and unwillingness to learn English.[1]

Using the dominant language as a measure to separate the white national self from its racial others is part of a characteristic practice in essentializing racial "traits" by inscribing racial meanings on the body and mind of those labeled "nonwhite" in the formation of the American national identity. Even though Asian Americans, like other racial "minority"[2] Americans, have been defined as the abject "other" of whites, their racial otherness in the United States differs from that of other minority Americans because of their supposedly inherent cultural otherness and subsequent political and cultural marginalization, and because of their apparently most successful assimilation. As David Eng puts it, Asian Americans are "alternately seen as the most foreign, racialized, and unassimilable in the era of exclusion (the myth of the yellow peril) and the most invisible, colorless, and compliant in the post-1965 era (the model minority myth)" (24). Either excluded from or absorbed into mainstream America, the image of Asian Americans as the "perpetual foreigner" remains prevalent.

Social inscriptions of otherness on the body and mind of Asian Americans are so pervasive that Asian American poets are often confronted by questions about the relation between their visible difference and their poetry. At a reading I heard Myung Mi Kim give on November 2, 2001, at the State University of New York at Buffalo, a member of the audience asked a question in words to this effect: Given your visible otherness, are you trying to reclaim your Koreanness, or dwell in English? Kim replied that her poetry was about the impossibility of either. Kim's answer rejects the either-or position, along with the assumptions underlying the question, which defines Kim's bodily difference as the marker of her racial and cultural otherness and singles out this otherness as a dilemma for Kim's poetic endeavors. While implying an essential Korean ethnicity, the question polarizes Kim's ethnic identity with English, evoking the problematic relationship between the racially marked cultural other and the dominant language, which has been used, among other things, as a tool to colonize, exclude, or assimilate the other.[3]

For Kim and many other Asian American poets, there is no fixed ethnicity to reclaim, no "home" to dwell in in English. Rather than seeking refuge in English, Asian American poets reinvent new ways of saying and hearing in that language, rendering it inflected with "alien" sounds or "foreign" accents. "I hear / interrogation in vague tongues," declares Li-Young Lee's persona (*City* 17). "*Nantoka nantoka sora / like sorrow, sorrow, sorrow*," Kimiko Hahn's persona calls out in Japanese and English (*Earshot* 22). Parodying Chinese Americans' fake pidgin produced by Hollywood, John Yau's lyric speaker mockingly claims, "I was the wood doctor / who made mouse calls" (*Edificio Sayonara* 82). The persona of the Vietnamese American poet Truong Tran says, "in the language of my severed tongue / referring to you / could not be done / by simply saying / *you / cha / thầy / cậu*" (45). "What is English now," asks Myung Mi Kim, "in the face of mass global migration . . . ? How can the dictions(s), register(s), inflection(s) as well as varying affective stances that have and will continue to filter into 'English' be taken into account?" (*Commons* 110). In an interview, Kim states, the fact that "we're each implicated in a machinery that works to maintain the loci of power," makes it even more necessary "to pose how we might participate in inventing how 'change' takes place" (Y. Morrison 75, 77). Asian American poets' participation in the dialogue concerning how change in American poetry takes place entails reinventing the lyric I, "contaminating" the English language, and imprinting otherness in their poetics.

## The "Lyric I" and the Crisis of the Self

Contemporary Asian American poetry is at once a part of and apart from a profound change in American poetry, one which Marjorie Perloff refers to as "the transformation of Romantic (and Modernist) lyric into what we now think of as postmodern poetry." For Perloff, the salient characteristics of postmodern poetry include its capacity to deal with the "political, ethical, historical, philosophical," and its urge to "make contact with the *world* as well as the *word*" (*Dance* 180–81). Above all, what marks postmodern poetry's significant break with Romantic and Modernist lyric, Perloff suggests, is the elision of the "lyric I." In her discussion of postmodern poetics, Perloff calls critical attention to Language poets' "appropriation of found objects" which "works precisely to deconstruct the possibility of the formation of a coherent or consistent lyrical voice, a transcendental ego" (*Poetic License* 12). The absence of the first person singular and the fragmentation of the lyric voice seem to have become defining characteristics of postmodern poetry, reflecting what Frederic Jameson calls the "formal consequence" of the "disappearance of the individual subject," the late capitalist dissolution of the "bourgeois ego," resulting in part from the hegemony of popular mass culture (*Postmodernism* 16, 15). Asian American poets, however, resist the dissolution of the individual subject even as they challenge the conventions of the traditional "lyric I" as the poet-I.

Being perceived and positioned as the undesirable other, the outsider, or the foreigner, Asian American poets cannot identify with the poet as defined by Ralph Waldo Emerson: "The poet is the sayer, the namer, and represents beauty. He is a sovereign, and stands on centre" ("The Poet" 321). This sovereign poet as the central man postulates an authoritative position that is at once unavailable and deplorable to Asian American poets. Far from being at the center, David Mura finds himself and other Asian Americans invisible in American culture: "where am I, / the missing third?" (between the polarized images of whites and blacks) asks his persona (*Desire* 5). Likewise,

Marilyn Chin's persona asserts her doubly marginalized status as an Asian American woman: 'So here lies Marilyn Mei Ling Chin, / . . . / She was neither black nor white, / neither cherished nor vanquished, / just another squatter in her own bamboo grove / minding her poetry —" (*Phoenix* 18). Speaking from multiple positions as a Chinese-English American, an art curator, a critic, a professor, and a poet, for whom the nominative position of the Emersonian poet is a point of departure, John Yau states: "I am the Other — the chink, the lazy son, the surrealist, the uptight East Coast Banana, the poet who is too postmodern for the modernist, and too modern for the postmodernist. You have your labels, their falsifying categories, but I have words. I — the I writes — will not be spoken for" ("Trees" 1994, 40).

While participating in transforming Romantic and Modernist lyric into "postmodern poetry," Asian American poets open up the poetic space for the other and its alterity, highlighting the ethics, politics, and aesthetics of otherness in their investigation of subjectivity, language, and self-other relationship. Their poetry calls into question a homogeneous, stable, totalizing definition of the "lyric I" as the self-centered, unitary, autonomous Cartesian self, speaking in a masculine, authoritative voice, reducing the other (including women and nature) to objects of its knowledge. Rather than seeking to get rid of the "lyric I," Asian American poets transform its attributes, reinvent its functions, and reconceptualize its relationship with the other.

For racialized minorities such as Asian Americans whose individuality has been denied and whose subjectivity has been deprived, the "I" in lyric poetry can serve as a viable site for restoring individuality and subject agency. The elocutionary subject position of the "I" enables the repressed other to rearticulate its otherness by revealing an undefinable interiority and an unsettling alterity exterior to the dominant systems of thought and values. For the socially constructed abject other to assert an interiority that resists social inscriptions is to undermine both the normative categories and those which are perceived as deviant from the norm. In articulating an inner self and otherness that elude socially inscribed meanings of the raced and gendered body, the lyric speaker as the other in Asian American poetry gives voice to an alterity irreducible to any categories of socially constructed otherness.

At the same time, Asian American poets enact an ethical relationship with the other through the subject position of the lyric I, responding to the other as a responsibility without assuming mastery over the other's alterity. In so doing, they confront the ethical, political, and aesthetic questions regarding the other and its relationship to the self embedded in language and subjectivity.

Moreover, contemporary Asian American poetry demonstrates that the agency of intervention and the ethics of alterity need not be enacted exclusively through the lyric I. It can be executed through various ways of using language, voice, and form. Thus my examination of the poetics and ethics of alterity in Asian American poetry entails investigating the displacement and disappearance of the first person singular as the organizing principle of the lyric poetry, as well as the transformation of the traditional attributes and functions of the lyric I, including its underlying concept of the individual subject defined in terms of autonomous consciousness.

Instead of following the beaten path of critiquing the lyric I's self-enclosure, self-indulgence, and authoritative voice of a universal, masculine, autonomous subjectivity, I pursue an alternative route by examining the relation between self and other as a primary condition for the constitution of the individual subject, and for an ethics regarding otherness. I contend that a radical challenge to the traditional lyric I must involve reconceptualizing the Cartesian self and its relation to the other, whose alterity undermines the Cartesian certainties in the self-sufficiency of reason that reduces the "not-me" to objects of knowledge, or to categories defined as the other of the self. Asian American poetry compels a rethinking of the speaking subject in lyric and of the effects resulting from the transformation of the lyric I and lyric voice.

Criticism of postmodern American poetry, which endorses the debunking of the self and privileges the dissolution of the I in the poem, leaves the traditional Western concept of the self intact, and forecloses the possibilities for rethinking the lyric I as a site where established notions of the Cartesian I are contested, transformed, and reinvented by minority American and women poets. Yusef Komunyakaa, for example, asserts that the I in lyric poetry need not be "self-centered" or "egotistical"; the lyric I can travel "beyond the personal" and embody a "we" (145). Conceived as such, the lyric I becomes an enabling subject position that entails multiple possibilities for colonized peoples. As Rafael Pérez-Torres contends in his study of Chicano poetry, "When performed by those . . . colonized or post colonized groups who have been denied representation and subjectivity, the reclamation of a self proves a resistant act" (164). Giving voice to the oppressed or the silenced through the lyric I also characterizes the importance of the speaking subject for Native American poets. In his introduction to an anthology of twentieth-century Native American poetry, Brian Swann observes, "The individual voice . . . would seem to be at its strongest when it is not just 'individual' . . . but also 'representative.' Often the individual speaks for, is spoken through" (xix). Likewise, the I in Marilyn Chin's poem, "The End of A Beginning," declares to be "the beginning of an end" in Chinese American history (*Dwarf Bamboo* 3). In her study, *Tell This Silence: Asian American Women Writers and the Politics of Speech*, Patti Duncan argues that "because of their continuing status as outsiders in a nation that perceives them as 'foreigners'," Asian American women writers "engage unique relationships with the subject position of the writing 'I'" (73). To break the silence of racial and patriarchal oppression "is to reclaim one's language and oneself" (77). The transformation of the self-enclosed lyric I in "minority" American poetry challenges definitions of the lyric in terms of a homogenized and universalized speaking subject.

Criticism that regards the elision of the I in postmodern poetry as the marker of real poetic invention overlooks the political and creative agency of the subject, particularly that of the other whose voices have been silenced in patriarchal discourses, in the process of colonization, and in the construction of Eurocentric literary canons. In her critique of Harold Bloom's lament over the imminent death of poetry, Perloff writes, "the poetry whose death we are about to witness is equated with lyric, with Romantic subjectivity. The possibility that poetry might deal with anything outside the enclosed self is immediately brushed aside" (*Dance* 174). Although Perloff rightly argues that the lyric is not a "timeless and stable product to which various theoretical paradigms can be 'applied' so as to tease out new meanings" (*Poetic License* 29), her emphasis on the disappearance of the lyric I as a defining characteristic of postmodern poetry, in contrast to Romantic lyric, forecloses the possibility of reinventing the lyric mode through transformation of the conventional lyric I.

Limited by her choice of James Wright's "Snowstorm in the Midwest" as an example of a formulaic late Modernist lyric modeled on the Romantic "epiphany poem" (*Dance* 168–69), Perloff sees alternatives to inward-turning lyric only in experimental poems such as Language poems, postmodern collage poems, and long narrative poems like Edward Dorn's *Gunslinger*, a four-book epic of the "Wild West."⁴ Quoting Dorn's remarks in an interview that "I was interested in getting rid of I. . . . I didn't want to have any truck with that first person singular excuse which I find one of the most effective brakes on current verse practice," Perloff contends that Dorn's urge to get rid of "what [Charles] Olson called 'the lyrical interference of the individual as ego'" illustrates "Dorn's central distrust of the metaphysical tradition based on the primacy of Being as presence, the Cartesian separation of man from the objects of his knowledge. . . . Thus the realm of inherent human values, of a logocentric universe is called into question, and with it the centrality of persons" (*Dance* 167). Contrasting the disappearance of the Cartesian I in Dorn's poem with the presence of the lyric I in Wright's poem, Perloff concludes that all the "hall-marks of the late modernist lyric" as shown in Wright's poem "will become less prevalent as our conceptions of the relation of self to world become more closely adjusted to the phenomenology of the present." She adds, "In understanding that present, a narrative that is not primarily autobiographical will once again be with us, but it will be a narrative fragmented, dislocated, and often quite literally non-sensical" (*Dance* 169).

Perloff's focus on the decentering of "persons" and the replacement of a primarily autobiographical narrative by fragmented, dislocated, and nonsensical narratives as characteristics of postmodern poetry casts the lyric I into a fixed category, and excludes the autobiographical lyric poems by minority poets, such as Asian American poets, from her consideration of the transformation in American poetry. In so doing, the capacity of postmodern poetry for dealing with the social, political, ethical, and philosophical is greatly limited. Perloff's dismissal of the lyric I as anything other than the transcendental ego, the self-enclosed Cartesian subject, or the Romantic inward-turning poet-I, seems in part the result of a homogeneous notion of both the lyric I and of the self. In other words, the assumptions underlying both the concept and dismissal of the lyric I are grounded in a homogenized concept of the self and its relation to the other and the world. Such a concept obscures the possibilities of alternative subjectivity and attributes of the lyric I.

Even when critics such as Norman Finkelstein question the implications of eliminating the lyric I, and emphasize that "the status of the self in poetry is nothing other than the social and political responsibility of the poet" (8), the self-other relationship as a politico-ethical concern is not addressed.[5] In his essay, "The Problems of the Self in Recent American Poetry," Finkelstein raises provocative questions about the social and political dimensions of the self, noting what is at stake when the notion of the individual is abandoned in postmodern poetry such as Language poetry. Emphasizing the individual subject's potential agency of intervention, Finkelstein questions "the political if not poetic efficacy" of experimental poets' repudiation of the self and denunciation of expressivity (8–9). Although Finkelstein's emphasis on the social and political dimensions of the self challenges the political and poetic efficacy of undoing the lyric I, his view on depersonalized utterance is too dismissive of its possibilities of intervention. Moreover, Finkelstein's defense of selfhood and subjective agency does not offer alternatives to the attributes and functions of the traditional lyric I. Rather, Finkelstein examines the status of the lyric I in contemporary American lyric in terms of a paradigm shift from a unitary subject to fragmented subjectivity as a totalizing model of the self that is unmarked by the difference of race, gender, class, sexuality, or ethnicity. Reiterating Frederic Jameson's theory of "the dynamics of cultural pathology," Finkelstein contends that the problematized status of the lyric I and the lyric voice in American poetry can be understood in terms of the distinction between the modern and postmodern "cultural pathology," which is characterized by a shift from "the alienation of the subject" to "the fragmentation of the subject" (4). Even though "the postmodern self shatters into fragments," Finkelstein contends, its traces are still discernable in "the most intriguing texts by language poets" as well as by poets writing in a more traditional lyric mode, such as Mark Strand and W. S. Merwin. Like Perloff's definition of postmodern poetry, Finkelstein's formulation of the distinction between modern and postmodern subjects does not take into account the raced and gendered subject and its relation to the lyric I. Nor does it address the self's relationship to the other.

The subjectivity of the silenced and marginalized other will continue to be overlooked or repressed in critical investigations of the lyric I if critical discourses continue to assume totalizing accounts of postmodern poetics in terms of a privileged, exclusive concept of the postmodern subject. Asian American critics call into question a wholesale definition of the postmodern self in terms of fragmented subjectivity. Responding to Finkelstein's discussion on the status of the lyric I, Shelley Sunn Wong points out, "A distinction between the lyric 'I' of mainstream American poetry and that of Asian American poetry needs to be made because of the way the assumption or maintenance of an autonomous 'I' results in different social and political ramifications." Critiquing the much valorized fragmentation and multiplicity of the postmodern subject and the disputed lyric I, Wong poses the questions: "Was the Asian American subject ever not 'fragmented'? Was, then, the lyric 'I' ever available to the Asian American writer?" (138). On a similar note, Traise Yamamoto calls critical attention to the problems of celebrating indeterminacy and fragmentation in resisting "a unified, essentialized subjectivity" (80). She argues that "for the raced subject, an ontology and epistemology based on fragmentation not only pose serious political problems but also tend to subvert the attempt to integrate the several and disparate aspects of being and bring them to bear on a sense of self" (75). Poststructuralist theories about subjectivity and difference "understood as an abstraction separate from the context of the specific conditions of racism and sexism," Yamamoto contends, "will always modulate into the absurdity of privileging precisely that which has been used to deny subject-status and agency to the marginalized and oppressed" (80).

Both Wong and Yamamoto raise provocative questions about the relation between raced (and gendered) subjectivity and its role in the formation and transformation of lyric poetry in which the self as the speaking subject and organizing principle is thrown into crisis. However, Wong's rhetorical questions about the Asian American subject do not challenge the traditional formulation of the lyric I, or offer an alternative model of the lyric speaker.[6] Nor does Yamamoto's emphasis on the necessity of the I that "confers" agency for Japanese American women's selves "through the autobiographical act" (113) propose a different mode of subjectivity beyond the binary of the public versus the private self.

Other Asian American critics have expanded the exploration of the raced and gendered subject by situating the formation of the Asian American self and its subject position within complex social power structures, including race relations and capitalism within and outside the U.S. nation-state. David Leiwei Li contends, "Strangled between the authentic white subject and the oppositional black subject," the

Asian American's "claim to distinctive self and national embodiment will have to be fought out not only between the East and West, Asia and America, but also between black and white, labor and capital" (10). In a similar vein, but with an emphasis on the complexity of raced subjectivity, Viet Thanh Nguyen argues that rather than simply constituting a mode of resistance, Asian Americans participate "in political struggles over the meaning of citizenship and subjectivity within the American body politic, assuming a variety of possible positions that range from opposition and contestation to acquiescence and consensus with the dominant body politic" (11). David Eng offers further insights into the ambivalent and contradictory subject positions of Asian Americans with a focus on the formation of the Asian American male subject through a psychoanalytical approach that integrates various critical theories. Calling into question "the notion of a pure political agency" of the racial minority subject, Eng investigates "the ways in which the more immaterial, invisible, or unconscious effects of racism are internalized by the minority subject as a social system of self-regulation and self-domination" (24). These critical perspectives have significantly advanced discourses on subjectivity beyond homogenizing definitions of the postmodern subject.

The otherness of Asian Americans addressed in these provocative studies, however, is still implicated in the binary, hierarchical power structures and raced social relations within or outside the U.S. nation-state. In other words, these critical investigations do not offer alternative concepts of either the subject or the other, except as effects and agents of ideologies and operations of social, political, and economic systems. Understood within this framework, the Asian American subject is defined only in relation to the "white subject" or the "black subject," and the otherness of Asian Americans remains a stigma for exclusion or containment.

Kandice Chuh in her recent book *Imagine Otherwise: On Asian Americanist Critique* (2003) seeks to go beyond critiquing the social construct of Asian Americans' racial and cultural otherness by suggesting a different approach to disrupting the social inscriptions of Asian Americans' difference and its reduction to a stable cultural otherness. Chuh argues that Asian Americanists' work must entail undermining "persistently the multicultural, positivist narratives of otherness that suggest a concrete knowability." For Chuh, this task "demands a deconstructive account of 'Asian American,' a move toward embracing the a priori subjectlessness of discourse" (26). By proposing a move as such, Chuh hopes to counter knowledge produced by "a subject-driven discourse where subjectivity bears the legacy of Enlightenment" (29). Furthermore, Chuh suggests that critical approaches that demonstrate "the impossibility of any objectivity, the irreducible inadequacy of any totalizing approach . . . or disciplining of knowledge" would help resist the process of objectification in which Asian Americans' difference becomes a "knowable" object (28). At the same time, Chuh explores the possibilities of "an Asian American studies that accounts for difference through a model of what Avery Gordon (1997) has described as 'complex personhood' rather than multicultural otherness" (29).

It seems then the lyric I in poetry could serve as a fitting model for articulating a "complex personhood" as Chuh has proposed. Yet, this model of a subject-driven discourse would contradict Chuh's proposition for "a move toward embracing the a priori subjectlessness of discourse." In naming "multicultural otherness" as an object of knowledge to be contested, Chuh calls critical attention to the political and epistemological questions of otherness. Nevertheless, the Enlightenment subject and its role in constructing the knowable other, though rejected, are not debunked by Chuh's proposition. The fundamental differences between the 'complex personhood' of racial minorities and the subject bearing the legacy of Enlightenment remain obscure and undertheorized.

Similarly, some feminist poets or critics seek to intervene in the lyric conventions based on the lyric I as the self-sufficient Cartesian subject, without dismantling the problematic attributes of the I as the Enlightenment subject. As Linda Kinnahan observes in her thought-provoking study, *Lyric Interventions: Feminism, Experimental Poetry, and Contemporary Discourse* (2004): "While the 'I' is radically altered through its regendering, the lyric subject popularly supported by the poets of the women's movement nonetheless retains primary conventions inherited from a patriarchal tradition or allowed to women by that tradition: the unitary 'I,' often autobiographical, expressing experience . . . through accessible language." But for other feminist poets, Kinnahan adds, "these conventions of the lyric 'I' were seen to obstruct rather than enable social transformation" (4). Mindful of divergent attempts to transform the lyric, Kinnahan takes a broader approach to women's reinvention of lyric poetry. She emphasizes, "The challenges that women might make to lyric conventions and the possible value they might find in reconstituting elements of the lyric involve a politics of form manifesting experimental reformulations of theory and feminism, of literary history and gendered subjectivity" (19). By exploring the "gendered self and its lyric expressions" in terms of the lyric I and of language and form, Kinnahan brings gendered politics, aesthetics, and subjectivity into critical discourses on modernist and postmodernist poetry.

Other feminist critics such as Trinh T. Minh-ha, the late Gloria Anzaldúa, and Inderpal Grewal explore various models of subjectivity. They emphasize the necessity for new forms of subjectivity which are radically different from the self-contained, sovereign subject that is formulated within the tradition of Western metaphysics. Trinh proposes a plural, ambivalent I which unsettles "every definition of otherness" (1990, 395). Anzaldúa postulates a hybrid self defined by "a mestiza consciousness" which breaks down "the unitary aspect of each new paradigm" (79–80). Grewal argues for "new forms of subjectivity that are radically different from the European imperialist and state-nationalist subject that is binarily constructed and essentialist" (233). The new models of subjectivity they formulate are defined as heterogenous, multiple, and inclusive, in contrast to the unitary, imperial, masculine subject constructed in a binary self-other relationship, in which the other is always lesser than and subordinate to the self. In other words, this new subject is grounded in multiple identities and social positions, which unsettle the binary construct of self in relation to its other.

Nevertheless, in emphasizing the plurality of the I and its socially constructed identities and positions as the basis for this new form of subjectivity, these critics have also left the concept of that self grounded in Western metaphysics undismantled, because their formulation of the subject does not undermine, even though it opposes, the Western philosophical tradition in which the so-called imperial subject is rooted. Moreover, in rejecting the self-other relationship as a binary construct, and in undertheorizing the role of the other in their formulation of the new subject, these critics overlook the possibilities of an alternative concept of otherness which can constitute a new kind of self-other relationship underlying the social, ethical, political, and philosophical questions regarding the other in the formation of the individual subject and literary genres.[7]

This study offers a reconceptualization of both self and other through analysis of Asian American poets' transformation and displacement of the traditional lyric I, and through investigation of their branding of otherness in the lyric voice, the English language, and the poetic form. Asian American poets enact an ethics of alterity in their articulation of the self, in their response to the other, and in their deployment of lyricism and poetics. In her discussion of Marilyn Chin's poems, Adrienne McCormick argues that "Chin's 'I' poems" that bridge the creative and the critical "do not merely reflect the rich and varied modes of Asian American feminist literary theory which predate her work, but are themselves acts of theorizing" (37). The same thing could be said of other Asian American poets' reinventions of the lyric, which pose challenging theoretical questions about not only the creative or the critical, but also the philosophical and the ethical.

## Levinas and the Ethics of Alterity

This study of the ethics and poetics of alterity draws largely from the writings of the philosopher Emmanuel Levinas. Levinas's concept of self and other challenges Western ontology which, he argues, has failed to allow the other to be other. Tracing the autonomous subject to the Cartesian self based on self-sufficiency of consciousness, which reduces the world and the other to the object of its intentions, Levinas critiques the metaphysical tradition underlying the pervasive concept of the self and its other in patriarchal, colonial, and Orientalist discourses.

Departing from Western metaphysics, Levinas's ethical philosophy of alterity offers an alternative conception of both the self and the other. Levinas contends that the other is other because of its irreducible, absolute alterity beyond the intentionality of the I, outside the *totality* of representation, knowledge, or the subject's familiar system of thought and values. As a result, the subject is incapable of assuming mastery of the other whose presence disturbs the subject, and whose otherness resists being contained within discourses or representation. This premise of the other undermines the subject's intentionality, challenges the sufficiency of reason, and disrupts the subject's self-enclosure. The subject becomes vulnerable and unable to bring the world and the other into the light of its reason to be grasped and mastered.

Levinas's concept of the other is fundamentally different from the social, cultural, or discursive constructs of the other in a binary hierarchy. The other in binarism is defined by the dominant; its otherness is part of the same social system or frame of thought. In this case, the otherness of the other is reduced to the opposite of the dominant, yet is completely knowable and assimilable; it is constitutive of the binary hierarchy or totality. Countering this otherness, Levinas insists that the other's alterity is infinitely elusive. In his essay, "Meaning and Sense," included in *Collected Philosophical Papers*, Levinas writes: "The other who faces me is not included in the totality of being expressed. . . . He is neither a cultural signification nor a simple given. . . . But the epiphany of the other involves a signifyingness of its own independent of this meaning received from the world" (*CPP* 95). The otherness of this other then is absolute, irreducible to social, ideological, or cultural inscriptions of meanings.

At the same time, the presence of the other disturbs and jostles the "mundane" cultural meaning because it is "not integrated into the world." Levinas refers to this presence of the other as an event, which can be understood as "the epiphany of a face" that is "a *visitation*," signifying the presence of an ungraspable, uncontainable otherness (*CPP* 95). A presence as such understood in terms of a face emphasizes the elusive, unknowable, and irreducible otherness of the other. "A face *enters* into our world from an absolutely foreign sphere," Levinas contends, "that is, precisely from an absolute, that which in fact is the very name for ultimate strangeness." Thus, Levinas emphasizes that a face is "not simply a *true representation* in which the other renounces his alterity" (*CPP* 96). Levinas's contention suggests that the concept of "true representation" assumes that the other is completely accessible, knowable, and representable as is characteristic of discourses and representations that construct the otherness of race, gender, and culture. Totalizing knowledge of the other, which claims authentic or realistic representation of the other, actually distorts or reduces the alterity of the other.

It is precisely because of its proximity, exteriority, and transcendence that the other disturbs the solitude of the self, disrupts its self-absorption, and challenges the sufficiency of its consciousness. In the same essay, "Meaning and Sense," Levinas emphasizes the inadequacy of consciousness when the subject encounters the other. In fact, "Consciousness is called into question by a face. . . . Visitation consists in overwhelming the very egoism of the I which supports this conversion. A face confounds the intentionality that aims at it" (*CPP* 97). Once supreme consciousness is called into question, "The I loses its sovereign self-coincidence, its identification, in which consciousness returns triumphantly to itself to rest on itself." Furthermore, "The calling into question of oneself is in fact the welcome of the absolutely other" (*CPP* 97). As Richard A. Cohen puts it succinctly in his introduction to *Face to Face with Levinas*, "In relation to the other the self is reconditioned, desubstantialized, put into question. Put into relation to what it cannot integrate, the self is made to be itself 'despite itself.' . . . Hence one is radically passive in a superlative passivity equal to the superlative alterity of the other person." Furthermore, Cohen notes, "The other's alterity is experienced as a command, an order which as it orders ordains the self into its inalienable selfhood" (7). Herein lies the ethics of a self-other relationship. For Levinas, the encounter with the other initiates an ethical relation between self and other, a relation that dismantles egoism of the subject and collapses binary hierarchy.

The encounter with the other, moreover, affirms the unique selfhood of the self as subject, obliging the self to respond to the other as responsibility. What establishes the self as a unique, individual subject is not its consciousness, but its ethical relationship with the other: "To be an I means then not to be able to escape responsibility, as though the whole edifice of creation rested on my shoulders. But the responsibility that empties the I of its imperialism and its egoism, even the egoism of salvation, does not transform it into a moment of the universal order; it confirms the uniqueness of the I. The uniqueness of the I is the fact that no one can answer for me" (*CPP* 97). This concept of the self as a subject constituted by an ethical relationship with the other provides a viable alternative to the Enlightenment subject of reason, to the self-centered lyric I, and to its fragmentation or dissolution in postmodern poetry.

In addition, Levinas's concept of the self-other ethical relationship is grounded in the primacy of language, in the mode of language-response to the other, which acknowledges the other while rendering the self open and vulnerable to the other. Levinas stresses the significance of *saying* in the subject's language-response to the other in speech that is oriented toward the addressee, but which can prevent the other from being absorbed as knowledge or reduced to the object of the intentionality of the I. For Levinas, ethics is embedded in language. As Jill Robbins observes, Levinas's work "describes the ethical relation to the other as a kind of language, as responsibility, that is, as language-response to the other who faces and who, 'in turn,' speaks." According to Levinas, Robbins adds, "ethics is something that 'happens' in language" (*Reading* 54). In his essay, "Language and Proximity," Levinas writes, "Language, contact, is the obsession of an I 'beset' by the others. Obsession is responsibility. . . . Language is fraternity, and thus a responsibility for the other" (*CPP* 123). Levinas emphasizes that the language-response to the other is not a transmission of knowledge, but a language gesture that renders the self open and vulnerable to the other. He calls this mode of using language "saying" that is fundamentally different from the "said." In his dialogue with Richard Kearney, Levinas emphasizes: "Language as *saying* is an ethical openness to the other; as that which is *said*— reduced to a fixed identity or synchronized presence — it is an ontological closure to the other" ("Dialogue" 29). Thus Levinas valorizes saying over the said, and "signifying" over "signs" in the self's language-response to the other, in which speech that is oriented to the addressee can prevent the other from being reduced or absorbed into the prescribed or the self-same totality (*OB* 48). Levinas's emphasis on maintaining alterity as an imperative for an ethical relation to be enacted in language offers new insights into Asian American poetics of alterity, including the poets' incorporation of foreign accents and words in their poems.

Another important aspect of Levinas's concept of alterity that enables a radical break from the notions of the lyric I as a self-sufficient subject of reason is the concept of time. In his dialogue with Richard Kearney, Levinas says: "The relationship with the other is *time*: it is an untotalizable diachrony in which one moment pursues another without ever being able to retrieve it, to catch up with, or coincide with it." This noncoincidence of time and nonpresence of the self in the other's time is a primary condition for the self-other relation, in which the other cannot be absorbed into a union with the self. Levinas adds, "Time means that the other is forever beyond me, irreducible to the synchrony of the same. The temporality of the interhuman opens up the meaning of otherness and the otherness of meaning" ("Dialogue" 21). Time, then, is pluralized, rather than homogeneous" temporality is multiple, comprising other times of the other. This concept of time in relation to the other breaks open the lyrical moment as the isolated moment of here and now, in which the lyric I is alone with itself. Hence Levinas's concept of the other in terms of time can shed light on the multiple temporal-spatial relationships in Asian American poetry, which are characteristic of Asian American poets' signifying of otherness beyond the One, the same, or the binary definitions of self and other.

However, for those who are familiar with Levinas's remarks about poetry, it might seem inappropriate for a study in poetry to draw so heavily on his philosophy. But Levinas's perspective on poetry by no means pits the aesthetic against the ethical. In *Difficult Freedom*, Levinas suggests that the aesthetic experience in poetry can deprive us of our subjective agency. He writes, "Violence is also in *poetic delirium* and enthusiasm, when we offer our mouth to the muse who speaks through us, in the fear and trembling of the sacred which tears us away from ourselves" (7). Overwhelmed by aesthetic experience, we can become mere puppets of forces that control us: "The numinous or the sacred envelops and transports man beyond his powers and wishes . . . [It] annuls the rapport between persons by making them participate, albeit ecstatically, in a *drama* not brought about willingly by them" (*DF* 14). Paralyzed in this way, the subject loses its own subjective agency, unable to enact its responsibility. Thus Levinas's critique here on the "*poetic delirium* and enthusiasm" should not be equated with an anti-poetic stance.[8]

If the subject is constituted by its relation to the other as responsibility, to lose one's subjectivity would mean to relinquish one's responsibility. Levinas's remarks about the ethical questions regarding subjective agency in another work, *Totality and Infinity*, further clarify his ideas about the relation between literature and ethics. "When I maintain an ethical relation," Levinas writes, "I refuse to recognize the role I would play in a *drama* of which I would not be the author or whose outcome another would know before me. I refuse *to figure* in a *drama* of salvation or of damnation that would be enacted in spite of me" (79). For Levinas, to maintain one's subjective agency is an ethical responsibility because, in doing so, one is refusing complicity, resisting assimilation and subjugation by discursive manipulation or representational tactics.

This concept of resistance to imposition or subjugation as an imperative in maintaining an ethical relation between self and the dominant power has significant implications for Asian American poets.

For Asian Americans to "refuse to recognize the role I would play in a *drama* of which I would not be the author or whose outcome another would know before me" is, in a sense, to refuse the role of the silenced or subjugated other. It seems that the loss of subjecthood for the raced or oppressed other is directly related to the loss of their alterity as the other in discourses that violently reduce their otherness to a completely knowable object through transparent representation. Given the implied correlation between epistemological violence in discursive representations of the other and the repression or erasure of alterity of the other, it stands to reason that Levinas deplores the loss of subject agency for exercising one's ethical responsibility.

Although Levinas might seem to be ambivalent about literature, his philosophy of the ethics of alterity remains consistent. As his remarks about Marcel Proust's work indicate: "The mystery in Proust is the mystery of the other." Levinas argues that the unknowable otherness within the self, the dialogue with the other, renders Proust's writing unique and ethical, for it establishes a direct relationship with the other as other ("The Other in Proust" *PN* 102). Assuming knowledge or mastery of the other would "destroy the nearness, the proximity, of the other. A proximity that, far from meaning something less than identification, opens up the horizon of social existence." Thus Levinas concludes: "Proust's most profound teaching — if indeed poetry teaches — consists in situating the real in a relation with what forever remains other — with the other as absence and mystery. It consists in rediscovering this relation also within the very intimacy of the *I* and in inaugurating a dialectic that breaks definitely with Parmenides" ("The Other in Proust" *PN* 104–105). Significantly, an ethical relationship with the other must reject the self's assumption of knowledge of the other, or the self's assimilative impulse to be one with the other, which underlie the monism of Parmenides, as well as assimilationist ideology and practice that repress, absorb, and erase otherness.

For Levinas, the discovery of a relation with the other as other signifies a departure from the Western philosophical tradition of ontology. In *En découvrant l'existence avec Husserl et Heidegger*, Levinas contends: "Western philosophy coincides with the unveiling of the other in which the Other, by manifesting itself as a being, loses its alterity. Philosophy is afflicted, from its childhood, with an insurmountable allergy: a horror of the Other which remains Other. It is for this reason that philosophy is essentially the philosophy of Being;

the comprehension of Being is its final word and the fundamental structure of man" (188 qtd. in Davis 32). Levinas suggests that in its attempt to domesticate the other in terms of the unity of being and totality of truth that suppress alterity, traditional Western philosophy has failed to think of the other as other. Even when the other was interpreted "as a threat and a degradation" by Jean Paul Sartre, for instance, Levinas points out, the other "was still considered, as in all Western ontology, to be a modality of unity and fusion, that is, a reduction of the other to the category of the same" ("Dialogue" 17). Understood from this perspective, the production of raced, gendered, or cultural otherness has deeper roots than discourses of patriarchy, racism, colonialism, nationalism, or Orientalism. An effective disruption of otherness as such must entail a dismantling of the self and its other conceived within the Western metaphysical tradition.

## Critical Approaches

My investigation of an Asian American poetics of alterity in relation to the lyric I will engage with both the Levinasian otherness or alterity and the otherness constructed by ideology and social power relations. The lyric I in Asian American poetry, more often than not, is a socially and culturally defined other, represented as the outsider, the foreigner, deviant from the norm, and positioned as marginal or subordinate. At the same time, Asian American poets reclaim otherness as irreducible alterity, as a form of resistance and intervention, which entails new perspectives on self and other, and generates new possibilities for using language, image, and poetic form. Thus, Asian American poets negotiate with a different and complex otherness, including that of the immigrant, the exile, the woman, the person of color, the homosexual, the model minority and yellow peril, as well as that otherness which is unknowable and resists all categories. Their exploration and articulation of otherness through innovative poetics can be better understood through Levinas's concept of the other and his ethics of alterity.

Moreover, Asian American poets explore a politics of otherness that transforms, rather than simply resists, the homogenizing dominant culture. Hence, while using Levinas's complex ethics of alterity as the central theoretical and methodological framework for my investigation of the poetics of alterity in Asian American poetry, I also draw from other theoretical perspectives developed in feminist discourses, cultural studies, critical race theories, and gay and lesbian studies, as well as Asian American literary studies. My exploration of the ethics and poetics in Asian American poetry concentrates on three aspects of otherness: 1) otherness which is an effect of power, such as the socially constructed otherness of women and racial or ethnic minorities, who are forbidden to be equal participants with members of the dominant group; 2) otherness which is self-chosen as a form of resistance and critical intervention; and 3) otherness which is irreducible to socially constructed identities, and whose absolute alterity challenges the sufficiency of consciousness, unsettles the autonomy of the self, disrupts the production of totalizing knowledge, and transforms the homogenizing dominant culture.

In addition, I would argue that the ethics and poetics of alterity in Asian American poetry enact more than a critical intervention in the discourses on subjectivity and otherness. In her provocative study, *An Ethics of Dissensus: Postmodernity, Feminism, and the Politics of Radical Democracy*, Ewa Płonowska Ziarek contends: "To respond to conflicts, injustice and domination requires not only a critique of power/knowledge but also a therapeutic working through of the unspeakable racial traumas and the elaboration of an alternative ethics based on the responsibility for the Other's oppression. Without such responsibility, the politics of difference risks deteriorating into an indifferent struggle of antagonistic force" (215). It is precisely by responding to otherness in the contexts of social injustice and oppression, and by paying aestheticized attention to the other as a "caress" to the other's trauma, that Asian American poets render their innovative poetry politically viable and socially accountable.

## Overview of Chapters

This study is divided into seven chapters, not including the introduction or conclusion. Each chapter focuses on a single poet, investigating in depth the poet's articulation of specific categories of otherness, and the poet's development of a particular poetics of alterity through transformation of the traditional lyric I, the lyric voice, and the lyric form. The organization of the chapters follows a trajectory of the ways in which the lyric I and lyric voice are deployed and displaced, moving from autobiographical and confessional poems where the lyric speaker is central, to surrealist and Language poems where the poet-I as the lyric I is replaced by multiple voices of the other, and the lyric voice gives way to impersonal, hybrid, and other-sounding patterns of language(s).

Chapter 1, "Li-Young Lee: Your Otherness Is Perfect as My Death," examines the aesthetics and implications of a corporeal lyric I who is a refugee, an immigrant, and a poet in exile. The corporeality of the self in Lee's poems is related to his persona's vulnerability and impulse to investigate the otherness of the other; it also underlies his lyric speaker's openness to and desire for the other which remains elusive.

Chapter 2, "Marilyn Chin: She Walks into Exile Vowing No Re-turn," investigates the ways in which Chin gives voice to Asian women and working-class Chinese immigrants through a multicul-tural and bilingual lyric I and a hybrid poetics of otherness which en-rich and rupture the idiom of Eurocentric American lyric. While em-ploying hybridity to dismantle binary constructs of identities of race, gender, nation, and culture, Chin confronts the ethical and aesthetic challenges in maintaining proximity and distance between self and other in her predominantly autobiographical lyric poems.

Further investigating the possibilities for ethics of alterity in au-tobiographical lyric, Chapter 3, "David Mura: Where Am I, the Miss-ing Third?," discusses Mura's use of the autobiographical and fictional I to give voice to the excluded, condemned, and exiled other. My reading of Mura's poems emphasizes the aesthetics of lyricism and the agency of the lyric I as a crucial component of the ethics and politics of Mura's poetry.

With a concentration on yet another different mode of autobio-graphical lyric characterized by intertextual collage, Chapter 4, "Kimiko Hahn: The Passion of Leaving Home," discusses Hahn's appropriation and reinvention of the lyric mode for articulating an embodied female subjectivity, eroticism, and aesthetics by incorpo-rating French feminist theories and autobiographical materials with Chinese and Japanese women's languages and literary traditions in her poems. Hahn's incorporation of French and Anglo American fem-inist theories in her poems about the intertwining of race, gender, sexuality, language, and aesthetics makes a valuable contribution to feminist critical discourses on otherness.

Further exploring Asian American poets' reinvention of autobio-graphical lyric, Chapter 5, "Timothy Liu: Each of Us Harboring What the Other Lacked," expands still further on the themes of otherness and the ethical, political, and aesthetic questions it poses, by taking up an openly gay poetry to foreground the agency of the lyric I. While my reading of Liu's poems focuses on the transformation of the masculine subjectivity and language through homoeroticism that breaks away from binary constructs, particularly those of gender and sexuality, the holy and the profane, my discussion of particular poems also addresses questions of time and alterity. Although these questions are embedded in any self-other relationship, I approach them from the perspective of Liu's homoerotic desire and his confrontation with mortality and AIDS.

Chapter 6, "John Yau: The I of Changes, the Destroying I, the Its of the I," moves into the debates over the demise of the self, the efficacy of poststructuralist concepts of the subject, and postmodern poetics for minority discourses. A poet, a critic and curator of art, a long-time resident in New York City, Yau is closely associated with contemporary artists and poets, including the New York School of poets and Language poets. His familiarity with various avant-garde schools in the arts and poetry is reflected in his poems, which at once evoke and depart from surrealism, abstract expressionism, and Language poetry. Further complicating the constitution of the subject, Yau interrogates both the possibilities and limits of the lyric speaker in articulating a self that is elusive, unstable, at once public and private, and irreducibly other. Yau's poetics and poetry invite comparison with Marc Chagall, not simply because Chagall incorporates contemporary concepts and techniques of various postimpressionist schools of painting, and yet resists being identified with any, but most importantly because Chagall refuses to abandon Jewish themes and identity with the other for abstraction or formal experiments. Like Chagall, Yau confronts the ethical and political questions of otherness through technical innovation, choosing to remain the other at the margins of avant-garde circles. Yau's work undermines the apparent separation between minority discourses and radically experimental poetry.

Chapter 7, "Myung Mi Kim: Speak and It Is Sound in Time," further investigates the possibilities for minority poets to participate in developing postmodern experimental poetics and in using this poetics to engage with issues most often dealt with in minority discourses. This chapter explores the ways in which Kim's poems respond to a range of historical, political, and aesthetic issues by resolutely breaking away from the centrality of the lyric I/eye, and by relying on multiple fragmentary voices and the primacy of sound patterns of language to signify "contamination" of English by Korean and to articulate the experience of Korean diaspora, resulting from Japanese colonization, American military intervention, and transnational capitalism.

The focus of my reading of each poet moves from transformation of the lyric I to the displacement and disappearance of the first person singular in language-centered poems. This line of inquiry highlights the fact that while calling critical attention to overlooked issues in postmodern and minority discourses, and exploring a viable model for the application of Levinas's ethics of alterity in literary criticism, this study responds to the impetus of increasingly globalized encounters across many kinds of boundaries. These encounters with the other at home and abroad make ethical questions of alterity especially urgent. The exigencies of these questions compel this study whose concerns, though beyond poetics, are bound up in poetry.

# CHAPTER ONE

# Li-Young Lee

YOUR OTHERNESS IS PERFECT AS MY DEATH

At a 1993 symposium on Asian American literature spon-
sored by the Academy of American Poets, Li-Young Lee stated:
"When I write, I'm trying to make that which is *visible*— this face,
this body, this person —*invisible*, and at the same time, make what is
*invisible* —that which exists at the level of pure *being*— completely
visible" (qtd. in Hummer 5). While evoking his experience as a raced
and ethnic other, Lee's statement articulates a poetics that resists so-
cial inscriptions of racial meanings on the bodily surfaces through
exploration of interiority that is elusive, multifaceted, and protean.
As Levinas states, "The inner life is the unique *way* for the real to ex-
ist as a plurality" (*TI* 58). Lyric poetry enables Lee to counter racial or
ethnic stereotypes through articulation of the raced other's irre-
ducible, ungraspable inner life erased in socially constructed uni-
form collective identities of race or ethnicity that are naturalized by
discourses and representations which inscribe supposedly knowable
essential differences on the body. Thus by rendering the racially
marked body invisible, and making visible its interiority, Lee sub-
verts precisely the logic that encodes the body with ideologies which
privilege one particular type of body over others for humanity, citi-
zenship, civil rights, and political responsibilities.[1] At the same time,
Lee rearticulates the raced and gendered body through a corporeal
aesthetics that renders universal the body marked for exclusion, ex-
ploitation, and subjugation, redefining universal humanity monopo-
lized by the white body and white male subject. His strategies and
aesthetics for rendering the unseen visible and the racial markers in-
visible offer a unique and viable alternative to predominant modes of
representing the body in Asian American literature.

Given its social and political valence, the body has been a con-
tested site of competing ideologies in Asian American literature and
criticism. Expanding on the well-established notion of the body as

"*the* cultural product" (Grosz *Bodies* 23), Viet Thanh Nguyen in his incisive study, *Race and Resistance: Literature and Politics in Asian America*, emphasizes that the Asian American body is "a historical product" "invested with both symbolic and economic capital" (17). In attempting to claim "the humanity of their individual bodies and . . . the legitimacy of their collective political body," Nguyen argues, Asian Americans "seek to turn the body from being negatively marked by a history of racist signification to being positively marked and marketable in the arena of multiethnic identification and consumption" (18). Moreover, he finds in Asian American prose writings "not a teleological development of the body but instead the development of multiple versions of bodily signification that exist simultaneously"(19), including the Eurasian hybrid body, the wounded body, the remasculinized body, and the queer body produced in the contexts of resistance to racism and colonialism. Despite this diversity, however, Nguyen notes a problematic "internal division of Asian America . . . between the symbolic poles of black and nonblack, into bad subjects and model minority"—a division that can reinforce the imposition of Asian Americans' racial position by the dominant society (30). Nguyen's contention suggests, among other things, that Asian Americans' reinscription of the racially marked body within the existing binarized representational systems of racial identities allows problematic and limited strategies for political affiliations and critical intervention. Lee's corporeal aesthetic offers an alternative approach to the raced body and embodied subject through what Elizabeth Grosz calls "a certain resistance of the flesh, a residue of its materiality left untouched" by social inscriptions (*Bodies* 118).

Exploring the problems and contradictions of the visible and invisible aspects of Asian Canadian and Asian American identities, Eleanor Ty in her recent book, *The Politics of the Visible in Asian North American Narratives* (2004), offers further insights into Asian North American novelists' and filmmakers' reinscription of "their visibility" that is paradoxically bound up with their invisibility "in dominant culture and history." She argues that "in reinscribing the meaning of the visible markings on their bodies, the authors succeed in making visible to the public or to historical records the experiences and stories of those who have heretofore been invisible to majority culture" (12). One major strategy of these authors "is to recreate selves that have been effaced by the screen of the visible. For some, writing, producing a film, or telling a story becomes a struggle to avoid disappearing into oblivion; for others, it is a way to deal with the various selves that have been called into existence through spectacles of otherness" (12–13). While many of Lee's autobiographical poems accomplish similar tasks, they explore and make visible a different kind of invisibility — the interiority of the other who is reduced to transparent, inscrutable, and knowable spectacles.

An infinitely plural, various, and mysterious inner life of the supposedly homogenous, knowable other disrupts disciplinary, systematic productions of knowledge of otherness naturalized through bodily images represented as manifestations of essence. In a conversation with David Mura, Lee observes that racism can operate as "a type of arrogance, an unwarranted assumption of knowledge of the Other" (qtd. in Mura "Dim Sum Poetics" 98). To counter such assumptions, Lee insists on maintaining what Levinas calls "the ethical inviolability of the Other" (*TI* 195) through his lyric speaker, who is enthralled by the unknowable other whose alterity appeals, fascinates, and eludes. "Your otherness exhausts me, / like looking suddenly up from above here / to impossible stars fading," says Lee's persona to the loved other. In fact, Lee's persona makes no attempt to grasp the other's alterity as knowledge: "And your otherness is perfect as my death" (*City* 55). At the same time, Lee simultaneously debunks racial stereotypes and the disembodied lyric subject through his lyric speaker, who is a socially defined and violated other — "one of the drab population," who is a refugee, an immigrant, speaking English with an accent, and whose "blood motley . . . ways trespassed upon" (*City* 52). A particularized lyric I as such in Lee's poems renders his claim to universal humanity especially provocative and subversive.

Bearing visible features of the raced ethnic other, Lee and his family experienced painful racial discrimination in the United States. When Lee's father became the minister of a small town in Pennsylvania after completing his studies at the Pittsburgh Theological Seminary, his all-white Presbyterian congregation referred to him as "*Our heathen minister*" (Lee *Winged Seed* 130). The bodily and cultural differences of Asian Americans in the United States have been regarded as markers of their essential and completely knowable otherness that deviates from the norm of white America. In his prose-poem memoir, *The Winged Seed: A Remembrance* (1995), Lee recalls his childhood experience of being regarded and treated as an alien other. "Perceived as feeble-minded, I was, like my siblings, spoken to very loudly, as though the problem were deafness" (*Winged Seed* 78). And Lee was taunted by schoolmates with racist hearsay about his family: "*They say your house is always dark like no one lives there. . . . They say all you people have the same first and last names and your mother can't tell you apart. . . . They say you keep snakes and grasshoppers in a bush on your back porch and eat them. They say you don't have manners, you lift your plates to your mouths and push the food in with sticks. . . . They say you don't believe in God, but you worship the Devil*" (*Winged Seed* 86). Underlying the circulation of such knowledge of the other is the kind of racism Lee speaks of — "a type of arrogance, an unwarranted assumption of knowledge of the Other." In his poems, Lee challenges this kind of arrogance, while offering an alternative way of responding to the other through an embodied, vulnerable subject who refuses to claim knowledge of or oneness with the other.

Given the social and cultural contexts of the United States and the poetic conventions of Western lyric, Lee's articulation of the corporeality of the lyric I in his poems has complex implications and functions. It breaks down the mind-versus-body dichotomy underlying Wordsworthian lyric poetry, in which the lyric I is a disembodied subject. Defined by an autonomous consciousness, the traditional lyric I is self-contained, self-enclosed, and self-centered, operating as the organizing principle of the poem. Its confidence in the sufficiency of its intentionality reduces the world and the other to the object of its knowledge. Rejecting these attributes and functions of the traditional lyric I, Lee insists on exploring the corporeality of his lyric persona. It is precisely because of its corporeality that Lee's lyric I is mortal, vulnerable, and resolutely implicated in the social, and inevitably bound to the world and others.

However, Lee refuses to assume sameness as or unity with the other. The other whom Lee's lyric I addresses maintains its irreducible otherness — an alterity that undermines the illusion of the autonomy of the self, pluralizing its world and rendering its intentionality insufficient for knowing the other. The self in Lee's poetry demonstrates a reconceptualized lyric I and its relations to the world and others through a corporeal aesthetics.

## Corporeal Subject and Aesthetics

The lyric I in Lee's poetry articulates a self whose subjectivity is embodied and constituted by its relationship with the other. This concept of the self and its impact on Lee's poetics can be better understood in terms of Levinas's philosophy of an ethical self-other relation which is grounded in the embodied subject's language-response to the other. For Levinas, the encounter with the other is an epistemological challenge, and an ethical event. He argues that alterity challenges self-contained Cartesian subjectivity, and disrupts its circular knowledge that reinforces the self-same: "The strangeness of the Other, his irreducibility to the I, to my thoughts and my possessions, is precisely accomplished as a calling into question of my spontaneity, as ethics." For Levinas, this "calling into question of the Same by the Other" operates as "the ethics that accomplishes the critical essence of knowledge" (*TI* 43). Moreover, Levinas suggests that the concept of the subject has to break away from the traditional philosophy of ontology in order to allow alterity to pose a challenge to sameness, and for the same to "welcome" the other and to be transformed by otherness. In his "Translator's Introduction" to Levinas's *Otherwise Than Being*, Alphonso Lingis explains the necessity for this break: "Levinas opposes the ontological philosophy which accounts for subjectivity as a locus or moment engendered by the inner movement of Being for its own exhibition. He intends to show subjectivity as the locus where alterity makes contact, a locus finally created by this movement of alterity" (xvi). This notion of subjectivity as the locus where the subject encounters alterity disrupts the lyric I's solipsism and its mastery of the self and other, which characterize the lyric I in the Wordsworthian lyric tradition.

Lee's poems enact encounters with alterity through a mode of speech which is similar to what Levinas calls "saying." For Levinas, saying is an ethical response when an encounter with the other takes place in speech. "To say is to approach a neighbor." (*OB* 48). Saying in this sense departs from the kind of lyric I's self-proclaiming as an autonomous creative subject,[2] and from the Emersonian poet's authoritative naming of himself and others. Levinas emphasizes that saying as an expressive mode of speech addressed to the other differs fundamentally from the kind of self-affirming discourse in which "[t]he relationship with the other would then extend forth as an intentionality, out of a subject posited in itself and for itself" (*OB* 48). In contrast, saying entails "the risky uncovering of oneself . . . the breaking up of inwardness and the abandon of all shelter, exposure to traumas, vulnerability" (*OB* 48). As such, saying disrupts the lyric I's solipsistic "inward turning" that Harold Bloom considers characteristic of Wordsworthian Romantic poetry, of which the "true subject," he contends, is "the poet's own selfhood" (*Agon* 287). Rather than turning into the self, saying is an act of responding to the other, an opening of the self to otherness, which renders the self passive, vulnerable, and susceptible in its encounter with alterity.

In addition, Levinas adds that saying reverts "the ego into a self" which has the "form of a corporeal life devoted to expression and to giving." The corporeality of the self, then, is a condition for the subject's relation with the other to be one-for-the-other. For only when the subject is embodied can suffering and offering be possible. "Then the for-the-other involved in saying must not be treated in terms of consciousness . . . , [nor] thematizing intentionality," Levinas stresses (*OB* 50–51). In this sense, saying is intricately bound to the subject's corporeality and sensibility, which make the subject vulnerable and susceptible in its encounter with the alterity of the other. The corporeal subject differs fundamentally from the traditional lyric I defined in terms of consciousness as the essence of the disembodied subject. The corporeality of the subject in Lee's poetry makes possible a self-other relationship that not only breaks open the confinement of the self-centered lyric I but also breaks down the dominance of the I over the other, and renders impossible the subject's mastery of otherness. The lyric I in Lee's poems, moreover, is often an autobiographical I whose identities are associated with those of exiles, refugees, and poor immigrants. Thus the saying of this lyric I as a socially and culturally marked other also has the effect of resisting assimilation, countering social inscriptions of the body, while articulating an alterity irreducible to the dominant culture's categorizations of the other in terms of a privileged norm represented by the white body and the English-speaking, European American culture.

One of his early poems, "Persimmons," is a salient example of what Lee achieves through a corporeal aesthetic and a poetics of alterity that rearticulates socially defined otherness. Rather than becoming merely an image representing the lyric speaker's ideas, feelings, or insights, persimmons in Lee's poem remain irreducible and undefinable in their materiality as an evocative and mobile element that brings into the poem otherness and multiple perspectives. The poem begins with the speaker's memory of an earlier experience of alienation and humiliation as an ethnic other in the classroom:

> In sixth grade Mrs. Walker
> slapped the back of my head
> and made me stand in the corner
> for not knowing the difference
> between *persimmon* and *precision*.
> How to choose
>
> persimmons. This is precision.
> Ripe ones are soft and brown-spotted.
> Sniff the bottoms. The sweet one
> will be fragrant. How to eat:
> put the knife away, lay down newspaper.
> Peel the skin tenderly, not to tear the meal.
> Chew the skin, suck it,
> and swallow. Now, eat
> the meat of the fruit,
> so sweet,
> all of it, to the heart.
>
> Mrs. Walker brought a persimmon to class
> and cut it up
> so everyone could taste
> a Chinese apple. Knowing
> it wasn't ripe or sweet, I didn't eat
> but watched the other faces. (*Rose* 17–18)

In contrast to his confusion of the spellings or pronunciations of the two English words, the speaker performs the eating of a persimmon with precision, showing what cannot be named or reduced to semantics or definitions, while suggesting another way of knowing through sensuous experience. The speaker's pleasure of eating persimmons renders particularly ironic Mrs. Walker's naming of an unripe persimmon "a *Chinese apple*" and his classmates' unpleasant experience of tasting it that confirm their misleading knowledge of "Chinese" apples (*Rose* 18). An arrogance of assuming authority of knowledge of the unfamiliar is embedded in Mrs. Walker's mis-identification of the fruit, which is evocative of the dominant culture's construction of otherness according to its normative sameness. By posing epistemological and ethical challenges to how knowledge about difference is produced, Lee renders the apparently transparent ethnic cultural elements in this poem particularly subversive.

But critics have overlooked this aspect of Lee's poem. Steven Yao in his discussion of "Persimmons" observes that a "sense of profound alienation and otherness . . . arises from a confrontation with mainstream ignorance and cultural insensitivity." But by the end, Yao contends, the poem achieves a "triumphal narrative of integration and synthesis wherein the poet . . . enters fully into (indeed, contributes to the formation of) multicultural American society by mastering its operative language, as evidenced by the poem itself" (5). The claim of a multicultural American society that entails political and economic equality for racial and ethnic minorities, I would emphasize, must critically examine the ways that difference or otherness is perceived and treated. Rather than simply performing an integration of mainstream and ethnic cultures, Lee's poem effectively exposes the arrogant, reductive naming of difference, by showing the unnamable voluptuousness of persimmons and demonstrating both the alterity and humanity of his Chinese American persona and his parents through their relationships with persimmons, thus rendering their ethnicity uncontainable and unknowable.

Refusing to reduce persimmons to an object of knowledge, Lee illustrates the various ways in which his persona and his parents appreciate them, revealing their individual interiority. In so doing, Lee further departs from the centrality of the lyric I, as his persona turns to the particularity of each of his Chinese parents' ways of relating to persimmons.

> My mother said every persimmon has a sun
> inside, something golden, glowing,
> warm as my face.

> Once, in the cellar, I found two wrapped in newspaper,
> forgotten and not yet ripe.
> I took them and set both on my bedroom windowsill,
> where each morning a cardinal
> sang, *The sun, the sun.*

Finally understanding
he was going blind,
my father sat up all one night
waiting for a song, a ghost.
I gave him the persimmons,
swelled, heavy as sadness,
and sweet as love.
This year, in the muddy lighting
of my parents' cellar, I rummage, looking
for something I lost.
My father sits on the tired, wooden stairs,
black cane between his knees,
hand over hand, gripping the handle.
He is so happy that I've come home.
I ask how his eyes are, a stupid question.
*All gone*, he answers.

Under some blankets, I find a box.
Inside the box I find three scrolls.
I sit beside him and untie
three paintings by my father:
Hibiscus leaf and a white flower.
Two cats preening.
Two persimmons, so full they want to drop from the cloth.
He raises both hands to touch the cloth,
asks, *Which is this?*

*This is persimmons, Father.* (Rose 18–19)

The multiplicity of meanings and materiality of persimmons, and the sensibility and spirituality of the speaker's immigrant parents challenge mainstream America's reductive view of difference.

Using persimmons as the organizing principle, Lee relies on free association to develop the theme of the poem, moving from particularities of the speaker and his parents to a universality that makes invisible the "Chineseness" without erasing the individuality and cultural difference of the Chinese. The closing lines of the poem in the voice of the father offer another example of execution of precision in making a brush painting of persimmons, while rendering universal this culturally specific experience through his human spirituality and corporeality:

> Oh, the feel of the wolftail on the silk,
> the strength, the tense
> precision in the wrist.
> I painted them hundreds of times
> eyes closed. These I painted blind.
> Some things never leave a person:
> scent of the hair of one you love,
> the texture of persimmons,
> in your palm, the ripe weight. (Rose 19)

The sensuous experience of the father's painting of persimmons and his statements about enduring memories of scent, touch, and feelings enhance his loss of eye-insight and the corporeal mutability of his body that refuses racial or ethnic markers.

The significance of the corporeal in Lee's poem must also be understood within the social, cultural, and discursive practices where the body is constitutive of subjectivity and identity. The feminist philosopher Elizabeth Grosz, in her book *Volatile Bodies: Toward a Corporeal Feminism*, undermines the primacy of consciousness in the conception of subjectivity, and displaces the privilege of the mind by foregrounding the body as "a site of social, political, cultural, and geographical inscriptions, production, or constitution" (23). Understood in these terms, the body loses its "naturalness," and with it, the naturalized differences of gender, race, class, and sexuality. Grosz argues: "Bodies are fictionalized, that is, positioned by various cultural narratives and discourses, which are themselves embodiments of culturally established canons, norms, and representational forms." However, Grosz contends, "there must be a certain resistance of the flesh, a residue of its materiality left untouched by the body's textualization" (118). She emphasizes that the body is not simply a "sign to be read, a symptom to be deciphered, but also, a force to be reckoned with" (120). Rather than merely a passive surface, the body can be a form of resistance to social inscriptions and cultural conformity.

Similarly, the sociologist Bryan Turner in his book, *The Body and Society: Explorations in Social Theory*, investigates the body as a site of individual resistance and agency, as well as a site of social regulation and normalization. He contends that "The body is a site of enormous symbolic work and symbolic production. Its deformations are stigmatic and stigmatizing, while at the same time its perfections, culturally defined, are objects of praise and admiration. Because of its symbolic potential, the body is also an object of regulation and control." As a discursive and public site, Turner argues, "the body is both an environment we practise on and also practise with. We labour on, in and with bodies" (185). The body, then, is not merely the effect of social regulations and cultural representations; it also participates in producing ideological and political effects.

The idealized body in the cultural environment of the United States is a normalized, naturalized embodiment of a privileged race, gender, and class. Further exploring the ideas embedded in Grosz's and Turner's contentions, David Palumbo-Liu observes that the idealized body "is a cultural text that does not simply stand alone as an idealized presence; it is a corporeality imbricated within an economy of representation and power, which is itself situated within the logic of race and class in the United States" (*Asian/American* 119). As one of his numerous examples, Palumbo-Liu cites from Franz Boas's report entitled "Changes in the Bodily Form of Descendants of Immigrants" included in *Abstracts of Reports of the Immigration Commission* (1911). The summary introduction to the report begins: "The Immigration's anthropological investigation had for its object an inquiry into the assimilation of the immigrants with the American people as far as the form of the body is concerned." According to the report, "the east European Hebrew, who has a very round head, becomes more long-headed; the south Italian, who in Italy has an exceedingly long head, becomes more short headed; so that in this country both approach a uniform type, as far as the roundness of the head is concerned" (*Immigration Report* 2: 505, qtd. in Palumbo-Liu *Asian/American* 85). The report concludes: "This fact . . . shows that not even those characteristics of a race which have proved to be the most permanent in their old home remain the same under the new surroundings; and we are compelled to conclude that when these features of the body change, the whole bodily and mental make-up of the immigrants may change. . . . The influence of American environment makes itself felt with increasing intensity, according to the time elapsed between the arrival of the mother and the birth of the child" (qtd. in Palumbo-Liu *Asian/American* 85–86). Nevertheless, Palumbo-Liu points out that "the notion of America as a catalytic space," and the bodily transformation as a sign of assimilation, are only applicable to eastern European and Mediterrean immigrants. "[I]t seemed to go without saying," Palumbo-Liu writes, "that 'orientals,' whom the Commission agreed should be excluded from the nation, were not susceptible to such transformation, no matter how intense or lengthy their exposure — both the physiognomic and the psychic gaps to be crossed were too great" (*Asian/American* 86). The Commission's study of the immigrants' body is predicated on the assumption of a natural correlation between corporeal characteristics and mental makeups. The body regarded as a mode of expression of mentality or a psychical interior becomes a marker of essentialized racial difference.

In the context of the body politic of the U.S. nation-state, Lee's investigation and re-articulation of the corporeality of the body in his autobiographical poems achieve the effect of specifying the raced and gendered bodies of the self and others, while undermining their socially constructed identities. His poems displace the privilege of interiority as the locus of subjectivity, thus severing the naturalized bond between the surface of the body and its interiority. In poems such as "Irises," "Dreaming of Hair," and "Always A Rose" collected in his first volume, *Rose* (1986), Lee's investigation of the corporeal is an exploration of the invisible, an encounter with alterity. The corporeal self in these poems is at once connected to and separate from other bodies, including flower-bodies. This relation of connection without fusion between self and other renders an ethical relationship to otherness possible.

Apart from a corporeal aesthetic, Lee's displacement of the I as the organizing principle of the poem, as shown in "Persimmons," helps the establishment of an ethical self-other relationship. Lee develops these two major aspects of his poetics in his longer poems such as "Always A Rose" and "Rain Diary," which are extended explorations of his central themes. An irreducible material body and an embodiment of love, the rose in "Always A Rose" lends itself to multiple associations, heterogeneous meanings, and encounters with alterity, while its materiality is bound to decay and death. Lee's employment of the rose as the organizing principle of the poem allows others to enter the poetic space through their responses to and associations with the rose. With reference to the rose left for the dead, Lee's persona speculates how each member of his family would respond to it, thus acknowledging the individual particularity of each:

Of my brothers
one would have ignored it,
another ravished it, the third
would have pinned it to his chest and swaggered home.
My sister would rival its beauty,
my mother bow before it, then bear it
to my father's grave, where
he would grant it seven days,
then return and claim it forever.
I took it,
put it in water,
and set it on my windowsill. (*Rose* 37)

By introducing family members into the poem as individuals, each having a different relation to the rose and a unique inner life, Lee breaks away from what Charles Altieri calls a formulaic mode of contemporary Asian American autobiographical poetry. In his 1995 essay, "Images of Form vs. Images of Content in Contemporary Asian-American Poetry," Altieri states that "Most Asian-American poetry and almost all criticism of that poetry now concentrates on images of content — as testimony to typical conditions in first- and second- generation immigrant cultures and as the actual work of coming to terms with contradictions and demands" in negotiating with culturally and socially constructed conflicting identities and marginalization in mainstream America ("Images" 72). Lee's poetry resists this categorization. Rather than negotiating with Asian Americans' culturally and socially constructed identities and their marginalization in mainstream America, Lee refutes these identities and resists their impositions through autobiographical lyric which rearticulates the socially and culturally defined body. In investigating the corporeality and articulating the spirituality of those whose bodies and subjectivity are racially marked, Lee's autobiographical lyric insists on addressing the human condition of love, suffering, mortality, and desire for immortality — familiar themes of universal humanity in Western lyric — through a new sensibility and poetics that reinscribe the universal in terms of heterogenous particularities.

Just as he resists reducing the rose to a conventional metaphor, or to an image of his lyric speaker's ideas, Lee refuses to represent the body as merely a social, cultural, or historical product. In section 3 of "Always A Rose," for instance, the speaker contemplates his connections to other human bodies, to animal bodies, and other bodies in nature through association with the materiality of the rose, erasing negative markers of the raced body:

3.
When with arrows, night pierces you, rose,
I see most clearly
your true nature.
Small, aurora, your death is large.
You live, you die with me, in spite
of me, like my sleeping wife.

. . . . . . . . .


My arms and legs are the rain in its opulence,
my face my mother's face.
My hair is also hers.
She inherited it from the horses
who recovered it from the night.
Here is what is left: a little brown, bits of black, a few specks
    of light.
Here are my shoulders and their winglessness,
my spine, the arc of love.
And here on my belly
is a stripe of skin, hairless
and the color of old blood.
Beginning at the navel, it descends into the tangled hairs.
Vestige, omen, this is the stain
which at my birth my father
traced with his finger
while pronouncing in dread
that I was born half girl.
So I was given the remedy of the rose,
made to eat you whole, swallow your medicinal taste. (*Rose* 39)

In its corporeality, the speaker's body becomes one of vastly different kinds of material bodies in the world. The irreducibly corporeal body of the speaker is a site of multiple connections, distinctions, regulations, and encounters. It binds the speaker to the forsythia-body, the pine-body, the parents-body, and the horse-body among other bodies, yet it also separates the speaker from all other bodies. In his reading of this poem, Johnny Lorenz notes that as "a palimpsest of ancestry," human "faces are, in a sense, versions of a text, but versions that suggest the impossibility of exact origins," as Lee's lines — "my face my mother's face. / My hair is also hers. / She inherited it from the horses / who recovered it from the night" — suggest. "In these lines," Lorenz contends, "Lee reads his own face as a recurrence, and he reimagines the shadowy ruins of origin through a private myth-making: his ancestors are horses. . . . While a face reproduces itself, never exactly, as a family inheritance, it is also the returning mark and cause of otherness" (158). But genealogy and its link to naturalized racial otherness are precisely what Lee undermines in these lines. Rather than "the returning mark and cause of otherness," I would argue, Lee's surrealistic assertion of the face here challenges and removes the social inscriptions of the raced, gendered, cultural, or national otherness by disrupting family lineage and unsettling bodily hierarchy, linking his and his mother's bodies to animal and vegetable bodies. In contrast to his dismantling of socially constructed categories of bodies, Lee's reference to the father's horror at his son's apparently bodily anomaly suggests that when interpreted in a cultural framework, the uniqueness of the speaker's body can become a deviation from the norm of gender identity; his bodily surfaces can become a sign of blemish or omen. But this physical anomaly of the individual is regulated, or normalized, with material remedy through eating.

With the apparently autobiographical reference to eating roses as remedy, Lee introduces into the poem another theme — opening the self to the other and transforming the self through otherness — which underlies the motif of eating in this and Lee's other poems. The concept of accepting otherness into sameness for the sake of self-transforming differs significantly from that of assimilation, which suggests coercing the other to conform to the dominant norm. As the poem develops, eating becomes an act of confronting suffering, of trying to understand the self and others, and of investigating otherness:

4.
Odorous and tender flower-
body, I eat you
to recall my first misfortune.
Little, bitter
body, I eat you
to understand my grave father.
Excellent body of layers tightly
wound around nothing,
I eat you to put my faith in grief.
Singed at the edges, dying
from the flame you live by, I
eat you to sink into
my own body. Secret body
of deep liquor,
I eat you
down to your secret. (*Rose* 40)

Eating as a response to otherness renders the self vulnerable and susceptible to the other because of the self's corporeality. Thus eating serves more than a cognitive function; it enacts openness to and contact with the other through what Levinas might call "sensuous exposure" to alterity. As Alphonso Lingis points out, "sensibility as savoring" for Levinas "is a susceptibility to being affected, in which not only a reception of messages, but the living of life is at stake." Hence, "Levinas wants to locate, beneath the sensuous exposure to material and as its basis, the exposure to alterity" ("Translator's Introduction" *OB* xxvii). Lee's emphasis on his lyric subject's corporeality and sensuous exposure to alterity prevents the lyric I from assuming mastery of or domination over the other.

By relating the lyric I's body to the rose body, while maintaining the otherness of the rose and investigating the alterity of death, Lee disrupts the hierarchy of the raced and gendered body, as well as the body-versus-mind binary in Western philosophy, which Grosz critiques. Hence not only does Lee's corporeal aesthetics undermine the essence of gender in the coding of mind and body in Western philosophy and lyric poetry, it also subverts the assumed racial essence fixed on the raced bodies as indicated in the *Immigration Report* on the assimilation process of particular ethnic groups. Lee's exploration of his persona's body and the rose-body suggests that there are no inherently fixed meanings of the interior which correspond to bodily surfaces, as essentialist discourses on race, gender, and culture would suggest.

In fact, Lee goes beyond undermining social inscriptions of the raced and gendered body. Relying on the multiplicity of the rose, including its embodiment of love and beauty, the speaker in section 5 offers a rose to numerous others, particularly those who have suffered from poverty or discrimination, and who have been banished from one country and remain marginal or invisible in another:

> And there is one I love, who hid her heart behind a stone.
> Let there be a rose for her, who was poor,
>
> . . . . . . . . . . . . . . . .
>
> And there is one I love, smallest among us –
> let there be a rose for him –
> who was driven from the foreign schoolyards
> by fists and yelling, who trembled in anger in each
>     re-telling,
> who played alone all the days,
> though the afternoon trees were full of children.
>
> . . . . . . . . . . . . . . . .
>
> exiled from one republic and daily defeated in another,
> who was shunned by brothers and stunned by God,
>
> . . . . . . . . . . . . . . . . .
>
>     For him a rose, my lover of roses and of God,
> who taught me to love the rose, and fed me roses, under
>     whose windows
> I planted roses, for whose tables I harvested roses,
>
> . . . . . . . . . . . . . . . .
>
> My father among the roses and thorns.
> My father rose, my father thorn. (*Rose* 41–42)

Through multiple associations with the rose, Lee directs the reader's attention to the lives of those who are poor, ostracized, and dislocated refugees and immigrants, especially to their interiority — a spirituality that renders their socially defined otherness or bodily difference "invisible."

Although Lee does not reject the conventional meanings of the rose, he refuses to allow the rose to become merely an image of the speaker's thought, or an object of the speaking subject's knowledge. The corporeality of both the speaker and the rose is central throughout the poem; the rose remains irreducibly material and other. As the speaker says to the rose: "Open me, thorn-flower!" "You sag, / turn your face / from me, body / made of other bodies, each doomed" (*Rose* 43, 44). Despite his connection to the rose-body, the speaker finds the secret of the rose inaccessible: "Still you say nothing. / So keep secret, secret" (*Rose* 43). The secret of the rose, the poem suggests, is the secret of death — the absolute unknowable other whose presence breaks the solitude of the subject, and undermines its intentionality.

Lee further develops his corporeal aesthetics in "Rain Diary" to explore deeper implications of the corporeal subject's relationship to death as the unknowable other. In this poem, death, like rain, arrives unexpectedly and leaves without a trace, stirring the lyric speaker and compelling him to explore its unknowable mystery. At the same time, the speaker wishes to expose the corporeal self to alterity to be transformed by this contact:

> I want the rain
> to follow me, to mark me
> with a stripe down my chest and belly,
> to darken my skin, and blacken my hair.
> I want to be broken,
> to be eroded like minutes and seconds,
> to be reduced to water
> and to little light.
>
> .  .  .  .  .  .  .
>
> I want to rise,
> the doors of the rain to open,
> I will enter, rain alive
> among my fingers, embroidered on my tongue, and brilliant
>     in my eyes,
> I want to carry it in my shirt pocket,
> devote my life to the discovery of its secret,
> .  .  .  .  .  .  .  .  .  .  .  .   (*Rose* 61)

Rather than assuming knowledge of the other, or seeking to master otherness, Lee's lyric I wishes to be "broken," "reduced," and changed through sensuous exposure to alterity. This embodied self-other relationship challenges the all-encompassing unity of the Emersonian "Over-Soul, within which every man's particular being is contained and made one with all other" ("The Over-Soul" 871). Nature and death as the unknowable absolute other in Lee's poems call into question the Emersonian definition of the "NOT ME" as a transparent object of knowledge like "an open book" ("Nature" 791, 802).

The encounter with death as the absolute other, Levinas contends, challenges the subject's mastery over the self and the exterior world. "What is important about the approach of death is that at a certain moment we are no longer *able to be able*. It is exactly thus that the subject loses its very mastery as a subject." For "an *event* can happen to us" without our assumption about or control over it. "This approach of death indicates that we are in relation with something that is absolutely other, something bearing alterity. . . . My solitude is thus not confirmed by death but broken by it" (*TO* 74). In facing death as the unknowable other, the traditional autonomous, solitary lyric I is no longer alone; its self-contained, self-sufficient consciousness can no longer assume mastery over everything that is not the self. In Lee's poems, death as the absolute other is inaccessible, ungraspable, irreducible to the subject's knowledge. Its alterity is beyond the subject's intentionality and defies its intellect and rationality. Levinas emphasizes that the other is outside any totality; its relationship with the self is not a harmonious fusion in which the other loses its alterity. Rather, the other "is not unknown but unknowable, refractory to all light. But this precisely indicates that the other is in no way another myself, participating with me in a common existence" (*TO* 75). This concept of the other underlies the corporeal aesthetic and recurrent themes of mortality and desire in Lee's poems.

## Desire for the Other

In Lee's poems about love, such as the title poem of his second volume, "The City in Which I Love You," it is through embodied subjectivity that the lyric I is attracted to the other and enthralled by the other's alterity. In his interview with Bill Moyers, Lee says that this poem is inspired by the "Song of Songs," one of his favorite works because of its "celebration of sexual love" and its "scope and grandeur and intensity" (Moyers 265). In his discussion of "The City in Which I Love You," Walter A. Hesford suggests a direct connection between Lee's appropriation of the "luxuriant imagery of the biblical Song" and his aesthetics of exuberant expression. According to Hesford, Lee at a reading "compared the poet to the woman who anoints Jesus' head with precious nard, her extravagant spilling proof that there is abundance in the world (see Mark 14:3–9)." Hesford adds, "Lee associates such giving over of oneself to extravagant expression with an Eastern *vis à vis* Western ethos" (39). Rather than attributing the affective exuberance of Lee's lyric to a binarized ethos, I would argue that an ethical self-other relationship is embedded in Lee's sensuous aesthetics, in his persona's erotic, metaphysical desire for the other.

According to Levinas, desire that is fundamentally different from need resulting from lack is crucial for an ethical self-other relationship. He argues, "Desire is desire for the absolutely Other." Unlike need, desire for the other cannot be satisfied. "A desire without satisfaction," Levinas adds, should be understood in terms of "the remoteness, the alterity, and the exteriority of the other" (*TI* 34). The proximity and alterity of the other are necessary conditions for the subject's desire. In the final section of *Totality and Infinity*, Levinas discusses erotic love as a most intense form of desire. Caress, not assimilation or possession, most appropriately characterizes the self-other relationship in desire. As Colin Davis explains in his book on Levinas: "In erotic love neither self nor Other is abolished; both are in fact confirmed, since the Other is desired as Other, not as an other to be reduced to the Same. The loved one is *caressed* but not *possessed*" (46). Lee articulates a self-other relationship as such through his lyric speaker's erotic desire for the other.

In "The City in Which I Love You," Lee employs a corporeal aesthetic and extravagant language as a gesture of responding to the other. Morever, as the title indicates, the city — a space of heterogeneity where one encounters strangers, including the exiled, the persecuted, the impoverished from around the world — embodies the range of diverse populations and the challenges they pose to homogeneity. Against this urban background, the poem's theme of love is particularly compelling in its ethical implications. Alluding to the quest for love and the celebration of both male and female erotic desire in the "Song of Songs," Lee uses a passage in chapter 3, verse 2 of the "Song" as the epigram of his poem:

> I will arise now, and go
> about the city in the streets,
> and in the broad ways I will seek . . .
> whom my soul loveth. ("Song of Songs" 3:2)

Incorporating the motif of the quest for love from the biblical "Song," Lee takes the reader on a journey of discovering the city in which his persona seeks his loved one. This journey is ultimately an ethical event of responding to the other with love, desire, and compassion without assuming oneness that erases the difference between self and other:

> And when, in the city in which I love you,
> even my most excellent song goes unanswered,
> and I mount the scabbed streets,
> the long shouts of avenues,
> and tunnel sunken night in search of you. . . .
>
> Past the guarded schoolyards, the boarded-up churches,
>     swastikaed
> synagogues, defended houses of worship, past
> newspapered windows of tenements, among the violated,
> the prosecuted citizenry, throughout this
> storied, buttressed, scavenged, policed
> city I call home, in which I am a guest. . . . (City 51)

This city which the speaker calls "home," yet in which he is "a guest," is not restricted to one particular city in the United States. The references to violence and crime, including "the guarded schoolyards, the boarded-up churches," and "swastikaed synagogues" allude to both the differences among the populations living in the city and to the responses to them with fear and hatred. Against this background of intolerance of and violence against the other, and associated with his feelings of dislocation and alienation as an immigrant in exile, the speaker's articulation of erotic love for the other is particularly poignant and significant.

In contrast to the impersonal, alienating background of the urban space, Lee rearticulates the erotic love in the "Song of Songs," enhancing the intensity and sensuality of the speaker's desire while calling attention to his vulnerability. In the biblical verse, the desire of both the male and female speakers is stated in more than one voice: "By night on my bed I sought him whom my soul loveth: I sought him, but I found him not" ("Song of Solomon" 3:1); "Thou has ravished my heart, my sister, my spouse; thou hast ravished my heart with one of thine eyes, with one chain of thy neck" ("Song of Solomon" 4:9). Even though there is only one male speaker in his poem, Lee is able to achieve the effect of what Levinas calls "an-nounc[ing] the ethical inviolability of the Other" (*TI* 195) through a corporeal aesthetic and language-act as saying which posits the female other as subject. While asserting his love and desire for the female other, Lee's persona entreats her to pursue him, offering his erotic love as a caress through voluptuous profuseness:

My tongue remembers your wounded flavor.
The vein in my neck
adores you. A sword
stands up between my hips,
my hidden fleece sends forth its scent of human oil.

The shadows under my arms,
I promise, are tender, the shadows
under my face. Do not calculate,
but come, smooth other, rough sister.
Yet, how will you know me

among the captives, my hair grown long,
my blood motley, my ways trespassed upon?
In the uproar, the confusion
of accents and inflections,
how will you hear me when I open my mouth?

Look for me, one of the drab population
under fissured edifices, fractured
artifices. Make my various
names flock overhead,
I will follow you.
Hew me to your beauty. (*City* 52)

The lyric I articulates his erotic desire for the other through precisely the kind of saying by which the speaking subject is rendered vulnerable and insufficient. This turning of the self to the other for the other makes it impossible for Lee's lyric I to assume domination over or possession of the female other. As Lee's persona pleads to her: "Hew me to your beauty."

Moreover, Lee's lyric persona in this poem is a socially and culturally defined other by the dominant culture in a nation-state where he is a "guest." By identifying himself as "one of the drab population under fissured edifices," whose voice is lost in "the confusion of accents and inflections," Lee again identifies the speaker as an immigrant, refugee, and exile. This identification of the lyric I with those who usually exist in the margins of mainstream American society, and whose individuality becomes obsolete under a collective racial or ethnic category, has the effect of restoring the humanity of those who are deprived of it. Hence the speaker in this poem is at once a particular and generic socially defined other whose unique individuality is irreducible to his collective identity. By referring to himself as one of the others ("Look for me, one of the drab population"), while emphasizing the self's difference from others ("they are not me forever"), Lee is able to relate the self to others without losing the individuality of the self or reducing the alterity of the other. This relationship enables Lee to respond to a wide range of particular others and their tribulations, as the speaker continues to articulate his association with and separateness from others, in his pursuit of the loved one through numerous cities where violence and persecution are taking place:

In the excavated places,
I waited for you, and I did not cry out.
In the derelict rooms, my body needed you,
and there was such flight in my breast.
During the daily assaults, I called to you,

and my voice pursued you,
even backward
to that other city
in which I saw a woman
squat in the street

beside a body,
and fan with a handkerchief flies from its face.
That woman
was not me. And
The corpse

lying there, lying there
so still it seemed with great effort, as though
his whole being was concentrating on the hole
in his forehead, so still
I expected he'd sit up any minute and laugh out loud:

that man was not me;
his wound was his, his death not mine.
And the soldier
who fired the shot, then lit a cigarette:
he was not me.

And the ones I do not see
in cities all over the world,
the ones sitting, standing, lying down, those
in prisons playing checkers with their knocked-out teeth:
they are not me. Some of them are

my age, even my height and weight;
none of them is me.
The woman who is slapped, the man who is kicked,
the ones who don't survive,
whose names I do not know;

they are not me forever,
the ones who no longer live
in the cities in which
you are not,
the cities in which I looked for you. (*City* 53–55)

The geographical span this poem covers, and the range of diversity
and multiplicity of people it describes evoke Walt Whitman's poems,
particularly those of *Leaves of Grass*. In his discussion of Whitman's
reinvention of the self and of the Romantic lyric I, Lawrence Buell
argues that the urban environment of New York City plays a crucial
role. In writing about the city and its populations, Buell notes,

Whitman converts diverse city dwellers "into an unprecedentedly sensitive barometer of the transformations of selfhood under urban conditions" (91). Buell considers Whitman's reinvention of the Romantic model of the lyric speaker one of his greatest innovative achievements: "One of Whitman's greatest innovations was to destabilize the autonomy of the Romantic persona more radically than any had attempted. The Whitmanian speaker becomes by turns atomized and omniscient, observer and participant, unitary and fragmented into a social collage, interchangeable with others. Animating this strategy were a 'democratic' ideal of equality and fraternity and a 'Transcendentalist' ideal of the inherent divinity of every person" (91). Buell emphasizes that "it is hard to imagine Whitman making his breakthrough of persona reinvention without benefit of urban context" (91). Against the background of the metropolitan urban space of New York City, where one encounters strangers from around the world on a daily basis, Whitman's poetic breakthrough entails an ethical response to the other. Buell points out that though Whitman is fully aware of, and even allows for, the instinct of self-withdrawal against urban violence, he insists on "reaching out" to make contact with strangers because "an urban inhabitance worthy of the name is not to be self-isolating and segmented, but carried on in the awareness of reciprocity with others" (98–100).

It seems that to articulate a sense of union, of oneness and sameness of self and others — strangers of various racial, ethnic backgrounds, of different gender, age, and class — is a major strategy through which Whitman's persona enacts his democratic ideal and responsibility for civility and community of an "urban inhabitance." This sense of oneness also characterizes Whitman's radical destabilization of "the autonomy of the Romantic persona." As the speaker of "Song of Myself" states:

> I celebrate myself,
> And what I assume you shall assume,
> For every atom belonging to me as good belongs to you.
>
> .   .   .   .   .   .   .   .   .   .   .   .   .   .   .   .   .   .
>
> This is the city . . . . and I am one of the citizens;
> Whatever interests the rest interests me . . . . politics,
>      churches, newspapers, schools,
>
> .   .   .   .   .   .   .   .   .   .   .   .

I acknowledge the duplicates of myself under all the
　　scrape-lipped and pipe-legged concealments.

. . . . . . . . . . . . . . . .

The weakest and shallowest is deathless with me,
What I do and say the same waits for them,
Every thought that flounders in me the same flounders in
　　them. (27, 65, 76)

Despite these assertions of a democratic ideal of equality and frater-
nity among all, the speaker's insistence on his oneness with and
knowledge of everyone seems to erase or suppress differences be-
tween self and other. By reducing otherness to self-sameness, the al-
terity of the other is absorbed or "violated" by this self-sameness.
This equating of self with other, though it articulates a radical demo-
cratic ideal in Whitman's time and place, seems to eliminate the eth-
ical distance between self and other.

Perhaps it is precisely in seeking to counter homogenizing one-
ness with the other — a unity in which otherness is absorbed or re-
pressed — that Lee's persona insists on the other's proximity which is
a premise for an ethical self-other relationship. Unlike Whitman's
persona, who identifies himself with various others, Lee's speaker ac-
centuates the difference between self and other. As the speaker re-
peatedly says, "That woman / was not me"; "that man was not me";
"none of them is me"; "they are not me." Even though he refers to
himself as "one of the drab population," Lee's lyric speaker refuses to
assume oneness with numerous others — "the violated, / the prose-
cuted citizenry" in cities around the world — whose suffering and
oppression he takes note of and gives voice to.

Rather than assuming unity with or knowledge of the other, the
speaker embraces the unknowable mystery of the other — an alterity
that fascinates, ravishes, yet remains elusive:

And your otherness is perfect as my death.
Your otherness exhausts me,
like looking suddenly up from here
to impossible stars fading.
Everything is punished by your absence.

. . . . . . . . . . . . .

Where are you

in the cities in which I love you,
the cities daily risen to work and to money,
to the magnificent miles and the gold coasts?

.   .   .   .   .   .   .   .   .   .   .   .   .   .

Between brick walls, in space no wider than my face,
a leafless sapling stands in mud.
In its branches, a nest of raw mouths
gaping and cheeping, scrawny fires that must eat.
My hunger for you is no less than theirs. (*City* 55–56)

As the speaker's desire extends from erotic love to hunger for the
spiritual, the immaterial in "the cities daily risen to work and to
money," the poem moves from erotic desire to a yearning that opens
the self to others and to alterity itself.

It is worth noting that the speaker emphasizes that his experience
of banishment, exclusion, and displacement enables him to love the
other whose otherness is "perfect" as his "death":

Like the sea, I am recommended by my orphaning.
Noisy with telegrams not received,
quarrelsome with aliases,
intricate with misguided journeys,
by my expulsions have I come to love you.

.   .   .   .   .   .   .   .   .   .   .   .   .

my birthplace vanished, my citizenship earned,
in league with stones of the earth, I
enter, without retreat or help from history,
the days of no day, my earth
of no earth, I re-enter

the city in which I love you.
And I never believed that the multitude
of dreams and many words were vain. (*City* 56–57)

Being a refugee, immigrant, new citizen of the United States, one of
"the drab population" with "accents and inflections," this lyric I trans-
forms the conventional lyric I as the poet-I who is at the center of the
society and its culture, replacing its autonomous consciousness, its
disembodied transcendental ego with an embodied subject, whose
blood is "motley" and "ways trespassed upon." Yet, this lyric speaker

is also a poet who "never believed that the multitude / of dreams and many words were vain."

By identifying a socially excluded and marginalized other with the lyric I as the poet-I, Lee dismantles racial and ethnic stereotypes that reduce the other's alterity to a threat or an abject otherness to be excluded, assimilated, or erased. At the same time, Lee's poem redefines otherness beyond social and ideological constructs in which the model minority and the "bad subject" are mutually constitutive and exclusive.

### Transforming the Universal through Otherness

Lee's exploration of the ethics and poetics of alterity entails more than a critical intervention in the social production or assimilation of otherness. In rearticulating the lyric I and the self-other relationship, Lee's poetry transgresses the confinement of both the racial subject and so-called ethnic literature, challenging the latter's seemingly inevitable thematic and stylistic limitations. Lee says in an interview that his family history of exile is not typical only of the Asian American experience. "I always thought that trying to find an earthly home was a human condition," Lee asserts. "It is arrogant of the dominant culture to think it's not part of a diaspora. My hope is that somebody who isn't Asian American can read it and say, Well, I feel that homeless, too." He adds that for Asian American writers to resist labels of group identities that confine them to "a little ghetto" is a necessary "transgression" (J. K. Lee 279).

Transgression as such in Lee's poems involves simultaneously employing and moving beyond autobiographical particularities and socially, culturally constructed identities in order to rearticulate socially constructed otherness. The complex functions of speaking as and to the other subverts the definition of otherness according to the dominant culture, and undermines an exclusive universality naturalized as the privilege of a particular race (white) and gender (male). Lee negotiates a politicized aesthetic of universality in such a way as to enact what Palumbo-Liu calls "a transformative operation upon the universal" which "has traditionally been articulated by a particular dominant class that has monopolized and naturalized it as their property" ("Universalisms" 203, 202). The content of the traditional universality, Palumbo-Liu points out, is "largely determined by precisely those who claim a particular affinity to that content, to the exclusion of those who do not." He adds: "To have access to it, the minor has been told to strip away the particularities of its identity that may not conform to that demanded by the Universal. It is precisely that *function* of the universal that has to be addressed, and one possible mode of intervention is to radically contest the *content* of the universal" ("Universalisms" 202). Lee's poems intervene in the monopoly of universality by breaking its attachment to any exclusive content, and refiguring the universal through those particularities which have been excluded from it.

Despite its autobiographical particularities, the lyric I in Lee's poems is not defined or confined by autobiographical details or by his socially constructed identities. In fact, Lee's use of autobiographical materials enables him to identify with the socially and culturally marked other, while subverting sexist and racist representations of otherness, by articulating a multiple, heterogenous, undefinable otherness and by enacting an alternative mode of responding to the other. Lee achieves a remarkable effect of radically contesting "the *content* of the universal" in the closing poem, "Cleaving," of his second volume, *The City in Which I Love You.* In this intensely lyrical poem, which responds more directly to the socially constructed abject otherness of poor immigrants and racialized others in the United States, Lee articulates a more complex relationship between self and other. At the same time, the corporeality of the body takes on a wider range of meanings and connotations. As in Lee's other poems, the lyric I is apparently autobiographical, but it refuses to be contained in its particularities. While maintaining his ethnic Chinese identity and making references to his family, the lyric speaker addresses larger human conditions such as diaspora and mortality. The poem begins with the speaker's observation of a Chinese butcher in Chinatown, whose condition of dislocation reminds him of his grandfather. The speaker's close attention to the delicate details of the Chinese butcher's face performs an ethical response to the other whose various differences resist homogenizing categories of race or ethnicity:

He gossips like my grandmother, this man
with my face, and I could stand

amused all afternoon
in the Hon Kee Grocery,

.  .  .  .  .  .  .  .  .

Such a sorrowful Chinese face,
nomad, Gobi, Northern
in its boniness
clear from the high
warlike forehead
to the sheer edge of the jaw.
He could be my brother, but finer,
and, except for his left forearm, which is engorged,
sinewy from his daily grip and
wield of a two-pound tool,

.  .  .  .  .  .  .  .  .  .

In his light-handed calligraphy
on receipts and in his
moodiness, he is
A Southerner from a river-province;
suited for scholarship, his face poised
above an open book, he'd mumble
his favorite passages.
He could be my grandfather;
come to America to get a Western education
in 1917, but too homesick to study,
he sits in the park all day, reading poems
and writing letters to his mother. (*City* 77–78)

While the "sorrowful" expression on the butcher's face at once re-
veals and conceals his inner world, the unique individuality of his fa-
cial structure shows similarities with and differences from other
Chinese faces, thus suggesting ethnic and individual diversity which
undermines racist stereotypes by "reconstituting the gaze of domi-
nant culture," to borrow Eleanor Ty's phrase (27). The speaker's ap-
preciation of the butcher's Chinese features and their individual
uniqueness provides a sharp contrast to Emerson's remarks about the
Chinese which Lee challenges later in the poem. Paying further atten-
tion to the Chinese butcher as a distinct individual, the speaker's com-
ment on the butcher's style of calligraphy on receipts is another way
of foregrounding the butcher's individuality, since calligraphy is

supposed to reflect the writer's personality and individual uniqueness. Reference to the butcher's absorption in his reading at his job indicates this Chinese immigrant's dislocation in the new country, where he is stuck with a job for survival, unable to pursue his own interests or develop his talent. In addition, association of this Chinese immigrant, reading in a butcher's shop, with the speaker's grandfather who came to "America to get a Western education / in 1917, but too homesick to study," sat "in the park all day, reading poems," partly suggests their feelings of exile and alienation in the United States, and partly indicates their alterity which resists assimilation by the dominant culture.

Moreover, the butcher's cleaving of the dead bodies of animals evokes human corporeality, vulnerability, and mortality, while its brutality resonates different kinds of violence throughout the poem. In the social space of the United States, the body which bears the social inscriptions of otherness can become a target for violence. But violence in this poem, as in Lee's other poems, is also related to a desire for change and for self-transformation. The paradox in the process of self-transformation through encounter with otherness is embedded in the double meanings of "cleaving"—the speaker clings to that which severs. At the same time, the ferociousness of cleaving associated with the butcher and the animal carcasses continues to reverberate throughout the poem, evoking human carnality and its susceptibility to brutality, decay, and mutability. Thus the poem simultaneously asserts an ethnic identity and a universal humanity without opposing one against the other. By refusing to render the ethnic and the universal mutually exclusive, Lee achieves the effect of "insert[ing] within the discursive performance of 'universal' a kind of double-task, an alienation effect, that will evince precisely the friction of minor/dominant negotiations and forestall the term's automatic referencing of the old constellations of meaning" as Palumbo-Liu says is the task of a minority discourse in transforming the universal ("Universalisms" 205). Lee's enactment of this twin task becomes more prominent as the poem develops.

Shifting from the animal body to the human body, the speaker's observation of the corporeal moves from the particular to the universal. As the body moves beyond its social and individual particularities, it takes on a universality that is at once material and spiritual. The speaker, then, connects this universality of human corporeality and spirituality to the Chinese butcher and to the exiled and poor immigrants:

> The noise the body makes
> when the body meets
> the soul over the soul's ocean and penumbra
> is the old sound of up-and-down, in-and-out,
> a lump of muscle chug-chugging blood
> into the ear; a lover's
> heart-shaped tongue;
> flesh rocking flesh until flesh comes;
> the butcher working
> at his block and blade to marry their shapes
> by violence and time;
> an engine crossing,
> re-crossing salt water, hauling
> immigrants and the junk
> of the poor. These
> are the faces I love, the bodies
> and scents of bodies
> for which I long
> in various ways, at various times,
> . . . . . . . . . *(City* 80)

Significantly, Lee arranges the lines in such a way that the universalized human body and soul are immediately associated through syntactic structure to poor immigrants' bodies on the junk — those human bodies which are marked as undesirable by their differences of race, gender, class, and nationality in the social space — thus breaking down the hierarchy of social inscriptions on the body. Through the lyric I's articulation of universal love for universal humanity embodied by poor immigrants, Lee produces precisely the kind of "alien effect" which Palumbo-Liu speaks of, one that forestalls universality's "automatic referencing of the old constellations of meaning." Just as those bodies are various, so are the ways of the speaker's love for them.

Equally significant is Lee's insistence on particularities and differences within the universal. Rejecting purity, homogeneity, hierarchy, and totality, Lee celebrates diversity and individual uniqueness:

> Brothers and sisters by blood and design,
> who sit in separate bodies of varied shapes,
> we constitute a many-membered
> body of love.
> In a world of shapes
> of my desire, each one here
> is a shape of one of my desires, and each
> is known to me and dear by virtue
> of each one's unique corruption
> of those texts, the face, the body:
> that jut jaw
> to gnash tendon;
> that wide nose to meet the blows
> a face like that invites;
> those long eyes closing on the seen;
> those thick lips
> to suck the meat of animals
> or recite 300 poems of the T'ang;
> these teeth to bite my monosyllables;
> these cheekbones to make
> those syllables sing the soul.
> Puffed or sunken
> according to the life,
> dark or light according
> to the birth, straight
> or humped, whole, manqué, quasi, each pleases, verging
> on utter grotesquery.
> All are beautiful by variety.
> The soul too
> is a debasement
> of a text. (*City* 81)

Lee's embrace of body and soul, and a variety of bodies as equals regardless of their socially defined values and meanings, is reminiscent of Whitman's articulation of a composite democratic self in "Song of Myself." But there are some significant differences between the lyric I in Lee's poem and that in Whitman's.

The "I" in "Song of Myself" is a composite, multitudinous, au-
thoritative self who contains heterogeneous others and speaks for
others: "what I assume you shall assume." Regarding all things and all
peoples on equal terms, and identifying himself with every type and
aspect of humanity, Whitman's lyric I embodies the ideals of an in-
clusive democracy. Yet, this self also seems to stand for a homogeniz-
ing nation that reduces alterity to the self-same, absorbing otherness
into oneness. The proximity of the other, the resistance of alterity
to transparency, which are crucial conditions for an ethical relation-
ship between self and other, are erased by the claims of sameness
Whitman's lyric I makes. Rather than being transformed by the other,
Whitman's lyric I assimilates the other. His lyric speaker's turning
toward the other always returns to the self, to "home" — the familiar,
the already known.[3]

The lyric I in Lee's poem resists such fusion with the other as
Whitman's all-encompassing self claims. While evoking a Whitman-
esque democratic universality, Lee departs from the assimilative ten-
dency of Whitman's composite self by insisting on the distance be-
tween self and other. He maintains this distance through articulation
of a metaphysical desire for the other. Asserting an insatiable hunger
for otherness, Lee's lyric I establishes an ethical relation with alterity,
in which the other maintains its distance and difference. "A desire
without satisfaction," Levinas contends, is one which precisely "*un-
derstands* the remoteness, the alterity, and the exteriority of the
other" (*TI* 34). This desire for the other characterizes the love Lee's
lyric I articulates, which enacts an ethical relationship with the other,
"without this distance destroying this relation and without this rela-
tion destroying this distance," as Levinas says of the necessary con-
dition for alterity to resist totality (*TI* 41). Far from assuming unity
with, or mastery over the other, the self in Lee's poem is compelled
by unfathomable plenitude of the other and the world to sing and
explore:

and I feel urged to utterance,
urged to read the body of the world, urged
to say it
in human terms,
my reading a kind of eating, my eating
a kind of reading,

my saying a diminishment, my noise
a love-in-answer.
What is it in me would
devour the world to utter it?
What is it in me will not let
the world be, would eat
not just this fish,
but the one who killed it,
the butcher who cleaned it.
I would eat the way he
squats, the way he
reaches into the plastic tubs
and pulls out a fish, clubs it, takes it
to the sink, guts it, drops it on the weighing pan. (*City* 82)

While resonating with violence and death, the motif of eating takes on another dimension of meaning when equated with reading. In a study of the metaphysics and politics of eating in Chinese and Chinese American literature, Gang Yue notes that "the Chinese term 'eating,' encompasses a far broader semantic and discursive field and possesses more generative and transformative capacities than its English counterpart" (ii). Lee incorporates and expands on the Chinese concept of *eating* to articulate a multidimensional relationship between self and other, and between self and the world. As his lyric speaker asserts, "my reading a kind of eating, my eating / a kind of reading," eating, then, suggests not only an openness to the other, a hunger for otherness, but also an effort to understand, rather than define, the other. And reading, as a kind of eating, connotes more than a mode of interpretation; it indicates rendering the self vulnerable and susceptible to the other, by opening the self to the other, taking in what is not-me without reducing otherness to the self-same. Eventually, eating/reading in Lee's poem is associated with self-transformation through encounter with otherness.

The otherness of the other, moreover, compels Lee's lyric I to respond to it through saying as responsibility. The speaker's attempt to understand otherness in order to sing it, and his articulation of desire for the other, as well as his emphasis on the universal corporeality of himself and the immigrants, takes on more impetus as he begins to challenge Emerson's authority in defining the Chinese according to an exclusive universal standard for measuring human desirability:

> I would eat it all
> to utter it.
> The deaths at the sinks, those bodies prepared
> for eating, I would eat,
>
> .  .  .  .  .  .  .
>
> the death-far-from-home, the death-
> in-a-strange-land, these Chinatown
> deaths, these American deaths.
> I would devour this race to sing it,
> this race that according to Emerson
> *managed to preserve to a hair*
> *for three or four thousand years*
> *the ugliest features in the world.*
> I would eat these features, eat
> the last three or four thousand years, every hair.
> And I would eat Emerson, his transparent soul, his
> soporific transcendence.
> I would eat this head,
> glazed in pepper-speckled sauce,
> the cooked eyes opaque in their sockets. (*City* 83)

In contrast to the speaker's affectionate reading of the Chinese butcher's face, and in the context of racist violence referred to earlier in the poem — "that wide nose to meet the blows / a face like that invites" — Emerson's remarks about Chinese features are shown to be implicated in racist ideology.[4] The individual and collective bodies become raced in the social space and body politic of the United States. Slavery, genocide, and colonization have been justified by racializing the other's body according to the norm — a universality monopolized and naturalized as the property of a privileged category of whites.

Emerson's authoritative inscription of undesirable otherness on the Chinese body reveals a form of epistemological violence, which often underlies material violence against the other. Reducing the appearance of the other to a visible object of knowledge is a violation against alterity. Jill Robbins's insight in Levinas's ethics sheds light on the ethical dimension of this kind of epistemological violence. For

Levinas, Robbins contends, "there is violence in reducing a face to an object or thing seen" (*Reading* 57). Levinas contends that to evaluate the other as a transparent image is to "deface" the other (*IIRTB* 49). "The face is not of the order of the seen, it is not an object, but it is he whose appearing preserves an exteriority which is also an appeal or an imperative given to your responsibility" (*IIRTB* 48). But, Levinas points out, "the expression of racism" turns "qualitative differences and attributes into a value, as in the appreciation of things that one would possess or reject." To deface the other in this way, Levinas emphasizes, "is not to encounter the face of the other, not to respond to the uniqueness of the other" (*IIRTB* 111). Lee's incorporation of Emerson's words in his poem exposes Emerson's "defacing" of the other, and challenges the disembodied subjectivity underlying Emerson's claim of the Over-Soul. Lee undercuts the superiority of the mind over the body embedded in Emerson's concept of the self and the "NOT-ME" by indirectly emphasizing human corporeality and mortality through juxtaposition of Emerson's "soporific transcendence" with a cooked fish head, both of which Lee's lyric speaker would "eat." Through the motif of eating, Lee stresses the fact that as we eat "our deaths are fed / that we may continue our daily dying, / . . . . / As we eat we're eaten" (*City* 85). The inevitability of human mortality underlies the violence and passion of Lee's lyric utterance: "Else what is this / violence, this salt, this / passion, this heaven?" (*City* 86). It is precisely through corporeality and mortality that Lee's lyric I establishes an ethical relation with the other by responding to the other's suffering and uniqueness, and taking the other into account. As the speaker's detailed observation of the Chinese butcher's features indicates, Lee seeks to articulate difference that is not subordinated to identity, but is rather outside the dominance of the One, the self-same totality. In so doing, he enacts what Palumbo-Liu calls "a transformative operation upon the universal."

Further, in contrast to Emerson's "transparent soul," which "gives itself alone, original, and pure" ("The Over-Soul" 880), the soul for Lee "is a corruption / and a mnemonic" (*City* 82). For Emerson, the soul unifies and contains all under the sun: "that Unity, that Over-Soul, within which every man's particular being is contained and made one with all other" ("The Over-Soul" 871). But this all-encompassing universality seems to exclude from its rubric the Chinese with "the ugliest features in the world." Hence the pure, self-sufficient

Emersonian soul renders its unifying and homogenizing attribute an exclusive measure for a particular content of the universal, from which people with so-called undesirable features are banished or excluded. The body in Lee's poem then is a contested site not only of racial ideology and gender, class, and ethnic identities, but also of the content of universal humanity. Rejecting the unity and homogeneity of the Emersonian soul, Lee articulates an embodied, "cleaved" soul in a process of becoming:

> I thought the soul an airy thing.
> I did not know the soul
> is cleaved so that the soul might be restored.
> Live wood hewn,
> its sap springs from a sticky wound.
> No seed, no egg has he
> whose business calls for an axe.
> In the trade of my soul's shaping,
> he traffics in hews and hacks. (*City* 86)

The soul conceived in terms of a body being wounded so as to be remade, rejects binary oppositions such as body versus mind, subject versus object, and the corporeal versus the spiritual. In escaping dichotomy as such, the soul also loses its privilege of immateriality. Thus the soul, like the body, is vulnerable. Both the body and soul suffer and change as a result of encounters with the other; both are "passive" and not self-sufficient in relation to the other. Rather than pure, virtuous, and transcendental, the soul for Lee's persona "traffics in hews and hacks" as it is being shaped in its constant process of becoming.

The violence involved in the soul's making, like that in the motif of eating, is a condition for change, a result from opening the self to the other. An embodied self-other relationship as such breaks away from the kind of oneness embedded in Whitman's all-knowing, all-encompassing self and in Emerson's Over-Soul. Violence then in Lee's poem presupposes the vulnerability of the corporeal self and the irreducible alterity of the other, just as violence is an inevitable force that activates change of the embodied subject in the process of transformation. Lee further expands on the complex meanings of violence by situating the speaker's articulation of the self-other relationship in a much wider social and cultural context, as the closing of the poem returns to the Chinese butcher's cleaving and his sorrowful face:

> No easy thing, violence.
> One of its names? Change. Change
> resides in the embrace
> of the effaced and the effacer,
> in the covenant of the opened and the opener;
> the axe accomplishes it on the soul's axis.
> What then may I do
> but cleave to what cleaves me.
> I kiss the blade and eat my meat.
> I thank the wielder and receive,
> while terror spirits
> my change, sorrow also.
> The terror the butcher
> scripts in the unhealed
> air, the sorrow of his Shang
> dynasty face,
> African face with slit eyes. He is
> my sister, this
> beautiful Bedouin, this Shulamite,
> keeper of sabbaths, diviner
> of holy texts, this dark
> dancer, this Jew, this Asian, this one
> with the Cambodian face, Vietnamese face, this Chinese
> I daily face,
> this immigrant,
> this man with my own face. (*City* 86–87)

The speaker's gesture of cleaving to what cleaves him and of receiving the wielder's blade with a kiss, is a mode of what Levinas calls passivity, denuding, and self-exposure in response to the other. This gesture exposes the self to what hurts, frightens, and enriches for the sake of self-transformation. Moreover, since the body is a contested site for competing ideologies, the poem begins and ends with attention to racially and ethnically marked features. Reference to the Chinese butcher's face as a "Shang dynasty face" at once alludes to and counters Emerson's remarks about Chinese features, by going back "three or four thousand years" to the Shang dynasty (1765–1112 BCE).

This face, which at the beginning of the poem is related only to different types of Chinese features, at the end is identified with African, Arabic, Jewish, Cambodian, and Vietnamese faces — faces of those who are socially and culturally marked as the undesirable other. In so doing, Lee transgresses the culturally and socially imposed categories and boundaries among people without eliminating differences in a singular oneness, in which unity replaces alterity, and otherness is absorbed by sameness.

Lee's investigation of the face of the other opens what Robbins refers to as "the question of ethics" in her discussion of Levinas's ethics of alterity. According to Levinas, Robbins notes, "the face of the other is the very site and privileged figure for such an opening" (*Reading* 55). The face of the other which at once "gives and conceals" is similar to Levinas's concept of the *visage* which "is defined as the way in which the other presents himself" (Robbins *Reading* 61). Rather than reducing the face of the other to a petrified, homogeneous bodily surface as Emerson does, Lee responds to it in such a way so as to show the irreducible alterity of the other, while revealing the depths of this destabilized bodily surface by rendering the interiority of the other visible and perceptible without being completely accessible.

In so doing, Lee intervenes in the discourses on the racially and socially marked other through personal stories told in the voice of the autobiographical lyric I. This "I" "recommended by [his] orphaning," "quarrelsome with aliases" (*City* 56), is also a poet, "the only one / who's lived to tell" the story of his family who fled Sukarno's persecution in Indonesia, and wandered from one country to another before arriving in the United States (*City* 14). His family's story, however, is more than personal, as the autobiographical lyric I asserts: "But I own a human story, / whose very telling / remarks loss"; "I'll tell my human / tale, tell it against / the current of that vaster, that / inhuman telling" (*City* 26, 27). In the last section of the opening poem of his second volume, Lee invites the reader to discard the autobiographical details of his persona and to know him by heeding the song of his soul:

Know him by his noise.
Hear the nervous
scratching of his pencil,
sound of a rasping
file, a small

restless percussion, a soul's
minute chewing,
the old poem
birthing itself
into the new
and murderous century. (*City* 29)

By insisting on specifying the nonwhite, non-European immigrant identity of the lyric I as poet, and articulating his inner self that resists socially constructed identities, Lee disrupts social inscriptions of the racially and ethnically marked body. In seeking to intervene in raced cultural otherness, Lee also resolutely implicates the racial, social, and cultural other in the lyric utterance, thus transforming the content of the universal.

As he reinvents the identity of the lyric I and rearticulates the self's relationship with the other, Lee participates in a profound transformation of American lyric poetry and of American identity. It is part of "a transformative operation upon the universal," of which the white, masculine "central man" has been the privileged signifier (Palumbo-Liu "Universalisms" 203).

# CHAPTER TWO

# *Marilyn Chin*

## SHE WALKS INTO EXILE VOWING NO RETURN

In a 1995 interview with Bill Moyers, Marilyn Chin speaks of her poetic aspirations in terms of her sense of responsibility as a poet, a woman, and a Chinese American. "I see myself as a frontier. . . . And I feel that I'm a conduit for many voices. Historical voices, ancient voices, contemporary feminist voices. Women's voices mostly" (Moyers 67). An immigrant, a professor of creative writing, and a bilingual poet who has developed a poetics of cross-cultural encounters, Chin regards herself as part of a new beginning for Asian Americans, who used to be almost exclusively male laborers and domestic servants, forbidden by law to become naturalized citizens.[1] The frontier Chin explores is a racial, cultural, and poetic one. It entails departures from established cultural and literary traditions. One of these departures includes reinventing a lyric I whose identity is at once individual and collective, Chinese and American. The self as a frontier in Chin's poetry is a border zone where crossings over racial, cultural, and poetic boundaries inevitably result in encounters of otherness whose transformative impact is manifest in the hybridity of Chin's poetics — a mixing of elements from various poetic traditions across cultural and national boundaries, including an African American aesthetic, without erasing each's difference.

A poetics as such entails the kind of movement from "home" into "exile" which Levinas speaks of metaphorically by alluding to the difference between the Greek myth of Ulysses and the biblical story of Abraham: "*A work conceived radically is a movement of the same unto the other which never returns to the same.* To the myth of Ulysses returning to Ithaca, we wish to oppose the story of Abraham who leaves his fatherland forever for a yet unknown land" ("The Trace of the Other" 348). Chin's refusal to return home — the familiar, secure ground of sameness — is manifest in the hybridity of her poetry in terms of its form, content, and style. Like the Chinese poet who "walks into exile vowing no return" in her poem "Exile's Letter" (*Phoenix* 15), Chin leaves the home-ground of classical Chinese poetry and the familiar ground of traditional Western lyric in search of a hybrid poetics to explore the effects of the meeting of different cultures and peoples in the social context of the United States.

Thus the encounters in Chin's poems involve confronting socially constructed otherness and the alterity of the other. Speaking almost always from the position of a female subject, who is implicated in a complex history of patriarchy, racial oppression, and a multicultural heritage, Chin's lyric I often critiques the social exclusion of the other by the dominant culture, while articulating an irreducible alterity through language and poetic form. What seems to distinguish Chin's poetic style most from Li-Young Lee's and other Asian American poets' is her ironic, chastising, compassionate voice, at once humorous and fierce — a voice resulting mostly from the lyric speaker's ethical relationship with the other, one that constitutes the subjectivity of the self by its "non-transferable responsibility" for the other (Levinas "Apropos of Buber" *OS* 44). In her exploration of the Asian American experience, Chin confronts the paradoxes and tensions of acculturation, including the possibilities of inventing a hybrid identity and poetic style, which are embedded in her claim to be "a frontier."

## Self as Frontier

The self as a frontier in Chin's poetry is also an extension of and departure from other frontiers. In "The End of A Beginning," the opening poem of her first volume of poetry, *Dwarf Bamboo* (1987), Chin's persona refers to herself as "the beginning of an end, the end of a beginning" in working-class Chinese American history that begins not with the building of the transcontinental railroad in the United States, but with the building of the Great Wall in China. While this labor-intensive work serves as a contrast to the speaker's poetry writing, the vastly different historical contexts and geographical locations of Chinese labor, however, evoke something similar: at those territorial frontiers along the Northwest borders of China and at the West Coast of the United States attempts to stop the "invasion" of the "barbarian" others failed. The self who claims to be part of a collective history and identity in Chin's poem assumes a subjectivity in terms of its relation to and responsibility for the other — the Chinese laborers whose voices are buried with their bodies along the Great Wall and the railroad tracks. This responsibility which Chin's persona assumes involves a search for new poetic forms to articulate the personal and collective experience of Chinese Americans, and to transform mono-lingual homogeneity and Eurocentricism in American poetry through an unassimilable otherness.

Seeking to develop a female poetic voice and hybrid style, Chin employs a self-deflating humor to break away from the traditional mode of Western lyric, especially "the ponderous expressions of a Wordsworthian, brooding self."[2] In "The End of A Beginning," for instance, Chin escapes an authoritative masculine voice by speaking in the voice of a granddaughter, while asserting the self's connection to and position in the history of Chinese Americans:

> The beginning is always difficult.
> The immigrant worked his knuckles to the bone
> only to die under the wheels of the railroad.
> One thousand years before him, his ancestor fell
> building yet another annex to the Great Wall —
> and was entombed within his work. And I,
> the beginning of an end, the end of a beginning,
> sit here, drink unfermented green tea,
> scrawl these paltry lines for you. Grandfather,
> on your one-hundredth birthday, I have
> the answers to your last riddles:
>
> This is why the baboon's ass is red.
> Why horses lie down only in moments of disaster.
> Why the hyena's back is forever scarred.
> Why, that one hare who was saved, splits his upper lip,
> in a fit of hysterical laughter. (*Bamboo* 3)

In juxtaposition with the impossibly harsh conditions Chinese labor-ers endured, the image of the speaker sipping tea while writing po-etry enhances the speaker's claim to be "the beginning of an end, the end of a beginning" — a ruptured connection to the past that began with the brutal exploitation of labor in China, and continued with the history of working-class Chinese Americans. Moreover, this self as the end of a beginning of cheap Chinese labor in North America also suggests the beginning of a new Chinese American identity in the making of "these paltry lines" for the grandfather in the form of riddles that signify the cultural otherness of the grandfather and of the lyric I by emulating koans — nonlogical riddles and stories of Ch'an or Zen teaching, so designed as to put the student in a state in which he or she can abandon logic in order to leap into insights intuitively through unexplainable, nonrational methods.[3]

The self in Chin's poem is constituted by its relation to and responsibility for the grandfather and other working-class Chinese Americans. As the riddles in the closing lines suggest, the responsibility the speaker faces entails preserving an ethnic cultural heritage, despite the process of acculturation, through a poetics that resists assimilation by the dominant culture. Levinas's views on the formation of the self through an ethical relation between self and other shed light on the uniqueness of the lyric I in Chin's poems. Discussing the implications of Martin Buber's and Gabriel Marcel's philosophical reconceptualization of the relation between self and other, Levinas points out that in the radical shift from a subject-object relation of "I–It of knowledge" to one that is characterized by "the I–Thou of dialogue," a "new ethics" emerges. "But this new ethics," Levinas stresses, "is also a new way of understanding the possibility of an I." Breaking away from the ontological search for "a knowledge of the totality of being," Levinas proposes a rethinking of the subjectivity of the self in terms of its ethical responsibility for the other — "the ethical responsibility that also signifies that no one can take my place when I am the one responsible: I cannot shrink before the other man, I am *I* by way of that uniqueness, I am *I* as if I had been chosen" (*OS* 35). This uniqueness of the I based on the self's irreplaceable responsibility for the other as the crux of the subject and its ethical relation to the other, differs fundamentally from the Cartesian concept of the self and of the traditional Romantic lyric I. In claiming to be "the beginning of an end," and in offering her "paltry lines" to and for "Grandfather," the lyric I in Chin's poem asserts her subjectivity by assuming her irreplaceable responsibility for the other — her fellow Chinese immigrants and Asian Americans who are deprived of a voice, whose otherness has been reduced to the object of knowledge in discourses that define them in such a way as to justify their political exclusion and economic exploitation.

For Chin, the responsibility her poetic persona faces in claiming to be the "beginning of an end" in Chinese American history entails exploring a new poetics to signify an irreducible alterity that challenges racial or ethnic essence — the socially constructed categories of otherness. In articulating this otherness, Chin seeks to reinvent Chinese cultural heritage and to transform the Eurocentric aspects of mainstream American poetry through the alterity of the culturally marginalized other. John Gery in his essay, "'Mocking My Own Ripeness': Authenticity, Heritage, and Self-Erasure in the Poetry of Marilyn Chin," notes that because of her commitment to the art of poetry, "what has emerged, even in her poems of cynicism or despair, is a finely honed voice struggling toward self-definition, rather than one resigned to be seen *only* as other, or as others defined" (25). Chin's self-definition through a "finely honed voice," I would add, insists on articulating an otherness or difference that is not only intended to redefine the self, but also to transform mainstream American poetry. As Chin states in the introduction to an anthology of Asian American literature, *Dissident Song* (1991), which she edited with David Wong Louie: "It is our duty to usurp the canon from its monolithic, monolingual, monocultural, and henceforth monotonous fate. It is up to us 'ethnic' writers to save American literature from becoming suburban 'white noise'" (4). This task of transforming the dominant canon of mainstream American poetry through a poetics of otherness is also embedded in her persona's claim to be "the beginning of an end."

The poetic voice and style of "The End of A Beginning" illustrate that Chin's exploration of racial and cultural border crossings also involves developing a new poetics that departs from both Eastern and Western poetic traditions. In a later poem, "The Barbarians Are Coming," collected in her second volume, *The Phoenix Gone, The Terrace Empty* (1994), Chin articulates a compelling version of the self as a frontier where encounters with racial, cultural, and poetic otherness take place. The form and content of this poem demonstrate the possibilities of creating a new lyric by combining and transforming elements from different cultural traditions. Chin incorporates and revises the modern Greek poet C. P. Cavafy's poem, "Waiting for the Barbarians," and a passage from an ancient Chinese text of Daoism, *Chuang Tzu*, to express complex feelings about and different attitudes toward the other. Cavafy's poem is written in the form of a dramatized dialogue and linear narrative which lead to an epiphany at the end — the "barbarians" are used by politicians as a diversion from the state's problems. In this poem, the "barbarians" are a symbol for the outsider, a deceptive digression.[4] Chin borrows Cavafy's dramatization of the coming of the barbarians to reveal a state of mind, but she changes both the meaning of the "barbarians" and its function in her poem. Opening her poem with a description of the barbarians' approaching cavalry, Chin creates a sense of urgency, anxiety, and crisis:

> War chariots thunder, horses neigh, *the barbarians are coming.*
> What are we waiting for, young nubile women pointing at the
>     wall, *the barbarians are coming.*
> They have heard about a weakened link in the wall. *So, the*
>     *barbarians have ears among us.*
> So deceive yourself with illusions: you are only one woman,
>     holding one broken brick in the wall.
> So deceive yourself with illusions: as if you matter, that brick
>     and that wall.
> *The barbarians are coming*: they have red beards or beardless
>     with a top knot.
> *The barbarians are coming*: they are your fathers, brothers,
>     teachers, lovers; and they are clearly an other. (*Phoenix* 19)

Instead of an eagerly expected presence as in Cavafy's poem, the barbarians in Chin's poem are a "threat" to racial and cultural purity. The image of the wall marking territorial boundaries evokes the Great Wall of China built to stop the invasion of "barbarians." As the poem unfolds, it becomes clear that it is an illusion that the barbarians can be kept out by the wall: "they are your fathers, brothers, teachers, lovers; and they are clearly an other." The image of "one woman, holding one broken brick in the wall" dramatizes some Chinese immigrants' anxiety about and resistance to assimilation, and their illusion that individuals can preserve ethnic purity. The fact that women's bodies and sexuality are regulated and policed to secure racial purity and to maintain boundaries of nation, race, class, and culture renders the image of "young nubile women" at the wall facing the approaching barbarian cavalry particularly complex and forceful in confronting acculturation and interracial sexual relationship.

Chin's use of Asian women's body and sexuality as contested sites of ideologies and identities is a salient example of the strategy of using "sexuality to articulate the terms of citizenship and national belonging" in Asian immigrant writing, which Leslie Bow explores in depth. In her book, *Betrayal and Other Acts of Subversion: Feminism, Sexual Politics, Asian American Women's Literature*, Bow examines the ways in which "feminine sexuality" operates as a marker of "ethnic or national betrayal, particularly as sexuality mediates between progress and tradition, modernity and the 'Old World,' the United States and Asia." Within this context, Bow argues, "Asian American women writers not only mediate sexuality's construction as a determiner of loyalty but manipulate that construction as a tool of political persuasion, reconceptualizing 'disloyalty' as resistance to repressive authority" (11). Chin's assertion of interracial affiliations through sexual relationships across national and cultural boundaries, however, does not simply signify ethnic and racial "betrayal," nor resist racist and patriarchal repression only. Interracial sexual relationships in this and her other poems, such as "Barbarian Suite" and "A Portrait of the Self as Nation, 1990–1991" (*Phoenix* 22, 92–97), also negotiate the implications and consequences of Asian immigrants' acculturation, assimilation, and poetic hybridization. Chin says in an interview that she fears losing her Chinese language, "which would be like losing a part of myself, losing part of my soul." But "assimilation *must* happen. There's *no way* I can force my children to speak Chinese. There is *no way* that the pure yellow seed, as my grandmother called it, will continue." Moreover, Chin notes, "Just as I think it's impossible to keep Chineseness pure, I think it's also impossible to keep whiteness pure. I think *everything* must merge, and I'm willing to have it merge within me, in my poetry" (Moyers 70, 73). Assimilation for Chin as shown in her poem does not mean erasure or oppression of otherness by the dominant culture; rather it suggests a mutually transformative encounter between self and other.

This encounter and its implications for white America are also part of the dramatization of anxiety and illusion in the poem, as implied in the difference among the "barbarians," who are both white ("they have red beards") and Asian ("or beardless with a top knot"). Chin enhances the double meaning of the illusion about keeping the barbarians "out" by appropriating and revising one passage from *Chuang Tzu* by the Daoist philosopher Chuang Tzu in the last half of the poem. In this passage, Lao Tzu, the legendary founder of Daoism, is called "ill-bred" by a visitor who sees him being frugal with food, but Lao Tzu is indifferent to the name-calling. When asked why he remained indifferent, Lao Tzu said: "The titles of clever, wise, divine, holy are things that I have long ago cast aside, as a snake sheds its skin. Yester-day if you had called me an ox, I should have accepted the name of ox; if you had called me a horse, I should have accepted the name of horse. Wherever there is a substance and men give it a name, it would do well to accept that name; for it will in any case be subject to the prejudice that attaches to the name" (qtd. in Waley 17). Chin incorporates the Daoist attitude toward naming and names in her poem, while shifting the subject position from those who fear the barbarians to that of the barbarians and their attitudes toward being named the abject other:

> If you call me a horse, I must be a horse.
> If you call me a bison, I am equally guilty.
>
> When a thing is true and is correctly described, one doubles the
>     blame by not admitting it: so, Chuangtzu, himself, was a
>     barbarian king!
> Horse, horse, bison, bison, *the barbarians are coming*—
> and how they love to come.
> The smells of the great frontier exult in them.
>
> *after Cavafy* (*Phoenix* 19)

With this shift of perspective accompanied by a change in rhythm and intonation, Chin introduces the Daoist paradoxical attitude toward naming to expose the fact that the otherness of the other will always escape any names. Daoism regards categories of names as reductive and misleading, as Lao Tzu's remarks indicate. Hence to deny any naming or category as untrue to the thing described is to accept the belief that naming can define the essence of things, which is contrary to Daoism. Therefore Chin's barbarian I says defiantly: "If you call me a horse, I must be a horse. / If you call me a bison, I am equally guilty." Chin enacts the Daoist attitude toward naming to suggest that the otherness of the other is beyond any namable categories. At the same time, she destabilizes socially constructed categories of the other, col-lapsing the racial and cultural boundaries between self and other by switching the subject positions between the namer and the named.

The meaning of the barbarians as the other of the self thus dis-rupted, those who must be walled out as a threat at the beginning of the poem become a destabilized frontier at the end. It is worth noting that by the end of the poem, the identity of the barbarians has been called into question, and with it, the meaning and location of the frontier. The last line, "The smells of the great frontier exult in them," seems to suggest that the barbarians themselves are a frontier. In other words, the other is a frontier; encounter with the other is a venture into the unknown. While the self as a frontier in Chin's poetry indicates the otherness of the lyric I, this self suggests transgression of racial and cultural boundaries — a transgression that is embodied textually by Chin's blurring of boundaries for defining barbarians ("they are your fathers, brothers, teachers, lovers; and they are clearly an other") and by her incorporation of both Cavafy and Chuang Tzu without subordinating one to the other.

Chin challenges ideologies of racial and cultural purity through a hybrid poetic style that enforces her theme of transformative encounters with the other. She expands both her thematic and stylistic hybridity in her third volume, *Rhapsody in Plain Yellow* (2002), by incorporating the otherness of African American blues in her poems such as "Blues on Yellow," "Hospital Interlude," and "Millennium Six Songs." Speaking of her poetics, Chin says "I use the shake-and-bake method of composition, creating my own hybrid lyric by sampling echoes and references from both East and West" ("Translating Self" 310). The Western traditions for Chin include English, European American, and African American poetic traditions. She acknowledges her intellectual and aesthetic debts to African American leaders and writers, saying that she has learned from them the fact that "the self must represent a struggle that is larger than the self." She draws on "the uncompromising, in-your-face aesthetics of Amiri Baraka and June Jordan as well as from the formalized democratic anthems of Margaret Walker and Gwendolyn Brooks." In addition, she adds, "Then, there are the jazzy improvs and strong rhythms of Quincy Troupe and Yusef Komunyakaa. More recently, I've been studying the blues form, refined and codified by Langston Hughes" ("Translating Self" 311–12). Chin pays homage to African American aesthetics in "Blues on Yellow," and rearticulates her thematic concern of self as a frontier of encounters with otherness.

Placed on a frontal page of Chin's third volume, and immediately following the page of epigrammatic lines from William Carlos

Williams, "Blues on Yellow" spotlights encounters with the racial other as a challenge to both individuals and communities. Williams's lines read: "The stain of love/Is upon the world/Yellow, yellow, yellow" (qtd. in Chin *Rhapsody* 9). Improvising with the connotation of "yellow" as a marker of a socially constructed racial other, Chin's poem confronts the impact of the Chinese presence in the United States. The opening lines of "Blues on Yellow" allude to the Chinese immigrants' experience of exclusion, exploitation, and violence on the West Coast, in part as a result of their racialization as the undesirable other in the nation-space of the United States. The composition of the poem is modeled on the triplet structure of blues — statement and restatement followed by commentary response:

> *The canary died in the gold mine, her dreams got lost in the sieve.*
> *The canary died in the gold mine, her dreams got lost in the sieve.*
> *Her husband the crow killed under the railroad, the spokes hath shorn*
>     *his wings.* (*Rhapsody* 13)

Chin's use of the blues in dealing with Chinese American experience evokes a historical connection between African slaves and Chinese coolies. After the abolition of slavery, Chinese and Indian coolies were shipped to South America, the Caribbean, and the United States to replace slave labor. The coolie ships were modeled on slave ships.[5] Hence, Chin's appropriation of blues in dealing with Asian American experience "gives the blues song a new social context" ("Translating Self" 313), just as the aesthetics and historical context of blues add to the unsettling effects of her hybrid poetics.

Drawing on blues' humor and irony as strategies for survival and social critique, particularly for "talking back" to the dominant power, Chin moves from the deprivation of Chinese immigrants working in the gold mines, at the transcontinental railroad, and in the Chinese restaurants to the unsettling effects produced by the presence of the Chinese otherness in the rest of the poem:

> *O crack an egg on the griddle, yellow will ooze into white.*
> *O crack an egg on the griddle, yellow will ooze into white.*
> *Run, run, sweet little Puritan, yellow will ooze into white.*
>
> *If you cut my yellow wrists, I'll teach my yellow toes to write.*
> *If you cut my yellow wrists, I'll teach my yellow toes to write.*
> *If you cut my yellow fists, I'll teach my yellow feet to fight.*

*Do not be afraid to perish, my mother, Buddha's compassion is nigh.*
*Do not be afraid to perish, my mother, our boat will sail tonight.*
*Your babies will reach the promised land, the stars will be their*
    *guide.*

*I am so mellow yellow, mellow yellow, Buddha sings in my veins.*
. . . . . . . . . . . . . . . . . . . . *(Rhapsody* 13)

Echoing and extending the cooking motif (*"Something's cookin in Chin's kitchen"*) from the second stanza, the image of an egg — *"O crack an egg on the griddle, yellow will ooze into white"* — in the third stanza serves as a "political conceit about miscegenation" ("Translating Self" 313). Like other racialized minorities in the United States, Chinese were forbidden by law in several states to marry whites. Section 69 of California's Civil Code refused marriage licences to whites and "Mongolians, Negroes, mulattoes and persons of mixed blood." This law, implemented in 1880, was not repealed until 1948 (Yung 424). Evoking the anti-miscegenation law and its lingering effect on racial segregation, Chin employs the "uncompromising, in-your-face aesthetics" of African American writers not simply to assert interracial sexual relationships between Asians and whites, but also to suggest the inevitable, nonstoppable interpenetration of Asians into policed territories of white America.

American lyric poetry could be considered one of these territories, in which Chin is deliberately hybridizing Eurocentric lyric traditions with Asian and African elements. Thus, by insisting on rendering the lyric I as a raced and gendered subject, confronting Asian American history and incorporating the characteristics of blues in her poem, Chin seeks to transform the "white voice" and the formulaic testimonial or revelational models of American lyric through a politics of aesthetics.[6] For Chin, the self as a frontier then must involve reinventing the lyric I and rearticulating a self-other relationship that shape the poetic voice and form.

---

## "Saying" as Responsibility for the Other

One of the distinct aspects of Chin's poetics of alterity lies in her mode of saying as responsibility for the other in the context of Chinese Americans' everyday reality, including her own experience as a Chinese American. While seeking to inscribe subversive and transformative differences of the racial and cultural other in poems such as "The Cricket," "Narrow Roads of Oku," "Unreal Dwelling" (*Bamboo* 15, 5–8, 20), and "The Tao and the Art of Leave Taking" (*Phoenix* 30–31), which pay homage to East Asian aesthetics and poetic traditions, Chin confronts the contradictions in her desire to preserve an ethnic culture and the apparent inevitability of losing that heritage in the process of Asian Americans' acculturation and assimilation. She addresses this issue through the lyric I, whose subject position is characterized by an ethical relation to the other, embedded in the poetic utterance as an addressee-oriented language-response to the other in a dialogic I-Thou relationship in which the proximity of the other demands the subject's response.

For the self-other relation to remain ethical, the lyric I must not assume a homogeneous oneness with the other in which otherness is suppressed. This distance between self and other can be established and maintained through a speech act or "saying" in the Levinasian sense. Levinas further elaborates on his concept of *saying* in terms of an ethical relation to the other in his essay, "A New Rationality: On Gabriel Marcel," collected in *Entre Nous: On Thinking-of-the-Other*. In this essay Levinas applauds Gabriel Marcel's challenge to the value of "self-sufficiency" in classical thought and his proposal of a self-other relationship based on spiritual value and love. Engaging with the implications of Marcel's proposal, Levinas writes: "The spirit is not the Said, it is the Saying which goes from the Same to the Other, without suppressing the difference. It paves a way for itself where nothing is common. Non-indifference of the one for the other!" Levinas adds that what he means by "the non-indifference of Saying," is a new signifying mode in which difference of the other is not absorbed into the self-same commonality. Thus, saying entails "both relation and rupture," an "awakening of Me by the other, of Me by the Stranger, of Me by the stateless person." This awakening "signifies a responsibility for the other," which is "my expiation for the suffering, and no doubt for the wrongdoing of the other person. Expiation, assigned to me without any possible evasion and in which my own uniqueness is exalted, irreplaceable" (*EN* 63). In addition to disrupting the subject's self-sufficiency that sustains self-enclosure, saying then not only breaks away from discourses that subordinate the other to the subject's intentionality, but also signifies the subject's language contact with the other, and its responsibility for the other. Unlike the authoritative and nominative utterance of the traditional lyric I, this mode of saying is a response to the other as responsibility, which is characteristic of the lyric I's address to the other in Chin's poems such as "Art Wong Is Alive and Ill and Struggling in Oakland California" and "A Chinaman's Chance."

In these poems, Chin further develops her method of juxtaposing voices as a strategy for articulating both collective and personal experiences of working-class Chinese Americans, while establishing and maintaining an ethical relation between self and other. At the same time, she interweaves into this self-other relation her central themes concerning Chinese Americans' relationship to Chinese and American cultures in their process of becoming, in which the struggle for survival and material success seems to conflict with artistic and spiritual pursuits, while assimilation by the dominant culture threatens to eliminate Chinese Americans' ethnic cultural identity. In confronting these conflicts, Chin employs collage juxtaposition to allow multiple voices and contesting perspectives to engage in a dialogic interaction.

In "Art Wong Is Alive and Ill and Struggling in Oakland California," for instance, Chin juxtaposes four voices, representing four different perspectives on art, one of which is the lyric speaker's. Although differing from the other three, the lyric I's perspective does not dismiss or absorb the other's difference. This multiplicity of different voices renders impossible the dominance of the lyric I over the other. The poem begins with disparaging statements about a great Chinese painter, Chi Pai Shih, famous for his distinctive, remarkable paintings of insects, flowers, and plants. Those statements are juxtaposed with Chi Pai Shih's own remarks about his work:

Chi Pai Shih was born
in the Year of the Boar.
And a bore he was;
his footprints dirtied the snow.

*Thirty, I painted landscapes;*
*forty, insects and flowers;*
*fifty, I turned lazy as mud,*
*never ventured beyond*
*West Borrowed Hill.* (*Bamboo* 68)

It is worth noting that the speeches in these two stanzas are separate personal expressions which serve as contrasts to other perspectives on art and its relationship to Asian Americans. In her investigation of the artist figures in Asian American literature, Sauling Cynthia Wong finds "a large number of works exploring the idea of art as an Extravagant, *playful* act" that contends with "the forces of Necessity" (166, 168). She further notes that "in articulating the antithesis between work and play in *The Year of the Dragon* Frank Chin brings his and other affiliated Asian American representations of art into a vast Western discourse privileging play, which by some accounts spans the centuries from before Plato to Derrida. . . . Superficially, many features of the Asian American images of artists and their activities resemble the characteristics of play delineated in this discourse" (182–83). Although the antithesis between extravagance and necessity seems to be implied in Marilyn Chin's poem, her evocation of a Chinese painter and allusion to his credo, however, represents an alternative figure of artist that cannot be subsumed into a Western discourse on art that can be traced back from Derrida to Plato.

But rather than seeking to connect Chinese American artists to an origin or tradition of "home," Chin evokes Chi Pai Shih to enhance Chinese Americans' "exile" from their homeland. In response to the remarks in the two stanzas quoted above, the lyric speaker's following assertion suggests Chinese Americans' radical break with their ethnic cultural heritage. Vastly different from Chi Pai Shih's life of leisure dedicated to the creation and perfection of his painting, Chinese American life is burdened with the toil for survival, and "art," for the lyric speaker, is "dying" in a Chinese American restaurant:

Oh, Nonsense! Art
is a balding painter, humpbacked
as the dwarfed acacia
dying in his father's chopsuey joint.

His palette is muddy; his thoughts are mud.
He sits crosslegged,
one eye open, the other shut,
a drunken Buddha. (*Bamboo* 68)

This humpbacked, balding painter is at once an individual and an embodiment of a collective status of Chinese Americans, whose lives are spent in struggling to survive or thrive in the United States. Just as hard work in his father's "chopsuey joint" has weakened his body, Art's pursuit of the materialist American dream conflicts with his artistic ambition. In contrast to Chi Pai Shih's dedication to art, Art Wong's preoccupations are "fast cars and California gold." But Art seems to be more than a slave to materialist possessions. Sitting cross-legged like a "drunken Buddha," with "one eye open, the other shut," Art Wong embodies an unassimilable otherness despite his apparently typical American materialism. In fact, Art Wong's own words reveal an unlikely combination of carefree humor and koanlike paradox of Ch'an or Zen, ironized filial piety of Confucianism, and corrupt American dream, all of which coexist in him:

> I laugh at the sun; I take in air;
> I whistle in sleep, let cicadas within
> murmur their filial rapture
> My father's dream is my dream:
> fast cars and California gold;
> the singles bar is my watering hole. (Bamboo 68)

Art Wong's assertion about himself creates an ambivalence that suggests his cultural hybridity as a Chinese American. His Buddhist and Daoist spirituality undermines his apparent assimilation by the materialist American dream; his ironic remarks about "filial rapture" undermine his unabashed statement about inheriting his father's dream of material success. This statement is rendered more ambivalent by the reference to "the singles bar" as his lifestyle, which evokes the so-called working-class Chinese immigrants' bachelors' society resulting from U.S. exclusionary immigration laws that prevented the immigration of Chinese women. This ambivalent image of Art Wong enables Chin to avoid suppressing either the complexity of Chinese Americans' experience or the alterity of their otherness, showing a Chinese American identity that refuses any homogeneous categories.

Chin's persona embraces Art Wong's ambivalence, responding to his situation with sympathy and love. In the last part of the poem, the speaker's love for Art Wong suggests not only her concern for the other, but also her identification with the other's situation of loneliness and exile:

> And I . . . I am in love with him.
> Never ask why, for youth
> never begs the question.
> As long as boughs are green
> so is my love green and pure
> in this asphalt loneliness.
>
> I let down my long hair;
> my hair falls over his shoulders:
> thus, we become one. Oh, Willow,
> Cousin Willow, don't weep for me now.
> Consummate this marriage between
> Art and me, between
> the diaspora and the yearning sea. (*Bamboo* 69)

Just as this "marriage" is symbolic of the connection between diaspora and longing, Art Wong and the lyric I become an embodiment of the conditions and effects of Chinese diaspora. Even though the speaker says that in her act of love for Art Wong they "become one," this union stands for the coexistence of contradictions in Chinese American experience — artistic deprivation and pursuit for survival and economic success embodied by Art Wong on the one hand, and on the other, artistic aspiration and pursuit of spiritual fulfillment embodied by Chin's persona — rather than a fusion in which conflicts are neutralized and differences canceled out by sameness. Their embodiment of the collective experience notwithstanding, both Art Wong and the lyric speaker are concrete individuals with different aspirations in life. In a conversation with Maxine Hong Kingston, Chin mentions her own dream of becoming a poet in contrast to the immigrants' dream of buying houses ("Writing the Other" 1). In this poem, she exposes and explores the conditions underlying that contrast. Moreover, her persona's articulation of love for Art Wong, a painter, "ill and struggling," chasing after his father's materialist dream, signifies her response to the other as her unavoidable responsibility for the other, a responsibility that constitutes the unique subjectivity of the lyric I in her poem. This Levinasian uniqueness of the subject characterizes the lyric I and its saying in this poem and Chin's other poems.

More often than not, Chin enacts the lyric subject's response to and responsibility for the other in terms of social critique. Sometimes the critique is directed at assimilationist ideology, sometimes at racism and sexism, but it is almost always articulated along with conflicts in Chinese Americans' personal and collective experiences. In "Chinaman's Chance," for instance, Chin suggests that historical and social conditions for Chinese immigrants have made the survival of Chinese cultural identity particularly difficult. But Chinese Americans themselves, Chin also suggests, have a choice not to pursue the materialist American dream at the expense of their spiritual life. However, the poem moves from critique to affirmation of Chinese Americans' strength of survival despite their dislocation and experience of racial discrimination. The other whom Chin's persona addresses in this poem is a collective other, whose otherness entails irreducible alterity and a socially and historically constructed abject otherness. The title alludes to racist laws that aimed at excluding Chinese working-class immigrants from the United States and disenfranchising them economically and politically, thus making it impossible for them to have a chance to realize their American dream. Against this background, the poem explores the possibilities of reinventing the racial and cultural otherness of the self shaped by social and historical conditions.

The opening lines of the poem raise questions about the soul and the body in an ironic tone through allusions to Greek and Chinese philosophers. Plato's elevation of the soul over the body and Confucius's privileging of male over female become especially ironic when juxtaposed with the historical conditions of Chinese Americans. In contrast to the Greek philosophers' valuing of the soul, the bodies of Chinese young men were a valuable and excluded commodity in the labor market of nineteenth-century North America. Despite the privilege Confucianism bestowed on them, Chinese men became cheap labor and their lives worthless in a country where their exploitation was justified because they were "Chinamen," the racialized subordinate other:

If you were a Chinese born in America, who would you believe
Plato who said what Socrates said

Or Confucius in his bawdy way:
>      "So a male child is born to you
>       I am happy, very very happy."

\*   \*   \*   \*

The railroad killed your great-grandfather.
His arms here, his legs there . . .
*How can we remake ourselves in his image?*

Your father worked his knuckles black,
So you might have pink cheeks. Your father
Burped you on the back; why must you water his face?

Your father was happy, he was charred by the sun,
*Danced and sang until he died at twenty-one.*

.   .   .   .   .   .   .   .   .   .   .   .   .   .

Your body is growing, changing, running
Away from your soul. Look,

Not a sun but a gold coin at the horizon,
*Chase after it, my friend, after it. (Bamboo 29)*

The contrast in ancient Greek and Chinese philosophers' beliefs enhances the tension between spiritual and material pursuits for Chinese immigrants and Chinese Americans. Confucius's patriarchal primacy was futile for Chinese men who left home to die young, laboring under harsh conditions in North America. Plato's and Socrates' belief in the soul was superfluous when Chinese immigrants could not even survive physically. These philosophers' doctrines are no good, either, for a younger generation of Chinese Americans whose bodies are running away from their souls, while they are chasing after "a gold coin at the horizon"— the elusive American dream. In examining Chin's use of irony in her poems, Dorothy Joan Wang argues that irony suggests bifurcation, and Chin's employment of irony reproduces the multiple pressures and contradictions in the formation of Asian American subjectivities.[7] Wang's view highlights the fact that sardonic voices in Chin's poems are a means of social critique and technical strategy for dealing with the complexities of Asian American experiences and subject positions. The implied social critique in this poem is interwoven with an implicit chastisement of Chinese Americans for failing to honor the sacrifice of the older generation — "Your father worked his knuckles black, / So you might have pink cheeks. Your father / Burped you on the back; why must you water his face?" This failure, the speaker suggests, results from a preoccupation with material success, as she says sarcastically: "Look, / Not a sun but a gold coin at the horizon, / *Chase after it, my friend, after it.*"

Although the speaker identifies herself as a Chinese American by using "we," her switch from "we" to "you" distances her from other Chinese Americans, particularly those who would chase after the "gold coin at the horizon." With reference to the dead, broken image of "your great-grandfather" within the historical context of "Chinaman's chance," meaning no chance at all for Chinese immigrants who were categorized as the undesirable other by the dominant culture, the speaker's sarcastic remarks to you simultaneously assert a critique of social inequity and reveal her compelling sense of responsibility for other Chinese Americans. It is precisely this ethical distance between Chin's persona and other Chinese Americans that enables Chin to capture the complexity of Chinese Americans and to escape reducing them to a homogenous collective identity.

But the lyric self in Chin's poems, like that in Li-Young Lee's, is also an other in part because of its own cultural difference and socially constructed racial otherness. Hence in Chin's poems the lyric I's articulation of the self is also an assertion of Chinese American identity and alterity. As the pronoun switches from "you" to "we" in the second half of "A Chinaman's Chance," the speaker's ironic tone gives way to a meditative mood, and the references to suffering and sacrifice are replaced by cultural images. In accordance with her poetics of alterity, Chin uses imagery and riddlelike questions to generate the change of tone and transition in the poem:

Why does the earth move backwards
As we walk ahead. Why does mother's
Blood stain this hand-me-down shirt?

This brown of old tea, the yellow ring
Around the same porcelain cup. They stayed

Stone-faced as paired lions, prepared
As nightwatch at the frontier gate.

We have come small and wooden, tanned brown
As oak pillars, eyes peering straight
Through vinyl baggage and uprooted shoes.

We shall gather their leftovers: jimsons and velvets,
Crocuses which have burst-bloomed through walks.
We shall shatter this ancient marble, veined and glorious . . .

.   .   .   .   .   .   .   .   .   .   .   .   .   .   .   .   .   .   .   .

Night: black starred canopy, piece
Of Chinese silk, dank with must and cedar,
Pulled down from the source, a cardboard bolt. (*Bamboo* 30)

These Chinese images, though suggesting the endurance and survival of Chinese Americans' ethnic cultural heritage in the New World, indicate that this heritage is to be fractured and reinvented. As the speaker says: "We shall shatter this ancient marble, veined and glorious." Uprooted and dislocated in diaspora, Chinese Americans must remake the given in the process of becoming other than Chinese or model minority American. The emphasis on displacement in the closing lines foregrounds Chinese American alterity —"piece / Of Chinese silk . . . / Pulled down from the source, a cardboard bolt" — an otherness marked by its exile from "home" and its resistance to assimilation by the dominant culture in a new country.

The difference Chin maintains between her persona's attitude toward assimilation and those of others is an integral part of her poetic utterance in terms of saying as response to and responsibility for the other. In refusing to ascribe meaning to the other, or speaking for the other, Chin's signifying mode maintains what Levinas calls the "proximity" of the other. This proximity, "far from meaning something less than identification," Levinas emphasizes, "opens up the horizon of social existence" ("The Other in Proust" *PN* 104). A disruptive, unsettling otherness within the same, situated in the social reality and daily life experience of Chinese Americans, characterizes Chin's lyric I's speeches which are oriented toward the other.

*Sister of a Dozen, Cousin of a Million*

As she continues to explore the relation between self and other in terms of the subject's irreplaceable responsibility for the other in her poems, the other to whom Chin's lyric I responds becomes mostly Asian women, including her mother, whose experience and social status are a major concern of Chin's poetry. In her conversation with

Eileen Tabios, Chin says: "My Muse's major concern is the suffering of women, the suffering of my mother, first and foremost. My feminism is born out of personal and familial experiences" (Tabios 280). Shortly after immigrating to the United States, Chin's father left her mother and the family for a white woman. Chin says in her interview with Moyers that the white woman in her poems is "symbolic of the American dream," who has fragmented immigrant families. "This is the fragmentation that I write about over and over again," she adds, "hoping to resolve this pain, hoping to speak through my mother's suffering, hoping to be a conduit for her voice and for the voices of other Asian women" (Moyers 75). Chin investigates the interlocking effects of sexism and racism on Asian women, while exploring the consequences of Asian Americans' assimilation in poems such as the short sequences of "Where We Live Now" and "Exile's Letter (*Or: An Essay on Assimilation*)" collected in her first volume, *Dwarf Bamboo*, and a large number of poems, including a series of ten poems under the section title of "Homage to Diana Toy," in her second volume *The Phoenix Gone, The Terrace Empty*. In these poems, the lyric I speaks to a female other about the other's conditions.

Chin's most ambitious and accomplished poems about gender and race are those in which the lyric I is speaking as both the irreducible other and the socially marginalized other who engages in a dialogue which challenges dominant discourses. Speaking as an other involves breaking the form which reinforces the Same, and subverting the image that reduces and congeals the other into a fixed category. As Levinas contends, the manifestation of the other involves constantly undoing the form of the Same: "This way of undoing the form adequate to the Same so as to present oneself as other is to signify or to have a meaning. To present oneself by signifying is to speak" (*TI* 66). To speak as the other, then, is to disrupt totalizing and homogenizing knowledge. The lyric I as an enunciative subject position provides Chin with an enabling position for the self to speak as the other. Thus, the lyric I in Chin's poems is at once a particularized individual and an embodiment of a collective identity as the gendered and racialized other.

In an autobiographical poem, "How I Got that Name," subtitled "*an essay on assimilation*," for example, Chin's persona articulates her otherness by situating the formation of her subjectivity in the context of Asian American history and identity. Chin opens the poem by proclaiming her identity with an emphasis on its singular, individualistic Americanized name:

I am Marilyn Mei Ling Chin.
Oh, how I love the resoluteness
of that first person singular
followed by that stalwart indicative
of "be," without the uncertain i-n-g
of "becoming." Of course,
the name had been changed
somewhere between Angel Island and the sea,
when my father the paperson
in the late 1950s
obsessed with a bombshell blonde
transliterated "Mei Ling" to "Marilyn."
And nobody dared question
his initial impulse — for we all know
lust drove men to greatness,
not goodness, not decency.
And there I was, a wayward pink baby,
named after some tragic white woman
swollen with gin and Nembutal. (*Phoenix* 16)

Chin enhances the irony in the speaker's emphasis on the resolutely first person, singular proclamation of her Euro-Americanized name by evoking historically significant names such as "Angel Island" and "paperson," which resonate with the history of racial discrimination against Asian immigrants. Angel Island in the Pacific Ocean was the location for detaining Asian immigrants, a symbol of exclusion in contrast to what Ellis Island stood for on a different shore for immigrants from Europe.[8] The term paperson was used to refer to those male Chinese immigrants who immigrated to the United States with forged paper identities partly as a result of a big fire in Chinatown during the 1906 earthquake in San Francisco, but mostly because of the Chinese Exclusion Act implemented in 1882, which was not repealed until 1943. With those historical references, the autobiographical details in the poem reveal that the speaker's family are immigrants, and the father, obsessed with an American icon and anxious to assimilate, changed the daughter's Chinese name to "Marilyn." Thus the lyric I's particularized identity interlocks identities of gender, race, class, and culture in a particular social and historical context, rendering it impossible for the lyric I to assert a purely private self.

In accordance with this status of the lyric I, Chin switches the pronoun to "we" in the second part of the poem, thus further situating the self in the collective experience of Asian Americans, while engaging in a critical dialogue with the dominant culture. Speaking as we Asian Americans, the speaker alludes to and undermines the dominant discourse that contains them within a prescribed identity and social position. Despite the efforts of Asian immigrants like the father to assimilate and become white, Asian Americans are marked as the subordinate racial other and stereotyped as the model minority in the racial hierarchy of the United States. Chin employs irony and self-mockery to expose the naturalized stereotypes of Asian Americans:

> Oh, how trustworthy our daughters,
> how thrifty our sons!
> How we've managed to fool the experts
> in education, statistics and demography —
> We're not very creative but not adverse to rote-learning.
> Indeed, they can *use* us.
> But the "Model Minority" is a tease.
> We know you are watching now,
> so we refuse to give you any!
> Oh, bamboo shoots, bamboo shoots!
> The further west we go, we'll hit east;
> the deeper down we dig, we'll find China.
> History has turned its stomach
> on a black polluted beach —
> where life doesn't hinge
> on the red, red wheelbarrow,
> but whether or not our new lover
> in the final episode of "Santa Barbara"
> will lean over a scented candle
> and call us a "bitch."
> Oh God, where have we gone wrong?
> We have no inner resources! (*Phoenix* 17)

The irony in the self-mocking tone signifies a double-edged critique of both Asian Americans' urge to assimilate and the dominant culture's stereotyping of Asian Americans that cast them as the perpetual "foreigner"—"The further west we go, we'll hit east." The positioning of Asian Americans as the model minority subordinate to the power structure of racial hierarchy parallels the predominantly subservient image of Asian women in sexual relationships with white men in American popular culture such as shown in "the final episode of 'Santa Barbara.'" Reference to Asian American women being called "bitch" by their white "new lover" enhances the difference between Asian women and white women, and it also enhances the irony in the speaker being named after a white American woman, an American icon of beauty, desirability, and sexuality — qualities which are naturalized as white. Marked by their race, Asian American women can never be desired in the same way as Marilyn Monroe, even though both are cast as objects of male sexual desire.

Moreover, the speaker's critique of the model minority myth and assimilation ideology is accompanied by her emphasis on Asian Americans' resistance to assimilation and on their subversion of their stereotypes. At the same time she exposes the falsity and inadequacy of the dominant culture's assumed mastery of knowledge of the other. As the speaker asserts: "How we've managed to fool the experts / in education, statistics and demography —"; "We know you are watching now, / so we refuse to give you any!" By insisting on the fact that Asian Americans' alterity is exterior to the operating systems of the dominant culture, Chin's articulation of the self as other shatters the dominant culture's assumptions about and definitions of the other in terms of the Same. This articulation of the irreducible otherness of the other that subverts the social othering of Asian Americans enacts another aspect of an ethical relation which Levinas discusses in *Totality and Infinity*. "When I maintain an ethical relation I refuse to recognize the role I would play in a drama of which I would not be the author or whose outcome another would know before me" (79). In other words, to maintain an ethical relation between self and other, I must refuse complicity in the deprivation of my subjectivity or in the objectification of myself. Chin's exposure of the reductive and exclusionary social othering of Asian Americans refuses to accept the role of the model minority imposed by the dominant culture, thus maintaining an ethical relation with the other through social critique.

The last part of the poem further articulates the irreducible alterity of the gendered and racialized other by focusing on the response of this particularized lyric I, "Marilyn Mei Ling Chin," to the social environment. But rather than returning to the first person, singular pronoun, Chin uses "she" to create a necessary distance between the poet/speaker and "Marilyn," thus rendering "Marilyn" one of the characters in the poem, while identifying her as "sister of a dozen, cousin of a million" (*Phoenix* 18). Being implicated in her racial identity and her connections to other Chinese and Asians, this gender and ethnic specific individual continues to have ramifications for other Asian Americans beyond the particularized self. In contrast to the implications of the model minority — "We're not very creative but not adverse to rote-learning" — "Marilyn" is a poet and survivor against all odds. And her ironic remarks call critical attention to the problems of Asian Americans' position in a polarized black-and-white racial identity politics:

> She was neither black nor white,
> neither cherished nor vanquished,
> just another squatter in her own bamboo grove
> minding her poetry —
> when one day heaven was unmerciful,
> and a chasm opened where she stood.
> Like the jowls of a mighty white whale,
> or the jaws of a metaphysical Godzilla,
> it swallowed her whole.
> She did not flinch nor writhe,
> nor fret about the afterlife,
> but stayed! Solid as wood, happily
> a little gnawed, tattered, mesmerized
> by all that was lavished upon her
> and all that was taken away! (*Phoenix* 18)

In articulating the socially constructed otherness of the self, Chin's persona rejects the transcendence of the Cartesian self without eliminating the agency of the self's subjectivity. In fact, the subjectivity of the raced and gendered self in Chin's poems is the nexus of an ethical relation as responsibility for the other. As Levinas emphasizes, "only irreducible subjectivity can assume a responsibility" which "constitutes the ethical" ("Kierkegaard" *PN* 73). Chin's persona in this poem refuses to be defined either by Chinese patriarchs or by white

America. The self that is swallowed by but reemerges from the chasm between apparently opposing Western and Eastern cultures (as suggested in the iconic images of "a mighty white whale" that seems to allude to Melville's *Moby Dick*, and "a metaphysical Godzilla," the monster of many Japanese films) is a hybrid other who not only defies any reductive categories, but also embodies a new lyric subject who is an immigrant, a woman of color who is "sister of a dozen, cousin of a million," and a poet in exile — "just another squatter in her own bamboo grove / minding her poetry."

Hybridization of cultural identity that resists racial and cultural purity is a salient characteristic of Chin's poetics of alterity. Chin asserts the resolute difference of her hybrid poetics by evoking a canonical American poet, William Carlos Williams, and emphasizing the distance of her poetics from Williams's imagist aesthetics epitomized in his poem "The Red Wheelbarrow," which Chin alludes to in the middle of her poem. Her persona's assertion of her identity intertwined with Asian American history, culture, and social status in this and other poems resonates with her claim to be "the beginning of an end," which suggests a radical break in her poetry — "a movement of the same onto the other which never returns to the same," to quote again Levinas's remarks about radically conceived work. Hybridity in Chin's poetry could be understood in terms of a movement as such.

However, Chin's insistence on developing a poetics of alterity that reflects a hybrid cultural identity is overlooked by critics who identify Chin's poetry with dominant modes of American lyric conventions. In his essay, "Images of Form vs. Images of Content in Contemporary Asian-American Poetry," Charles Altieri singles out Chin's second volume as an example for his contention that most contemporary Asian American poems about the immigrant experience tend "to be written in a generic style, very close to dominant American modes of lyric feeling, so that it neither adequately represents specific cultural forces nor sufficiently posits challenges to that mainstream style" (73). Using "How I Got that Name" to illustrate his point, Altieri adds that despite their compelling personae and brilliant variations, Chin's poems "cannot escape the same old narrow range of reference and projected investments that one finds in the standard versions of the genre [testimonial lyric]" ("Images of Form" 75). But

Altieri's reading of "How I Got that Name" misses the poem's irony and sarcasm, among other things. Overlooking the social critique on the reductive definition and racial position of Asian Americans in the double entendre of the speaker's remarks about assimilation in "How I Got that Name," Altieri maintains that the expectation Chin sets up for the daughter/speaker to "resist the model minority label" only ends up in her finding "herself seduced by American popular culture." Eventually, Altieri considers Chin's articulation of the self at the end of this poem "an introduction to the volume willing to face up entirely to what we might call the sheer facticity of a self caught between cultures" ("Images of Form" 76). Despite the striking contrast which "Marilyn Mei Ling Chin" poses at the end of the poem to those Asian American stereotypes produced by dominant model-minority discourses referred to in the middle of the poem, Altieri concludes that resignation to "passivity" seems to force Chin "to continue the role of charming and submissive daughter" ("Images of Form" 77). Altieri's oversights seem to result from his homogenizing definition of the otherness of Chin's lyric I and of her poetics. He equates her poetry with "dominant American modes of lyric feeling" on the one hand, and on the other, insists on confining Chin's themes to "standard variations" on the testimonial lyric; and also relegates her poetics to her supposedly limited sense of the "decorum and artifice" as a "charming and submissive daughter" (77). Altieri's reading of Chin's poetry fails to investigate its otherness on its own terms, thus dismissing the complexity of both her themes and poetics and missing the challenges Chin's work poses.

As she continues to explore the possibilities for her poetry as a conduit for the voices of history, especially of Asian women, Chin seeks to further expand the capacity of the lyric I. In the title poem, "The Phoenix Gone, The Terrace Empty," different aspects of Chin's poetics, shaped by an ethical relation with the other as responsibility for the other, converge. Combining articulation of the self as other with social critique as responsibility for the other, Chin incorporates Chinese history and culture in her autobiographical poem, which evokes, but refuses to be identified with, the confessional mode of American lyric. In this poem, Chin locates the female self in a nexus of family history, Chinese patriarchy and feudalism and Chinese American experience, to resolve her feelings of "deep pain and guilt" for her mother, as a result of her father's betrayal and her mother's cultural dislocation (Moyers 75). In dealing with her mother's suffering, Chin associates it with other Asian women's experiences, while imagining her mother's life in China and locating it in the historical circumstances of her father's life in America. At the same time, Chin signifies the cultural otherness of her characters and their cross-cultural experiences through the form and imagery of her poem. The deliberately other-sounding title of the poem is borrowed from a poem by Li Bai / Li Po (701–62), a renowned poet of the Tang Dynasty (618–907). This poem is in part inspired by Chin's reading of some fragmentary notes by an imperial gardener about the imperial consorts in the Ming Dynasty (1368–1644), during her research at the Tai-Chung University library in Taiwan where Chin studied classical Chinese.

While the title of the poem, "The Phoenix Gone, The Terrace Empty," evokes classical Chinese poetry, the poem's images suggest historical changes and irretrievable loss, resonating the theme and mood of Li Bai's poem to which it alludes. Under the title, Chin adds an epigram in four Chinese characters with their English translation: "The river flows without ceasing." The sense of continuity implied in this epigram counterpoises the feelings of loss and of the end of an era implied in the title, thus creating ambivalence and tension, which help Chin achieve a compactness and intensity despite the range of historical references. At the same time, the poem's short, irregular, and measured lines seem to create a sense of flow that corresponds with the epigram, as well as the action of walking that takes place in the poem. These elements of multifaceted continuity and departure also characterize Chin's reinvention of the formulaic autobiographical American lyric. Although the speaker is often apparently an autobiographical I, Chin breaks away from the singularity and centrality of the lyric I in traditional Western lyric poetry by including multiple voices from different times and places.

The poem begins with an imperial consort speaking to herself, walking down the stairs in a garden cautiously because of her bound feet, thus calling attention to her body as an inscription of her gender identity and social status:

Shallow river, shallow river,
these stairs are steep,
one foot, another,
I gather the hem

of my terry-cloth robe.
Quietly,
gingerly,

. . . .

past the courtyard,
past the mulberries,

. . . . . . .

In the rock garden
the flagstones
caress my feet,
kiss them tenderly.

"Who in the netherworld walks on my soles
as I walk?
And opens her black mouth
when I cry?
Whose lutestrings
play my sorrow?
Whose silence
undulates
a millennium
of bells,
in which
all of history
shall wallow?" (*Phoenix* 46–47)

The consort's questions are actually the questions which Chin's poem raises and responds to through the voices of the consort and other Chinese women. These questions are directly related to Chin's poetry which "has a strong social and political context," and aims to be a conduit for "[h]istorical voices, ancient voices, contemporary feminist voices," and mostly for the voices of Asian women, including her mother, as Chin says in her interview with Moyers (Moyers 67, 75).

These questions also serve as a transition from the first passage to the third, which begins with Chin's persona walking in a garden at a different time and place from those of the imperial consort, but nonetheless connects the present to the past. Walking in the garden of "plum blossoms," Chin's persona thinks of "love / or the warm blur, / my mother," and remembers "hate, / the hard shape, / my father" (*Phoenix* 47). But both parents in her memory are "slow moving," like "water bison"—the beast of burden in the countryside of southern China, an image that leads her memory to her grandparents and their lives in a village in China, and then to her mother's past. As she shifts the focus of her poem from aristocracy to the working class, and from an ancient history to a comparatively recent past, Chin switches the location of her poem from the imperial court to the village, where the grandmother weaves and sings a lullaby about a girl who has run away from her mother, and where grandfather, an "itinerant tinker, heaves / his massive bellows" (*Phoenix* 48). At the center of this passage is the mother, whose youth and past happiness Chin tries to recapture:

> Do you remember
> the shanty towns
> on the hills of Wanchai,
> tin roofs
> crying into the sun?
> Do you remember
> mother's first lover,
> hurling
> a kerosene
> into a hovel?
> Ooooh, I can smell
> the charred sweetness
> in his raven hair.
> The hills ablaze
> with mayflies
> and night-blooming jasmine. (*Phoenix* 48)

In contrast to this impoverished and yet idyllic world of the mother's youth in China, the next passage focuses on the father's world in the United States, one obsessed with money:

> Open the gate,
> open,
> the gilded facade
> of restaurant "Double Happiness."
> The man crouched
> on the dirty linoleum
> fingering dice

is my father.
He says:
"Mei Ling, child,
Mei Ling, don't cry,
I can change our lives
with one strike." (*Phoenix* 48–49)

The sense of urgency and determination in the speaker's tone seems to suggest that Chin's persona is bracing herself to confront the unpleasant sight of her father and all that is associated with him. However, by giving voice to the father, Chin reveals a gentle side of him and his American dream of striking it rich in order to change the conditions of life for his family.

Refusing to reduce the other to the self-same, and in this case, the father to the persona's opinion of him, Chin introduces the aunt's voice to provide a different perspective on the father. In juxtaposition to the aunt's voice of sympathy, Chin brings in the ancestors' chastising voice, whose disapproval seems to be directed at both the father and the daughter. These voices make it impossible for either the father or Chin's persona to be judged within a single, totalizing value system. These voices also introduce more Chinese history and culture into the poem, and generate variations of tone and rhythm within the passage:

Do you know the stare
of a dead man?
My father the ox,
without his yoke,
sitting on a ridge
of the quay.
Auntie Jade
remembers:
"Hunger
had spooned
the flesh
from his cheeks.
His tuft
of black hair
was his only movement.
That Chinaman

had no ideals,
no beliefs,
his dreams
were robbed
by the Japanese,
his fortune
was plundered
by the Nationalists,
the Communists
seared his home.
Misery had propped
him there.
When you pray
to your ancestors
you are praying
to his hollowness."
*Amaduofu, amaduofu* —
child, child
they cried,
"Ten thousand years of history and you have come to this.
Four thousand years of tutelage and you have come to
    this!" (*Phoenix* 49–50)

With the question "Do you know the stare / of a dead man?" Chin turns away from the father's perspective to the daughter's by replacing his voice with hers. Her persona's reference to "the stare of a dead man" on the father's face, and her comparison of her father to "the ox, / without his yoke, / sitting on a ridge / of the quay" emphasizes the father's despair and dislocation in America. At the same time, the image of "the ox" — a beast of burden — again helps Chin highlight the working-class experience. As she says, "Ox is my Chinese lexicon for working class Chinese which is my people, my family" (qtd. in Tabios 298). By associating the father with the ox, Chin provides a social and historical context for the father's dislocation and unrealized American dream. She also allows Auntie Jade's voice to intervene in her persona's opinion of her father. The aunt's voice provides a historical perspective on the father's situation, and explains sympathetically to the resentful daughter: "Misery had propped / him there." In response to the aunt's remarks about the father's hollowness and about the daughter's prayer to her ancestors, Chin inserts a phrase of Buddhist chanting: "*Amaduofu, amaduofu,*" which is followed by the ancestors' chastising comments that seem to be directed at the failures of both the daughter and the father. The couplet form of these comments, with their long, incantatory rhythm, breaks down the swift tempo of the poem, thus enhancing its function of summing up the father's life, with which Chin's persona seems to have reached some sort of absolution. By the end of this passage, the father is no longer simply a hateful "hard shape" or a despicable gambler to the daughter.

Following the ancestors' remarks of disappointment about the father and the daughter, the poem moves to the daughter's negotiation with her family history and Chinese cultural heritage in "the new world." Again, Chin generates the transition with a question which simultaneously connects to the preceding passage and looks to the next:

> Shall I walk
> into the new world
> in last year's pinafore?
> Chanel says:
> black, black
> is our century's color.
> Proper and elegant,
> slim silhouette,
> .   .   ,   .   (*Phoenix* 50)

References to the speaker's walking "into the new world" in her "last year's pinafore" and "our century's color" resonate with the imperial consort's walk and her "terry-cloth robe," thus relating the daughter to the past and other Chinese women's lives. This short passage about the daughter serves as a transition from the father to the mother, whose voice is introduced in the following passage.

Insisting on responding to the other as a subject, an interlocutor in a dialogue, Chin allows the mother to speak to the daughter in her own voice. The mother's speech, however, is not a complaint about her life or about her husband's betrayal of her, but is rather a response to an other — the strange boyfriend of her daughter:

> "So, you've come home
> finally
> with your new boyfriend.

What is his name?
Ezekiel!
Odd name for a boy.
Your mother can't pronounce it.
And she doesn't like
his demeanor.
Too thin, too sallow,
he does not eat beef
in a country
where beef is possible.
He cannot play the violin
in a country
where rapture is possible.
He beams a tawdry smile,
perhaps he is hiding
bad intentions.
And that Moon
which accompanied his arrival,
that Moon won't drink
and is shaped naughtily
like a woman's severed ear." (*Phoenix* 50–51)

The mother's remarks about the daughter's boyfriend reveal her anxi-
ety about and suspicion of the other. By letting the mother articulate
her opinions and prejudice, Chin maintains an ethical relationship
with the other by refusing to erase the differences between mother and
daughter without casting their differences into a dichotomy of back-
wardness/Chinese mothers versus progress/Americanized daugh-
ters. Through her own voice, the mother emerges not as a mere victim
of sexism and racism, but as a subject with her own irreducible other-
ness, her culturally and historically conditioned prejudice, and her
separateness and difference from the daughter.

This distance between the mother and daughter helps maintain an
ethical self-other relationship as an I-Thou relation of equal subject
positions. In response to the mother's interpretation of the bad omen
of the moon as a warning against the daughter's boyfriend, a subse-
quent short passage evokes a traditional Chinese sign of the snake
biting her own tail, "meaning harmony at the year's end." But Chin
immediately inserts a different interpretation of the sign in the

daughter's voice: "Or does it mean / she is eating herself / into ex-tinction?" (*Phoenix* 51). The implication of female self-annihilation in the sign helps Chin to refocus the poem on women's suffering and subjugation by referring to Chinese women's bound feet again in the next passage, while continuing to incorporate the otherness of Chinese culture into the poem:

> Oh dead prince, Oh hateful love,
> shall we meet again
> on the bridge of magpies?
> Will you kiss me tenderly
> where arch meets toe meets ankle,
> where dried blood warbles? (*Phoenix* 51)

The "bridge of magpies" alludes to a Chinese myth about the forbid-den love between a cowherd and the youngest daughter of the Em-peror of Heaven, who are separated and kept apart by the Silver River (the Milky Way). Once a year in July magpies flock together to make a bridge over the river to help the star-crossed lovers meet. While al-luding to the forbidden love, Chin exposes the fact that women's love, body, and sexuality were regulated by patriarchal law that forced Chinese women to bind their feet in order to please men. The lines "Will you kiss me tenderly / where arch meets toe meets ankle, / where dried blood warbles?" evoke again the imperial consort and her complaint about the pain in her feet.

But the poem ends with a shift away from women's suffering and subjugation through the mother's voice:

> *The phoenix gone, the terrace empty.*
> *Look, Mei Ling,*
> *yellow crowfoot in the pond,*
> *not lotus, not lily.* (*Phoenix* 51)

The mother cites the line from Li Bai's poem to articulate her sense of inevitable change with the passage of time. In directing her daughter's attention to "yellow crowfoot in the pond," away from "lotus" or "lily," the mother seems to be reminding the daughter that she is at a differ-ent time and place, where the pond has "yellow crowfoot" rather than "lotus" and "lily," which allude to metaphors for Chinese women's bound feet that meet the aesthetic standard size of female beauty. Or the mother is simply articulating her own point of view, which differs from the daughter's. By ending the poem with the mother's voice and viewpoint, Chin raises questions about her attempts to speak for other women. As she says, "It was a moment of questioning the poem's role as a conduit of other women's voices" (qtd. in Tabios 307).

But this doubt does not prevent Chin from enacting her sense of responsibility for the other in her poetry. In "The Gilded Cangue," subtitled "(*Phoenix series #2/3*)," Chin further explores the necessity for giving voice to women's lives through lyric poetry, and the consequences of keeping silent about women's subjugation and suffering. For Chin, these questions concern the relations between art and life, as the speaker in the poem asks: "What is poetry if it could forget / the meaning of her life?" (*Phoenix* 56). In her conversation with Eileen Tabios, Chin expresses her feelings about the limitation of the centrality of the poet-self in mainstream American lyric poetry. "The American lyric is dominated by self and that doesn't satisfy me," she says. As minority poets, Chin adds, "We have to be greater than self." She believes that poetry "has to teach, to illuminate, to make the world a better place" (qtd. in Tabios 281). In seeking to fulfill the ethical responsibility of her poetry, Chin develops a hybrid poetics of alterity whose historical and cultural otherness challenges the Eurocentrism in Harold Bloom's formulation of the modern American lyric canon and in Marjorie Perloff's definition of postmodern American poetry which is characterized by the erasure of the lyric I.

Although written in a style and voice different from Lee's, Chin's poetry, like Lee's, responds not only to the other's alterity, but also to the other's suffering, oppression, and dislocation. The passion of Chin's lyric is characterized by the lyric I's attention to the other as an ethical responsibility materialized in the content, form, and language of her poems. Chin develops her poetics of alterity by choosing exile as her condition for reinventing the self and the lyric.

# CHAPTER THREE

# David Mura

## WHERE AM I, THE MISSING THIRD?

In response to Harold Bloom's essay, "They Have the Numbers; We, the Heights," which critiques poems such as those included in the 1996 *Best American Poetry* collection edited by Adrienne Rich, David Mura entitled his essay, "A Note from Caliban."[1] In referring to himself as "Caliban," Mura identifies himself with the racial other who is posited beyond the pale of the Western canon of which Bloom assumes the position of foremost guardian. This identification challenges the "honorable white" position of Asian Americans in race relations and confronts the politics of canon formation, calling into question Bloom's assumption of a universal aesthetic standard defined by only canonical white writers' works, a standard that minority writers, in Bloom's judgment, fail to achieve. By raising questions about the literary establishment's relation to racial ideology from the perspective of the other, Mura spotlights the correlations between the construct of an imperial subject of reason and its opposite other embodied by Caliban in Shakespeare's play. In so doing, Mura turns a constructed and subjugated abject other into a subversive, unsettling other, denaturalizing and redefining Caliban's otherness.

In Shakespeare's *Tempest*, Caliban, a native of the island, is subjugated and enslaved by Prospero, Duke of Milan, lover of books. For Prospero, Caliban's otherness is completely knowable even though he is everything that Caliban is not. In fact Prospero defines Caliban as the exact opposite of himself and what he stands for. Called variably "monster," "beast," and "hag-seed" by Prospero, Caliban is supposed to be half beast and half human, both African and Indian, born of an Algerian mother, whom Prospero refers to as the "damn'd witch" and "hag." Caliban's bodily difference is dehumanized and equated with a lack of intelligence and moral conscience. Although to Prospero, Caliban is "not honor'd with a human shape" and is "a born devil, on whose nature / Nature can never stick" (*Tempest* I, ii; IV, i); he is indispensable — "He does make our fire, / Fetch in our wood, and serves in offices / That profit us," says Prospero (*Tempest* I, ii). In this binary model of self-other relation, the self's identity is defined in opposite terms of the other, and vice versa; the self not only assumes superiority over the other, but also knowledge of the other. This arrogant assumption of knowledge of the other underlies racism and violates the ethics of alterity. As Levinas contends: "The possibility of possessing, that is, of suspending the very alterity of what is only at first other, and other relative to me, is the *way* of the same." Defined as the opposite of Prospero and everything he stands for, Caliban's otherness is merely a part of what Levinas calls "totality encompassing the same and the other" (*TI* 38). Given the fact that *The Tempest* was first performed in 1611, the relationship between Caliban and Prospero is indicative of race relations during the age of British overseas expansion and colonization. These relations ramify in the formation of race and racial positions in the United States. Speaking of Japanese Americans' social status in a 1999 interview, Mura says that his Japanese American identity is not simply constituted in relation to white America, but is "also formed in relation to African Americans" (Ling 114). Mura's identification with Caliban situates the construct of Japanese/Asian American identity within the racial ideology of the U.S. nation-state, as well as in a larger context of identity formations and power relations beyond national borders.

Through the elocutionary subject position of the lyric I, Mura investigates the subjectivity of the self as the socially marginalized other, and articulates the irreducible, intractable alterity of the other and of the self as other. Unlike the autobiographical I in Lee's and Chin's poems, this self in Mura's poems, especially those collected in his first volume, *After We Lost Our Way* (1989), is articulated mostly through various dramatic monologue speakers. Not until after he has confronted his own identity as a person of color, in *Turning Japanese: Memoirs of a Sansei* (1991), does Mura begin to explore his own subjectivity in his second volume, *The Colors of Desire* (1995). As he searches for an understanding of the effect of racial ideology on his sexuality and identity, including his attempts to assimilate and to disassociate himself from other Japanese Americans and minority Americans, Mura develops a poetics that at once draws on and departs from the lyric traditions of dramatic, interior, and confessional monologues. His poetry of self-exploration, like English Romantic lyric and the American confessional mode, involves an inward turn-ing, in which the poet's subjectivity is the central subject matter.

However, in its inward turning, Mura's lyric I does not keep the so-cially constructed self at bay. Rather, the subject's inward turning in Mura's poems is an act of the self's "exiling itself," of "turning inside out" to an other, which Levinas calls "saying" that indicates "the first visible chink in the psychism of satisfaction" ("Hermeneutics and the Beyond" *EN* 71). In disrupting the unitary subjectivity and self-sufficiency of the traditional lyric I, the lyric speaker in Mura's poems reveals the formation of the subjectivity of the self as a socially and discursively constructed other. Thus this otherness of the self as "Caliban" is not the kind of otherness which Levinas refers to as the infinite mystery of the other, irreducible to any categories. But in ex-ploring a sociohistorical category of otherness, Mura denaturalizes its essence, while redefining the debased other by undermining its constructed otherness and transforming it into the Levinasian con-cept of alterity through lyricism.

---

### *We Tearee Down Your Door!*

Evoking James Baldwin's remark that "No true account really of black life can be held, can be contained in the American vocabulary,"[2] Mura contends in an essay on Asian American poetry: "Any poet who wants to describe [minority Americans'] experience must somehow violate the accepted practice of the language, must bring into the lan-guage an alien vocabulary and syntax, rhythms that disrupt, images which jar, ideas which require a totally new relationship to the lan-guage and the reality it contains" ("The Margins" 171–72). Moreover, for Mura, investigating the multiplicity and complexity of Japanese Americans involves examining their social positioning as the other in relation to white America and other minority Americans. Like Chin, Mura explores the implications and costs of assimilation for his par-ents' generation, but as in the case of most Japanese American poets of his generation (sansei, third generation), much of his investigation deals with the impact of the internment during World War II on Japanese Americans' sense of self in a large number of his poems, such as "Letters from Tule Lake Internment Camp (1942–45)," "An Argu-ment: On 1942," and "A Nisei Picnic: From An Album" collected in his first volume, *After We Lost Our Way* (1989), and the sequence poems in his second volume, *The Colors of Desire* (1995), as well as the sequence of "Internment Epistles" that appeared in his third volume, *Angels for the Burning* (2004). While exploring the effects of dominant ideological interpellation on Japanese Americans, Mura shows their different responses to their imprisonment, including their complicity with and resistance to the state power, as suggested in the title of the poem "Letters from Tule Lake Internment Camp (1942–45)."

One of the largest internment camps, incarcerating more than 15,000 Japanese immigrants and Japanese Americans, Tule Lake was referred to by one of its internees, Yamato Ichihashi, as "the black-sheep camp" (Chang 240). It was the camp where the U.S. government sent those who had already been interned at various concentration camps but were considered "disloyal" to the United States. Among them were "no-no boys," who answered negatively to the two questions in the U.S. government's loyalty questionnaires given to all internees: "Are you willing to serve in the armed forces of the United States on combat duty, wherever ordered?" (Question 27); "Will you swear unqualified allegiance to the United States of America and faithfully defend the United States from any or all attack by foreign or domestic forces, and forswear any form of allegiance or obedience to the Japanese emperor, or any other foreign government, power or organization?" (Question 28).³ According to Ronald Takaki, about 22 percent of the nisei males eligible to register for the draft answered both queries with a "no." "Many of them said they were not expressing disloyalty but were protesting against the internment" which violated their "legal rights" and treated them "more like enemy aliens than American citizens" (*Strangers* 397–98). In his essay, "No-No Boys: Re-X-Amining Japanese Americans," Mura discusses the effects of racism on Japanese Americans. Rather than being regarded as heroes by Japanese Americans themselves, Mura notes, the no-no boys were sometimes "scorned by their own community." Some of them eventually "end[ed] up broken, crazy, silenced, left out of the pages of the history books" (144). In his poem, Mura inscribes the no-no boys' and other disloyals' presence in history, calling attention to resistance to the coercion of state power in contrast to other Japanese Americans' eagerness to prove their loyalty. The undesirable and containable otherness of Japanese Americans, then, is turned into a subversive otherness that challenges the dominant power's violation of the rights of the raced ethnic and national other.

As the title indicates, "Letters from Tule Lake Internment Camp (1942–45)" is written in the form of an epistolary monologue. By letting the monologue speaker address his letters to his wife at another camp, Mura alludes to the separation of the disloyals from their families by the government, thus incorporating another aspect of repressed history into his poem through personal experience. The poem begins with the speaker's assertion of his psychological response to his incarceration in a letter to his wife:

Dear Michiko,

Do songs sound different in prison?
I think there are more spaces between the words.
I think, when the song ends, the silence
does not stop singing. I think
there is nothing but song.

Matsuo's back, his bruises almost healed,
a tooth missing. His *biwa*
comes out again with the stars, a nightly
matter. He sends his regards. (*Way* 6)

In contrast to his dehumanizing treatment as a criminal, the speaker's voice and words sound surprisingly gentle and dignified. His remarks about songs, like his memory of the orchids and roses in his greenhouse back home referred to later in the poem, serve to reveal his humanity, his tenderness toward his wife, and the conditions of his confinement, deprivation, and isolation. The repetition of "I think" emphatically expresses the spirit of the individual in resistance to the tyranny of state power that threatens to efface Japanese Americans' individuality. At the same time, the other-sounding rhythm and sensibility these repetitive sentences produce incorporate into the English language an otherness that signifies the speaker's irreducible alterity. Similarly, the personal, humane touch in the speaker's reference to Matsuo contrasts with the brutality he receives.

Mura's employment of the capacity of dramatic monologue for presenting a situation and for revealing the speaker's personality and character also serves to expose the connection between fear of the other and violence against, even genocide of, the other. The speaker's monologue, addressed to his wife, associates their internment with concurrent unspeakable sufferings and frightening killings around the world. While this association alludes to the destruction of World War II, it also suggests a connection between Japanese Americans' incarceration in the internment camps and the concentration camps for Jews in Europe:

Dear Michiko,

Did you hear it last night?
So many cries
clinging to the wind?

Not just the grinding
of tanks, rifles and mortars,
or the sound of eyelids
closing forever, but something
hungrier, colder.

I'm frightened. So many dying.
What do our complaints
about blankets or late letters
matter? Or even our dreams?

But this was more than a dream.

It came across seas
and the mountains,
it smelled of ash, a gasless flame,
and I woke this morning
still tired, irritable, unable to rise.
. . . . . . . . . . . . .
I heard them again. The cries.

I wanted to answer: my lips
were cracked, dry.

Michiko,
am I going crazy?
Did you hear them? (*Way* 7–8)

The speaker's reference to the suffering and the killing of countless others on a massive scale during World War II, including the genocide of Jews and the dropping of atom bombs on Hiroshima and Nagasaki, suggests that Japanese Americans' internment was related to a similar kind of fear and hatred of the other which led to the atrocities committed in other parts of the world.

The most disturbing part of this poem is perhaps the implicit connection between the large-scale destruction during the war and the effects of the dominant ideology of a nation-state in constituting concrete subjects who act as agents of its ideology. The speaker's observation of some fellow internees discloses the impact of hatred for the other and the effect of the coercion of state power on Japanese Americans:

> I look around me and see many
> honest men who hide their beauty
> as best they can.
>
> .   .   .   .   .   .
>
> Why can't they see the door is inside them?
> If someone found an answer to that,
> they'd find an answer to why
> those who are hungry and cold
> go off to battle to become hungrier
> and colder, farther from home. (*Way* 6–7)

The speaker's inability to understand those internees who joined the U.S. army to fight in Europe reveals not simply the differences in Japanese Americans' perspectives on their relationships to the nation-state, and the differences in their response to internment, but also the contradictions in the government's treatment of the raced others, who were forced into a dilemma of national, racial, and ethnic identity conflicts. As Sau-ling Wong observes, while discussing the state's conflicting policies for assimilating and excluding Asian Americans: "they are expected at once to lose their offensive 'Asianess' and to remain permanently foreign" (91). This contradiction reflects the fear and intolerance of otherness, resulting from the homogenizing system that reduces and confines the other to the category of the abject other in relation to the self-same of the dominant norm.

Mura confronts the construct of the other by the state and Hollywood — the regime of identity productions — and reclaims the otherness of people of color in "Song for Uncle Tom, Tonto, and Mr. Moto." By placing a typical Asian stereotype with African and Native American stereotypes in American popular culture, Mura relates

Japanese American identity to other minority Americans, and situates their racial stereotypes in the historical context of colonialism and imperialism. The speaker of this poem assumes the voice of *Kitsune*, the trickster fox in Japanese folklore, to embrace an "offensive" culture of the other, to at once mimic and satirize the dehumanizing representation of "Japs" with a "sneaky inscrutable body" (*Way* 15), and to transform the subjugated, inarticulate, and subservient stereotypes of Japanese and other minority Americans into the image of an articulate, outraged rebel. The animal image of *Kitsune* as a Japanese American is reminiscent of Caliban, an embodiment of racialized and colonized peoples with whom *Kitsune*, the speaker, identifies:

> now, I, *Kitsune*, the fox,
> open this song –
>
> all the way from Shikoku and Shingu I axed the forest
> laid down spikes and pounded their heads, grabbed salmon
> like arrows leaping from streams, all the way from Kotchi,
>     from Akao
>
> .  .  .  .  .
>
> I am the dance the drum the sneaky inscrutable body
>
> .  .  .  .  .  .  .  .  .  .  .  .  .  .  .
>
> of a Jap who knows at last my brothers
> are creatures of adobe and Sand Creek and those who bowed
>     massa
>
> yes, sir, all the good niggers and the mute buffalo herds
> all the torrential unconsecrated nauseating flood, each
> singing the old imperial clichés — whip marks and sweat,
>     harvest, bone and blood
>
> .  .  .  .  .  .  .  .  .  .
>
> and yes I'm raving, asphyxiated and incurable
> and now proclaiming (*Way* 15)

This song of outraged "raving" that goes on from beginning to end without any punctuation at the end of each line until the last one has the effect of capturing the intensity of the speaker's rage, while conveying a sense of the enormity and extent of the wrongs committed against people of color accumulated through history, which are now pouring out with an irresistible urgency and profusion. According to Mura, the work of the black Martinican writer Aimé Césaire is the "abiding influence" on this poem. For Mura, Césaire's line is "denser and less elegantly paralleled than Whitman's." And while Whitman is a strict realist, Césaire "contains a surrealist and a mythic cast." But in writing "Song for Uncle Tom, Tonto, and Mr. Moto," Mura adds, "I'm not just influenced by his specific poetics or his use of the line; it's as much his post-colonial enterprise, throwing off or reinterpreting the culture and history of the colonizer and creating a new liberated culture for the colonial."[4] In responding to the other as responsibility for the other, Mura's poem employs an "alien vocabulary and syntax" to rearticulate the otherness of the subjugated Caliban which disrupts the dominant culture's construction of the raced other, of which Uncle Tom, Tonto, and Mr. Moto are a few examples.

While employing unusual syntactic structures with disturbing images and jarring vocabulary within the established form of monologue, Mura protests against the dehumanizing racist stereotypes of people of color through parody. His mimicry of racial stereotypes and his parody of ethnically accented words expose the deformation of minority Americans' images, while turning their debased otherness into an unsettling, unassimilable alterity. *Kitsune*'s monologue picks up speed and steam as his indignation intensifies with his protest against colonialism at home and abroad:

> and here in my uterine mind something is cleaving, beating,
>     growling
> .   .   .   .   .
> and it is rising in Soweto, in Wounded Knee
> in Savannah and savannah, in the Indonesian junk shops
> and the smell of the hanged man or the *shoyu*-stained tables of
>     *hana*[5]
> in the Andes and terrifying inner storms of the Caribbean
> sordid, visionary alleys of São Paulo, the alchemical, Amazonian
>     jungles
> and we are all good niggers, good gooks and japs
> .   .   .   .   .
> obsequious, ubiquitous ugliness, which stares at you baboon-
>     like, banana-like
> dwarf-like, tortoise-like, dirt-like, slant-eyed, kink-haired, ashen
>     and pansied
> .   .   .   .   .   .

yes, it us, it us, we, we knockeee, yes, sir, massa, boss-san,
    we tearee down your door! (*Way* 16)

Even though the speaker identifies with people of color in the United
States and around the world, his identification does not assume ho-
mogeneity. Rather, his emphasis on the diversity and heterogeneity
of "us" who have multiple cultural and linguistic backgrounds ex-
poses the homogenizing categories of the racial other. Reappropriat-
ing the debased otherness of Caliban, and speaking in the voices of
the raced others, *Kitsune* challenges the dominant culture's exclusion
of racial and cultural otherness and refuses to be kept in the assigned
marginal, subordinate positions. *Kitsune*'s song for the stereotyped
others defies standard pronunciations and the grammatical and syn-
tactical rules of English, deliberately bringing an "untutored" lan-
guage and prosody into English. Mura's use of the unsettling speech
and image of *Kitsune* in this poem can be understood in terms of what
Levinas calls saying, a speech act that resists the absorption of the
other into the One and the Same. *Kitsune*'s declaration in pidgin En-
glish, "we tearee down your door!," performs an otherness that at
once mimics and rejects racial stereotypes naturalized in Hollywood
films. Through the voices of a composite other, Mura's poem exposes
a correlation between representation of racial stereotypes and the
colonization or exclusion of raced others.

### Why Am I So Unworthy?

In the second part of *After We Lost Our Way*, Mura investigates so-
cial oppression and its effects on another group of people whose oth-
erness is defined and debased by the dominant culture. In a sequence
poem, "Pasolini," which consists of eleven dramatic monologues,
Mura rewrites passages taken from Norman MacAffee's notes to his
translation of Pier Paolo Pasolini's *Poems* (1982), and incorporates
materials from Pasolini's *Lutheran Letters* (1987) in order to reveal the
complexity of Pasolini, the poet, critic, playwright, film director, and
Marxist who was condemned by Italian society as a criminal because
of his homosexuality. Mura's interest in Pasolini results in part from
his identification with Pasolini because, like him, Mura is a poet, a lit-
erary critic, and a playwright who is actively engaged in social and

political issues. But more importantly, his writing about Pasolini is motivated by his recognition of the similarity between racial and sexual discrimination. In a 1990 interview with Lee Rossi, Mura said that "when I wrote about Pasolini, one of the identifications I felt was that the Japanese-Americans were condemned not for what they did but for who they were. . . . And I think the type of difficulties that a person has to face when society condemns him or her for who they are is something that I understood on some sort of intuitive level with Pasolini" (Rossi 265).

In identifying with the socially oppressed other, Mura, like Li-Young Lee and Marilyn Chin, faces a number of challenges. These challenges are embedded in the question Rey Chow raises: "Does 'otherness' itself automatically suffice as critical intervention?" (30), and the question Levinas asks: "What meaning can community take on in difference without reducing difference?" (*OB* 154). Mura seeks critical intervention and performs an ethical response to otherness through lyrical utterance, while situating otherness in the politics of race and sexuality. In his sequence about Pasolini, Mura juxtaposes multiple aspects of Pasolini's irreducible otherness with his humiliating identity as an immoral homosexual defined and condemned by society. This juxtaposition enables him to subvert the socially defined otherness of Pasolini, and to rearticulate Pasolini's otherness through the lyrical speech of the self.

In resisting the reductive, demeaning social construct of the other, the lyric I serves as a viable site for the othered subject to articulate its irreducible alterity that redefines his socially constructed otherness. Mura employs dramatic monologue to enact, as well as subvert, the construction of otherness through different characters and voices. At the same time the spatial capacity of the sequence form enables Mura to situate the monologues in a larger social world. In dealing with these multilayered complexities, Mura expands on the capacity of the dramatic monologue by interlacing multiple voices simultaneously, and by juxtaposing different monologues through their connections to the same topic. This interlocking of separate monologues has a provocative and destabilizing effect because the contending voices put into question any single perspective on Pasolini. The first dramatic monologue in the sequence, "To the Subject, No Address," addressed to Pasolini, apparently by the poet, captures the complexity of Pasolini, a controversial figure in Italian society:

> In photographs, you lean on your Romeo,
> sweater slipped on your shoulders, or leather
> pants, leather jacket, shoes with a leather
> so thin it tatters in the rain like paper,
> ruined by nights of sexual stalking . . . Defiant
>
> in interviews — "I shall continue to lead the ambiguous life" —
> crazy about Marx and *terza rima*, filming the
> Bogate slums of your novels, Chaucer, *Oedipus*,
> *Gospel*, *Sodom*, you chatted poolside at Cannes,
> lampooned fascists, slipped like a Pope through
>
> courts of intrigue, . . .
> > With cypress, nettles, poppies
>
> .   .   .   .   .   .   .   .   .   .   .   .   .   .   .   .
>
> poured a peasant boy's pity, your mother's
> face, Friulian dreams . . . *Far from hawk-shadows*,
> *green meadows, with the cries of a scavenger*,
> *I know now this longing, this weeping, this cry*,
> *is a simple thing — Yes, it's you, my Beatrice*,
>
> *my rose, my river of light . . . (Way 25)*

Rather than trying to define who Pasolini is, the speaker responds to his otherness by revealing and exploring its irreducible alterity. Refusing to reduce Pasolini to his homosexuality defined by the state and society, Mura juxtaposes seemingly conflicting images of Pasolini, as a Marxist and poet who has a preference for *terza rima*; a novelist who writes about life in the slums; an avant-garde filmmaker, whose films about sexuality and social problems are disturbing and challenging; an anti-fascist who moves with equal ease in the world of intellectuals and the world of politics; a peasant boy who grew up in the countryside and wrote poems in the Friulian dialect. While these details help to form a multidimensional picture of Pasolini, they also serve to render his otherness still more mysterious.

Pasolini's homosexuality, like his otherness, remains abstruse. The apparently peaceful, contented posture of Pasolini leaning on his Alfa Romeo sports car, is immediately undercut by his "nights of sexual stalking" — a piece of information whose meaning is called into question by Pasolini's defiant remark in an interview, "I shall continue to lead the ambiguous life." In contrast to the public's vigilant scrutiny of Pasolini's sexuality as suggested by the question in his interviews, the closing lines, spoken in the voice of Pasolini himself, seem to reveal Pasolini's identification of his longing for love with Dante's love for Beatrice. This yearning for someone who is "*my rose, my river of light*" may suggest both a connection and contrast with Pasolini's "nights of sexual stalking." The tenderness and spirituality in Pasolini's articulation of love, and particularly the religious connotations in his identification with Dante, subvert the public condemnation of Pasolini as abnormal and immoral because of his homosexuality. Moreover, Pasolini's lyric utterance about love, immediately following the reference to his mother's face, also suggests that for Pasolini, "Beatrice" is his mother, who looms large in his life, and is, in certain ways, the great love of his life. Mura alludes to Pasolini's exploration of and identification with Oedipus later in the sequence, particularly in the poem "A Violent Life." These ambivalent, multilayered meanings produced by Mura's employment of lyricism in Pasolini's interior monologue reveal a complex, elusive interiority that contrasts with the lists of facts about Pasolini's public image.

In rejecting transparency and fixity, lyrical speech has a similar effect like that of "saying" with regard to otherness. In a dialogue with Richard Kearney, Levinas points out the ethical dimension of language: "Language as *saying* is an ethical openness to the other; as that which is *said* — reduced to a fixed identity or synchronized presence — it is an ontological closure to the other" ("Dialogue" *Face* 29). Pasolini's lyrical utterance opens the self to the other and renders his own otherness irreducible to the facts in journalist reports. By incorporating Pasolini's lyric voice into this dramatic monologue, Mura juxtaposes two modes of discourse— one of journalism for conveying publicly accessible and sensational information about Pasolini through a distant, apparently neutral voice of reportage, and the other of lyricism for revealing Pasolini's interiority by using his own voice. In so doing, he situates the private speech of the lyric I in relation to the social, without rendering the private self completely accessible or knowable. The contrasts and contradictions between the public views of Pasolini and his private self create the dynamic, unsettling tension in the sequence, which make impossible any easy conclusions about him. This tension is central to Mura's strategy for simultaneously showing the social construction of Pasolini's otherness, and his unnameable, intractable alterity.

Lyricism in the speech of the private self articulated through the lyric I as the other in Mura's poems has the effect of resistance and subversion to totalizing Knowledge and the dominant power by revealing the elusive alterity of the self as other. Poetic language then, like Levinasian saying, can enact an ethical relation to the other. For Levinas, "ethics is something that 'happens' in language," to quote Jill Robbins again. Mura employs another strategy to juxtapose lyricism with public speech and to stretch the capacity of a single monologue by interlocking private and public speeches in such a way that the reader is compelled to constantly readjust his or her view of Pasolini that was formed from one particular perspective. This strategy also serves to expose and critique social oppression of individuals who do not conform to the norm of identity categories.

For example, in "Trials," another poem in the Pasolini sequence, Mura uses monologues to reveal the process and effects of Pasolini's identity construction as the other from both the perspective of the state and that of Pasolini. Locating Pasolini's private moment of lyricism in the process in which the state institution exercises its power, Mura suggests that a particular mode of discourse can be brutally oppressive on the other. With this method, Mura extends the possibilities of the lyric through collage juxtaposition of multiple perspectives and simultaneity within a single temporal-spatial moment, interweaving in one poem the trial lawyer's performance, the audience's response, and Pasolini's inner experience. This poem is divided into two parts. The first, subtitled "Offenses," is written in prose, which provides background information for the court trial scene. Against this background, the second part, subtitled "The Court, The Circus, The Dream," depicts a court scene by interlocking different voices, which demonstrates the social construction of Pasolini's identity as the other, and the way in which Pasolini's sense of self is affected by the public and state's condemnation of his homosexuality. These interlaced voices represent different perspectives indicated in the subtitle. For the court, Pasolini's trial is a matter-of-fact legal procedure; for the public, the trial is circuslike, a spectacle for sensational thrills; and for Pasolini, his trial is as unreal and absurd as a dream.

Mura's use of dramatic monologue for the prosecutor's voice serves multiple functions. Addressing the audience, the prosecutor's speech sets up the situation in court, presents the official position regarding the charges against Pasolini, and reveals the entanglement of art, politics, and sexuality. The diction and tone of the prosecutor's monologue suggest that his role is similar to that of a ringmaster in the circuslike court atmosphere:

> Ladies and gentlemen of this sandman circus,
> this grubby, tiny press-stuffed hall, all crammed
> with fascists, gossip queens, fairies, filmstars,
>     we charge this false *flâneur* of slums,
>         this so called novelist,
>       blind, pornographic poet genius –
> no, no, please hold your catcalls, your hot hisses –
> (Please rise, Signore, to your confetti dream.)
>
> . . . . . . . . . . .  (*Way* 32–33)

The prosecutor's public speech and the rowdy audience are juxtaposed with Pasolini's reaction to the situation through interior monologue. While the prosecutor's speech characterizes what Levinas would call the language of intentionality that seeks to define and fix Pasolini's identity with prescribed meanings to it, Pasolini's interior monologue, which reveals his humanity, undermines the official definition of his identity as the infamous homosexual. Pasolini's monologue also shows his alienation which is reflected in his uncanny, surrealist hallucination, in which Pasolini sees himself sitting in the defendant's seat like the helpless and inarticulate wooden puppet, Pinocchio. But instead of his nose growing for his lies and sins, something else *"sticks up/ from its crotch, as if Pinocchio / had misplaced his nose, and every time / he struggles to speak, all that comes forth / is the clacking of his wooden teeth"* (*Way* 33). The misplaced nose of Pinocchio suggests that Pasolini feels it is his sexuality more than anything else that is condemned and put on trial. This image of the self and Pasolini's reference to it in the third person express his sense of alienation from himself and the surrounding world, while indicating a "nomadic inwardness" that eludes the gaze of the public and the mastery of official discourses, as Levinas says of the alterity of the other (*EN* 71).

The self as other in Pasolini which Mura discloses through lyricism is a self who resists the official and social definition of his otherness. Hence Levinas's contention that "the epiphany of the other involves a signifyingness of its own independent of this meaning received from the world" ("Meaning and Sense" *CPP* 95) sheds light on the significant difference between the style of public speech by the prosecutor and the lyricism of Pasolini's monologue. Mura's interlacing of the prosecutor's dramatic monologue and Pasolini's interior monologue enhances this difference, while highlighting the possibilities of lyricism as a mode of resistance to social oppression. In contrast to the arrogant, demeaning, and denominating language in the prosecutor's speech, Pasolini's monologue is fragmentary and interior, responding to the surrounding situation and revealing his vulnerability:

> "'This,' Signore Pasolini proclaims, 'is
> a cultural new wave!' (*a brief aside*—
> To taste those spirochetes, syphilitic bits,
>     of course, that's the true culture he craves)—
>
> .   .   .   .   .   .   .   .   .   .   .   .   .   .   .   .
>
> *Hoots of laughter from the crowd, and*
> *When I, the puppet, turn to look at them,*
> *there's the face of my mother, a bruise*
> *on her cheek, her tears blue and streaming.*)—
>
> .   .   .   .   .   .   .   .   .   .   .   .   .   .
>
> "*Why am I so unworthy? devoid of love?*— (*Way* 33–35)

The juxtaposition of two different modes of speech, moreover, reveals Pasolini's otherness unknowable to the prosecutor and his self-same frame of reference. The prosecutor's disparaging remarks about Pasolini's ideas of the "cultural new wave" and his passion for Rimbaud, among other things, suggest that there is another context for Pasolini's otherness which is outside the value system of the prosecutor, the state, and the public. In addition, Pasolini's seeing of his mother's bruised face and "her tears blue and streaming" discloses another aspect of his private self irreducible to the state's denomination. The indication of the importance of his mother in Pasolini's life takes on a particular layer of meaning in juxtaposition to the prosecutor's condemnation of Pasolini's homosexuality and "other sins."

Articulated outside the logic and rhetoric of the prosecutor's discourse, Pasolini's private speech subverts the totalizing value system that condemns him. His questions — *"Why am I so unworthy? devoid of love?"* — do not challenge the truthfulness of the accusations, but rather the hatred of him because of his homosexuality. The thrust of his questions points to the central concerns of Mura's poems: the social constructions of racial and sexual otherness and their effect on individual subjects. In "Mirrors of the Self: Autobiography and the Japanese-American Writer," an essay about the relation between genre and race, Mura notes that the similarities between racial discrimination and sexual discrimination lie in the fact that the "condemnation and ostracism" directed at those who are discriminated against can result in their "deep suspicion of worthlessness [which] may begin to corrode the very center of the self" (216). In his poems about Pasolini and Japanese Americans, Mura investigates not only the effects of social condemnation and ostracism on those who are categorized as the other, but also the possibilities for intervening in such categorizations through the possibilities of poetic form and language for articulating the irreducible otherness of the other. He develops new strategies for articulating the self as other as he explores further the social and discursive constructions of otherness in his second volume, *The Colors of Desire*.

### Where Am I, the Missing Third?

Moving from investigating the oppression of the racial and sexual other to a more complex representational and discursive construction of otherness, *The Colors of Desire* is at once a continuation of and departure from *After We Lost Our Way*. Mura's major thematic concerns in his first book, such as the impact of the Japanese American internment, issues of assimilation, and the relation between one's sexuality and social identity, resurface in his second.[6] These thematic concerns are integrated into an extended exploration of the relation between sexual desire and racial identity, which Mura carries out within an autobiographical narrative of family history and the formation of the narrator's subjectivity and sexuality, which underlie all the poems in the volume. Through an investigation of the self, Mura seeks to expose and undermine the construction of otherness in cultural and discursive representations of gender, race, and sexuality, insisting on showing that these representations are racial positionings which help establish and maintain racial hierarchy as an organizing principle of a social order. In exploring the penetration of racial ideology in the formation of the individual's subjectivity and sexuality within power relations marked by gender and class differences, Mura confronts the challenges of finding an appropriate language and poetic form to reveal the process of this formation.

These challenges open up new creative possibilities for Mura, especially when there are no available models in mainstream American or Japanese American literature for what he seeks to accomplish in his poetry. While the experiences that European American poets write about are nothing like his own, there is little investigation of sexuality in Japanese American poetry or prose. Mura realizes that the lack of exploration of sexuality and the body in Japanese American literature, particularly writings about such experiences in the internment camps, may result from the impact of racial ideology that defines Japanese Americans' otherness for social exclusion. With this realization, he "began to sense that the deepest wounds in the Japanese American psyche, the deepest levels of repression [,] may have taken place within that [sexuality] realm" ("Mirrors" 260). Compared with the treatment of sexuality in Japanese literature, this repression of sexuality in Japanese American literature becomes particularly obvious. For many Japanese Americans, Mura adds, "the experience of the camps, their own sense of shame about being a racial minority, still remains in the closet; perhaps we should not be surprised then that their sexuality remains there too" ("Mirrors" 261). He believes that "the models of white middle-class America . . . , or even the aesthetics of mainstream contemporary American literature, can uncover only the briefest, surface aspects of Japanese American experience; there are depths and complications to that experience that require more sophisticated literary tools" ("Mirrors" 257). In developing adequate tools for mining the depths and complexities of Japanese American experience, Mura turns to European, Japanese, Caribbean, and African American writers for models. He incorporates Pasolini's technique of juxtaposing and interlocking multiple voices within a poem; he appropriates Marguerite Duras's cinematic representation and visual language in representing the body, and her blurring of the fictional with the autobiographical. He also draws on Yukio Mishima's autobiographical novel, *Confessions of a Mask*, in developing a confessional mode through employment of monologue and a particularized persona to express his sense of the forbidden boundaries of interracial sexuality.

But to understand the forbidden nature of his raced subject's sexuality, Mura needs an analytical vocabulary that includes race as a constituent component of subjectivity and sexuality, and a poetic language that confronts the dilemma of being a poet of color writing in English. He finds the former in Frantz Fanon's writings and the latter in Derek Walcott's poetry. Fanon's discussion of interracial sexuality in *Black Skin, White Masks* is especially pertinent to Mura's investigation of his persona's sexual desire for white women. Unlike the metaphysical, erotic desire that Lee articulates for the infinite other, the desire Mura investigates is need resulting from racial ideology. Mura perceives in Fanon's linking of sexuality to race and politics a powerful subversion of and intervention in racial hierarchy. In Walcott, Mura identifies with the conflicts and paradoxes such as those asserted in his poem "A Far Cry from Africa," which Mura quotes in his essay, "Mirrors of the Self." Torn between his rage against British colonial rule and his love for the English language, Walcott asserts the conflicts and challenges he faces as a poet and black African.

Mura faces similar challenges as a Japanese American poet, writing in English and in European American poetic forms about Japanese American experience. He used to regard his ethnic identity as "a source of shame or inferiority," and was more enamored of mainstream European American than Asian American, or any other minority American, literary traditions. In fact, he had tried to minimize his connection to any minority group for fear that he would be labeled a minority poet, whose poetry, "as seen from much of the American literary establishment," was "crude, unschooled, and untalented, filled with the understandable but regrettable clichés of oppression." He used to believe that to be taken seriously as a writer, he had to associate himself with canonized white male poets, rather than with "unskilled, anonymous minority poets" ("Intellectual Biography" 37, 40). When he eventually began to confront his identity complex, Mura realized that his identification with poets such as Robert Lowell and John Berryman was similar to his parents' identification with "the middle class whites of America." "We had come to so identify ourselves," says Mura, "with the Victors, with the rulers, that we had denied our own experience" ("Intellectual Biography" 41–42). He now emphasizes that in dealing with his own experience, he must "violate the accepted practice of the language, must bring into the language an alien vocabulary and syntax, rhythms that disrupt, images which jar, ideas which require a totally new relationship to the language and the reality it contains," evoking the words of James Baldwin in his essay on Asian American poetry ("Margins" 171–72). His poems demonstrate these efforts to search for new ways of using language and for a poetics capable of signifying the otherness of a Japanese American self.

This search, however, inevitably involves investigating and subverting the construction of racial otherness, which is implicated in the Japanese American experience. While exploring further the possibilities of monologue, sequence, and multiple voices, Mura develops new strategies such as collage composition, cinematic representation, and intertextual appropriation and revision to illustrate the ways in which sexuality and the body can be sites for articulation of and resistance to racial ideology. One of his strategies is locating the formation of his persona's identity and sexuality in the history of racism in the United States, and in the representation of racially marked bodies in American popular culture. In the title poem, "The Colors of Desire," Mura employs sequence to connect separate moments in history among the four sections of the poem. Hence descriptions and narratives about racism in the 1930s and 1940s in section 1 serve as a context for section 2, situated in 1957, when Mura's child persona encounters white men's racial slurs and suffers from his father's physical violence — a displacement of repressed anger resulting from racial discrimination against Japanese Americans and of the sense of helplessness. These sections form the background for section 3 when, in 1964, Mura's adolescent persona discovers white women's bodies in pornographic magazines as a seductive and forbidden site for people of color like him and his father. This section resonates with lynching, racial segregation in the South, Japanese American internment, and the transgressive interracial scene in a pornographic film described in section 1. With these multiple resonances, the speaker in section 4 examines the implications of his interracial marriage with a white woman. Thus the formation of his persona's subjectivity and sexuality is interwoven with personal and collective histories shaped by racial ideology.

In addition to making the most of the overall structure of the sequence, Mura also employs the cinematic technique of the jump-cut to include multiple moments in history within each section of "The

Colors of Desire" in order to link racial identity to sexuality. Section 1, subtitled "Photograph of a Lynching (circa 1930)," begins with the speaker's observation of white men in a photograph of a lynching in the southern United States. To foreground the formation of racial subjectivity, the speaker notes "at the far right" in the photo, "a boy of twelve smiles, / as if responding to what's most familiar here" (*Desire* 4). This disturbing scene reminds the speaker of a moment in 1942 when his father, still a teenager living in an internment camp in Jerome, Arkansas, "stepped on a bus to find white riders / motioning, 'Sit here, son,' and, in the rows beyond, / a half dozen black faces, waving him back, 'Us colored folks got to stick together'" (4). Mura tactfully brings this incident of the father's ambivalent racial identity and social status as a nisei to bear upon the sexuality and identity crisis of the sansei speaker through narrative and syntax that connect the passage about the father's bus ride to the next passage about the son's experience of watching an X-rated film thirty-five years later. He also links the black-and-white interracial sexual transgression in the film to the photograph of a lynching through his description of and comment on the coded representation of the black man, which Frantz Fanon has referred to as the "jungle" man, whom white men lynched for fear that his supposed sexual prowess threatened white racial purity:[7]

How did he know where to sit? And how is it,

thirty-five years later, I found myself sitting
in a dark theatre, watching *Behind the Green Door*
with a dozen anonymous men? On the screen
a woman sprawls on a table, stripped, the same one
on the Ivory Snow soap box, a baby on her shoulder,
smiling her blonde, practically pure white smile.
. . . . . . . . . . . . . . . . . . .
             And now he walks in —

Lean, naked, black, streaks of white paint on his chest
and face, a necklace of teeth, it's almost comical,
this fake garb of the jungle, Africa and All-America,
black and blond, almost a joke but for the surge
of what these lynchers urged as the ultimate crime

against nature: the black man kneeling to this kidnapped
body, slipping himself in, the screen showing it
   all . . . (*Desire* 4–5)

This performance enacts the forbidden sexual desire and transgression of racial boundaries through a sexual encounter in which the racially marked bodies are stabilized sites for identity construction. Mura investigates the reproduction of racial identities and the possibilities for disrupting this production through sexual relationships between white women and Asian American men in most of the poems collected in *The Colors of Desire*.

In the context of the racial ideology of the United States, white women for men of color are the embodiment of the American dream. Being associated with the dominant power, white women are also represented as the norm of female beauty and desirability, as shown in a number of Asian American writers' works, including Marilyn Chin's poems. In his autobiography, *American in Disguise* (1971), Daniel Okimoto associates his attraction to white women with his racial identity and social status in the United States:

In this white dominated society, it was perhaps natural that
white girls seemed attractive personally as well as physically.
They are in a sense symbols of the social success I was condi-
tioned to seek, all the more appealing, perhaps, because of the
subtly imposed feelings of self derogation associated with being
a member of a racial minority. . . . Behind the magnetism there
may have been an unhealthy ambition to prove my self-worth by
competing with the best of the white bucks and winning the fair
hand of some beautiful, blue-eyed blonde — crowning evidence
of having made it. (200–01)

Similarly, the blonde girl for the Chinese American man in Shawn Wong's novel *Homebase* (1979) is "the shadow, the white ghost of all my love life; she is the true dream of my capture of America. . . . She is America" (66). These Asian men's attraction to white women largely results from their awareness of their racial otherness marked as inferior and marginal. For them, white women are desirable because they embody privilege, beauty, and power. To be loved by white women and to have a sexual relationship with them gives them a sense of being accepted by the dominant culture, and having access to dominant power. As Michel Foucault contends in *The History of Sexuality*, "where there is desire, the power relation is already present" (81). Foucault argues that sex is "a complex idea that was formed inside the deployment of sexuality." Historically, he contends, sex "is subordinate to sexuality," and "sexuality is a result and an instrument of power's design" (152). Mura's poem exposes the naturalization of racial identity through deployment of sexuality in relation to power.

The performance of interracial sexual taboo generated by the prohibitions of racial ideologies reproduces racialized heterosexual norms and sexualized racial identities. Judith Butler's discussion of sexual prohibitions as "constitutive constraints" which make the "performativity" of gender and sexuality possible can shed light on the implications of the sexual performance in the X-rated film and Mura's representation of interracial sexual relationships in his poems. In *Bodies that Matter*, Butler argues that the "performative" dimension of the construction of sexuality is "precisely the forced reiteration of norms." In other words, Butler contends, constraint should be "rethought as the very condition of performativity"; "the law is not only that which represses sexuality, but a prohibition that *generates* sexuality or, at least, compels its directionality" (95). Mura's poem illustrates the effect of the performativity of racialized sexuality on his persona. For the sansei speaker, these images of "black and blond" in the pornographic film meant more than a transgression of sexual taboo; the absence of images of people like him in the deployment of sexuality has led to his sense of alienated racial identity. As Mura writes in his essay, "Mirrors of the Self," "a deep suspicion of worthlessness" resulting from racial discrimination "may begin to corrode the very center of the self" (261). A corrosion of the self as such underlies the self-hatred and neurotic sexuality of his persona in *The Colors of Desire*. As his sansei persona wonders "where am I, / the missing third?," black and white bodies haunt him night after night "like a talisman, a rageful, unrelenting release" (*Desire* 5).

The speaker's rhetorical question about the absence of Asian American male images in the representation of interracial sexuality points to the persistent issue of "feminization" of the Asian American male in the U.S. cultural imaginary, which David Eng refers to as "racial castration" in the formation of U.S. national identity in the image of white masculinity.[8] In a 1996 article entitled "How America Unsexes the Asian Male" published in *The New York Times*, Mura discusses the implications and effects of the Asian American male image in popular culture. He notes that the pathetic, ridiculous Japanese American character in the film *Fargo* is "only the latest in a long line of Asian and Asian-American male nerds." Such hopelessly unattractive images of Asian American men devoid of sexual appeal, Mura contends, "reinforce a hierarchy of power and sexual attractiveness" (C9). Investigating similar issues, Eng in his book, *Racial Castration: Managing Masculinity in Asian America*, argues that the racialization of Asian American masculinity is "an overdetermined symptom whose material existence draws its discursive sustenance from multiple structures and strategies relating to racialization, gendering, and (homo)sexualizing" (18). While examining this "symptom" and the conditions for its existence, Mura explores the ways in which an ethical, political poetics can disrupt the production of Asian Americans' racial otherness that sustains a racialized hierarchy of power relations.

In two experimental, intertextual sequence poems, "The Blueness of the Day" and "Lovers and Sons," Mura seeks to enact political subversion by repositioning Asian American men in their sexual relationships with white women. In so doing, he transforms Asian American men's naturalized racial otherness into a subversive and uncontainable alterity. In the last part of section 1, Mizuno, a Japanese American soldier, relates his sexual relationship with a white woman to his racial otherness through her eyes:

> And for a few minutes, I'll keep
> her face beneath me, almost dead, almost
> frightened of whatever she sees there:
>
> I've thought so often it's my skin, the folds
> of my eyes, the alien energy thrashing her thighs,
> but no, it's just my face, that implacable mask . . . (*Desire* 29)

The speaker's fear reveals more of his own "deep suspicion of worthlessness" that has corroded "the very center of the self," than the white woman's view of him. But his remarks about his face — "that implacable mask" — assert his otherness irreducible to the plasticity of the racially marked face. The nisei's claim to an otherness uncontainable by the socially inscribed body is profoundly subversive to racial ideology in which bodily image is a stable site for racial identity. Levinas emphasizes the absence of the presence of the other in the visible as a primary condition of alterity: "Because it is the presence of exteriority the face never becomes an image or an intuition" (*TI* 297). He argues that the manifestation of the other as the "face" must not be equated with the plastic form: "The face is a living presence; it is expression. The life of expression consists in undoing the form in which the existence, exposed as a theme, is thereby dissimulated. The face speaks. The manifestation of the face is already discourse" (*TI* 66). In other words, the alterity of the other is implicated in the language act; encounters with otherness generate saying.

For Mura, to undo the form in which the alterity of the other is reduced or erased involves undermining the stereotypical image of Asian American males by engaging with dominant discourses and breaking away from traditional lyric form. The abrupt ending of section 1 with the nisei soldier's remarks about his face indicates that the poet has reached an impasse in attempting to portray how Japanese Americans' racial identity is constructed through the gaze of white women. Mura seems to have found his treatment of Mizuno's interracial relationship through a single-voiced monologue from the Japanese American perspective inadequate.

Therefore, section 2, subtitled "Intermission (1991)," interrupts Mizuno's monologue to portray the poet's struggle in searching for an alternative method for signifying the otherness of Japanese Americans. Within the sequence, this intermission functions as a transitional point from the poet's struggle in looking for new materials and strategies to his discovery of a subversive intertextual appropriation and revision in sections 3 and 4, respectively subtitled "Sentences by M. Duras (dates unknown)" and "Marguerite (Pigalle, the Mediterranean, 1947)." Mura's imaginary treatment of the nisei soldier's sexual relationship with Marguerite Duras in these two sections is at once inventive and transgressive. In *The Lover*, an autobiographical novel about her own sexual encounter with a Chinese banker in the French colony, Indochina, Duras depicts the wealthy Chinese man in such a way that it produces and fixes his inferior racial identity and also his helplessness in his relationship with the white French girl, who "knows he's at her mercy" (*Lover* 35). Through the constructing gaze of the French girl, Duras renders the body of the Chinese banker weak, pathetic, and exotic, the otherness of which is at once an object of derision and desire: "The skin is sumptuously soft. The body. The body is thin, lacking in strength, in muscle, he may have been ill, may be convalescent, he's hairless, nothing masculine about him but his sex, he's weak, probably a helpless prey to insult, vulnerable. She doesn't look him in the face. Doesn't look at him at all. She touches him. Touches the softness of his sex, his skin, caresses his goldenness, the strange novelty" (*Desire* 38). This effeminized and exoticized Chinese male body becomes the site where Duras inscribes the other's racial, sexual, and gendered difference with an authority derived from the representational tactics of realism. As Homi Bhabha points out, "colonial discourse produces the colonized as a social reality which is at once an 'other' and yet entirely knowable and visible . . . . It employs a system of representation, a regime of truth, that is structurally similar to realism" (70–71). Mura undercuts the authority and effect of Duras's apparently realistic rendering of the otherness of the other in terms of an abject otherness by incorporating and revising her narrative while imitating her mode of representation.

In his invention of the nisei soldier's sexual relationship with Duras, Mura simultaneously parodies and displaces Duras's gaze of the Asian male body. In so doing, he reinscribes the raced and gendered Asian male body and shifts the Asian man's subordinate racial position in his relationship with a white woman. In Mura's poem, Duras finds the Japanese American soldier unlike her Chinese lover:

> *I thought your body would be soft like a woman's.*
> *Your cheekbones are so rounded, your eyes curled*
> *like sleep. You still wear the uniform. Why?*
>
> *I had a lover once like you. In that city where*
> *the Mekong dragged down half a continent, boats,*
> *water buffaloes, crates, chairs, tigers, palm trees,*
>
> *I was crossing on the ferry to school one morning,*
> *and out of a black limousine stepped a Chinese,*
> *in a white tussore suit, the suit of a banker . . .*
>
> . . . . . . . . . . . . . .
> *But you're not like him.*
> *There's this scar across your belly. Another on your lip.* (*Desire* 37)

Mura's re-representation of Duras's gaze of an Asian male body resists her voyeuristic mode of constructing racial difference, and frustrates the white woman's desire for domination over the stereotypical, helpless Asian man.

Mura also turns Duras, the observer, into the observed in another sequence poem, "Lovers and Sons," by replacing Duras's narrative voice with his. This change and the subsequent switch of subject positions enable Mura to shift the narrative and observation from one point of view to another, thus at once enacting and subverting not only Duras's voyeuristic and othering gaze, but also the Chinese banker's desperate desire. Resisting the white woman's gaze of mastery over his bodily difference, the Chinese banker in Mura's poem refuses to be transparently knowable:

> She strokes his body, the flesh so sumptuously
> soft, as of a long convalescence, drained by fever.
> And silken, without hair. Ambiguously shifting,
>
> his features are aloof, unreadable,
> like the sea of the tropics, the doldrums, a
> gold opalescence shimmering to the horizon.
>
> Touching her as always with a tentative calm
> that masks his fervency; weak, helpless,
> he knows his being will be eviscerated
>
> if she ever ends this moaning and motion
> of their bodies, this knowledge like nightmare,
> so far from pleasure, but never desire. (*Desire* 42)

In his intertextual revision, Mura subverts Duras's Orientalist representation of the Chinese man by insisting that the otherness of the other is elusive and irreducible, as indicated by the fact that Duras finds the Chinese banker's features "aloof, unreadable." This resistance to the reductive, authoritative construction of Asian men's effeminate stereotypes is similar to Lee's and Chin's articulations of Asian American otherness, which uphold an ethical relation to the other by enacting the subject's responsibility through language and poetic form. Mura's poem reclaims the Asian male's subjectivity by enabling the Asian male monologue speakers to refuse their "racial castration," and by undermining realist representations of Asian men as the "completely knowable" other.

However, Mura does not avoid confronting the impact of racial hierarchy on his persona. While appropriating and rewriting passages from Duras's *The Lover*, Mura integrates his persona's experience and sexuality, as well as his commentary, into the poem. Unlike the wealthy Chinese banker who wants to possess the white girl, Mura's persona says: "what I desire isn't to possess, but to be her — " (*Desire* 44). But Mura's persona emphasizes that he knows that the Chinese banker exists within him, and that he also shares his weakness and helplessness in his desire for the beauty, power, and privilege inscribed in the body and social status of white women.

At the same time, Mura is aware of the risk of reproducing a sexist discourse on race by representing the white woman's body as a site for his persona's sexual conquest in order to identify with power. He confronts sexism and gender difference along with racial identity and sexuality, thus dealing with another socially constructed category of otherness. Switching from narrative to meditative descriptions, Mura's persona moves from examining his sexuality shaped by racial hierarchy to confronting his sexism in his sexual relationships with white women:

> On a familiar ledge in my life I began to fashion
> a language for desire, for the soft caving
> inside me at the presence of sexual want,
> for my own weakness and loathing and shame,
> for the revenges I felt I needed against women,
> their impenetrable otherness, their beauty, their
> remoteness, and their skin, the whiteness of skin
> spread before me like a map of the ramparts.
> It was, I realize now, a type of madness, an ancient cruelty,
>
> . . . . . . . . . . . . . . . . . . . . . . . .
>
> In other words, reader beware. I was hardly
> as innocent or naive as I may make myself seem. (*Desire* 55)

The relationship between this white woman and the Japanese American poet is much more complex than one of domination versus subordination. The ethical relation between self and other in Mura's poems involves refusing to repress the other's voice or to erase the other's difference. Rather than reducing the white woman to her racial identity, Mura allows her to speak about herself and the Japanese American poet with whom she is having an affair.

By refusing to erase the subjectivity of the white woman, or the difference of gender and class in her experience, Mura is able to portray a more complex character whose view of her Japanese American lover is subsequently ambivalent and incomplete. As the monologue speaker in "The Affair: II — Her Version," the white woman reveals her experience of sexism through her memories of her parents' relationship and her mother's relationships with other men, which are characterized by violence and humiliation. Nevertheless, the white woman's remarks about her Japanese American lover suggest that those who suffer oppression and humiliation as a result of gender and class difference are not incapable of racial prejudice even in their intimate interracial sexual relationships.

Despite her prejudice, however, the white woman finds her Japanese American lover's otherness elusive. The limits and possibilities of the dramatic monologue enable Mura to reveal the intractable otherness of the raced and gendered other through the monologue speakers. The interior monologue of the white woman reveals that for her, the Japanese American poet "remains an enigma." Unlike any other affairs she has had, this one, with a racial other, is like an unexpected discovery of something new in what has been taken for granted, such as "the sympathy you suddenly feel/for someone you have always despised, from the very first moment of meeting." Her efforts in trying to understand and articulate her relationship with the Japanese American poet indicate the complexity of herself and her relationship with an Asian man, whose face she imagines will continue to haunt her in her old age. Even then, she would not be able to grasp his otherness. She imagines a moment in her future, when she is brushing away the ashes of her cigarette fallen on a print she is looking at, "his face, for a moment, will click into focus. And I will think of him. Like this. Like this" (*Desire* 69). The unreadable face of the Japanese American poet, like that of the other, remains in proximity, disturbing and demanding attention, but forever eludes.

Thus, Mura transforms the completely knowable otherness of the Asian male as an inferior other into the absolute alterity of the other through confessional monologues spoken from different subject positions. By shifting perspectives and subject positions, Mura performs the complex otherness of self and other, and strategically subverts totalizing representation of the otherness of race or gender. The ethics and poetics of alterity in his poetry demonstrate that critical intervention is possible through new signifying modes that contest racial stereotypes naturalized by what Stuart Hall calls "a racialized regime of representation" ("The Spectacle of the 'Other'" 249). As

Bhabha says of the subversive reinscription of racial identity in post-colonial literature: "What is interrogated is not simply the image of the person, but the discursive and disciplinary place from which questions of identity are strategically and institutionally posed" (47).

Mura counters discursive and disciplinary productions of stereo-typical identities by using the capacity of the lyric poetry to reveal the traumatic effects of racism, to rearticulate otherness, and to expose the deployment of sexuality and construction of identities in relation to power. Hall argues that power has to be understood "not only in terms of economic exploitation and physical coercion, but also in broader cultural or symbolic terms, including the power to represent someone or something in a certain way — within a certain 'regime of representation.'" In this respect, Hall emphasizes, power "includes the exercise of *symbolic power* through representational practices. Stereotyping is a key element in this exercise of symbolic violence" (259). The construction and production of an essential, knowable otherness of race, gender, and sexuality is part of the exercise and effect of symbolic power through seemingly realistic representational practices. The neurotic sexuality of Mura's persona in *The Colors of Desire* is in part an effect of "this exercise of symbolic violence." Mura's poems illustrate the effects of racial identity on sexuality through the gaze of both those discriminated against and those belonging to the dominant power, thus dealing with the impact of what Toni Morrison calls "racial hierarchy" on its victim and those who fabricate and perpetuate it, as well as those who resist and alter it (11).

Representing perspectives from both the victims and perpetrators of institutionalized prejudice, and seeking to intervene in the stereo-typing of otherness, Mura's approach to sexuality and race is similar to the kind of inclusiveness which Seamus Heaney advocates for poetry. Heaney states, "Poetry . . . whether it belongs to an old political dispensation or aspires to express a new one, has to be a working model of inclusive consciousness. It should not simplify. Its projections and inventions should be a match for the complex reality which surrounds it and out of which it is generated" (7–8). Mura achieves this kind of inclusiveness and complexity in *After We Lost Our Way* and *The Colors of Desire* by insisting on positioning the lyric I in relation to power, ideology, history, and the other. His poems suggest that poetry which refuses to empty history and politics out of itself, must also refuse to articulate only from the position of the victimized. In confronting the power of representation and the effects of symbolic violence, Mura's poetry deals with both the social, discursive constructs of the abject other and the Levinasian concept of the ethical relation with otherness as "absence and mystery" (*PN* 105). His poems suggest that before an ethical relationship with the other can be established and maintained, the symbolic violence done to the other must be redressed in order to articulate the elusive, irreducible, and unsettling alterity of the other. Employing strategically and creatively the possibilities of lyricism and of the speaking subject's position, Mura is able to not only expose and critique the repression and violation of the other, he also restores the other's inviolable otherness.

# CHAPTER FOUR

# Kimiko Hahn

## THE PASSION OF LEAVING HOME

In her essay "Memory, Language and Desire," Kimiko Hahn speaks of her conviction about the importance of desire as a necessary force in her poetry: "I believe even the most intellectually-oriented literature should throb with desire; not necessarily explicitly sexual but so informed." For Hahn, desire "looks toward the future"; the future is shaped by "political action." And "politics is an essential dimension to serious literary work" (68–69). In an intertextual poem, "The Izu Dancer," Hahn relates her female persona's desire of sexual transgression to her desire to reject women's institutionalized domestic roles of subordination. "I wanted to cross that fence / with the passion of leaving home," says the speaker, in order to reinvent the female self instead of fulfilling the roles of the daughter, the wife, or the mother prescribed by patriarchy (*Earshot* 9). The articulation of desire, especially female erotic desire, in Hahn's poetry is a political act, an aesthetic challenge, and an ethical responsibility. It involves a transformation of the masculine, disembodied lyric I and the poetic language and form established by patriarchal discourses and Eurocentric culture.

Unlike Marilyn Chin's articulation of her female persona's sexuality that engages with issues of assimilation and identities of race, nation, and culture, Hahn's exploration of women's desire and sexuality asserts an otherness that is outside of patriarchal cultural and discursive practices. Although Hahn's investigation of desire, like David Mura's, exposes the relations of race, gender, class, and sexuality to power, it is mostly committed to women's desire that signifies female subjectivity, subverts patriarchy, and reimagines a social order in which women are subjects equal to men. Rather than seeking to satisfy need, or to become one with the other, the desiring female subject in Hahn's poems maintains an ethical distance between self and other. In a way, women's desire for the other in Hahn's poems is similar to the metaphysical desire in Li-Young Lee's poetry, which is not exclusively sexual, nor can it be satisfied like need. For Hahn, women's desire, like a catalyst, can bring a number of transformations of women's status in patriarchy, including women's subordinate position and their marginalization in or exclusion from politics and creative productions of art, literature, and ideas in a patriarchal society. Hahn's notions of women's desire and its transformative forces are embedded in the title — "The Intelligentsia of the Chin Dynasty Desire Desire" — of one of Hahn's poems modeled on Chinese women's epistolary verses written in a language invented and used by a community of women only.

The desire Hahn seeks to articulate in her poetry can be understood in terms of Levinas's concept of metaphysical desire which "desires the other beyond satisfactions, where no gesture by the body to diminish the aspiration is possible." It is a desire "without satisfaction which, precisely, *understands* [*intends*] the remoteness, the alterity, and the exteriority of the other." In this desire, Levinas emphasizes, "there is no sinking one's teeth into being, no satiety, but an uncharted future before me" (*TI* 34, 117). The uncharted future which Hahn envisions for women, particularly women of color, is a future which cannot be achieved simply through political actions or social changes; its realization demands an ethics and aesthetics of alterity. Hahn seeks to enact this politics, ethics, and aesthetics in her poetry.

In seeking to develop a poetics to articulate women's desire, Hahn explores what Luce Irigaray calls "an art of the sexual" that will help "establish a new *ethics* of sexuality" (*Sexes* 3). Irigaray's concept of the ethics of sexual difference is influenced by Levinas's ethics of alterity. As Elizabeth Grosz notes, Levinas's "conception of alterity is central to Irigaray's understanding of relations between sexually different subjects" (*Subversions* 142). Extending Levinas's ethics of alterity into her investigation of culture, language, and sexuality mediated by patriarchy, Irigaray insists on rethinking gender relations and reconceptualizing a female subject which is not merely a variation of the self-sameness of the masculine subject, but one which recognizes the alterity of the female other.[1] In *Je, Tu, Nous: Toward a Culture of Difference*, Irigaray contends: "The status of sexual difference is obviously related to that of our culture and its languages." She adds that "sexuality, though said to be private, cannot possibly escape from social norms." Sexual norms that correlate with social norms in a patriarchal society, Irigaray argues, are predicated upon the domination of men over women (*Je, Tu, Nous* 15–16). Patriarchal power and culture are "marked in the deep economy of language. Sexual difference cannot therefore be reduced to a simple, extralinguistic fact of nature. It conditions language and is conditioned by it" (*Je, Tu, Nous* 20). Thus, "social justice cannot be achieved without a cultural transformation." Cultural transformation involves "changing the laws of language and the conceptions of truths and values structuring the social order" (*Je, Tu, Nous* 22). The social order in the United States is implicated in both patriarchy and racial hierarchy. For Hahn and other Asian American poets, a cultural transformation that aims to bring social justice and human dignity for all must challenge racism and Eurocentrism, as well as sexism.

Hahn develops a feminist poetics of alterity, which confronts the differences of race, gender, and culture in specific social contexts. She insists on incorporating Japanese language and literature, especially the traditions of Japanese and Chinese women's writings, into her multigeneric and cross-cultural poems. In addition to positing women as desiring subjects, Hahn's poems articulate a desire that is in large measure oriented toward an envisioned future of American culture which allows the other to maintain his or her otherness, a culture that produces a poetry whose "dominant element," Hahn asserts, "is diversity of subject, form and language" ("Memory" 69). For Hahn, as for Marilyn Chin, to meet the challenge of such a future involves redefining "Mainstream." An intervention as such, Hahn states, is "politically and aesthetically necessary. It should be our Desire" ("Memory" 69). Like Lee, Chin, and Mura, Hahn has to confront the socially constructed categories of otherness, while exploring in language, aesthetics, and form the possibilities for articulating an alterity which operates as a catalyst for cultural transformation.

### Refashioning a Language of Desire

In her poems Hahn searches for a language to articulate women's desire and subjectivity, to reclaim the female body, and to explore "a female culture or aesthetic" ("Three Voices" 10). For Hahn, using words innovatively to express women's sensibility and sexuality which challenges the patriarchal system that represses women's desire, and reduces women's otherness to inferior attributes that justify their subordination to men in a hierarchical binary, is artistically and politically necessary. The necessity to refashion a language for articulating women's desire and a female aesthetic is grounded, among other things, in the fact that gender and sexual difference is shaped by the values and meanings invested in networks of signification, as Irigaray argues. Advancing Irigaray's argument, Grosz offers further insights into the constituent conditions for the emergence of sexual desire which might seem to be a natural, corporeal mechanism of the private apart from the social domain:

> Sexual drives result from the insertion of biological or bodily processes into networks of signification and meaning; through this immersion, they become bound up with and intimately connected to the structure of individual and collective fantasies and significations. The drive is a result of corporeal significances, the binding of bodily processes and activities to systems of meaning. This signifying and fantasmatic dimension is necessary for the sexual to emerge as such and for the establishment of desire. The domain of sexual drives is doubly implicated in representation and signification. (*Bodies* 55)

Given the fact that sexual drives result from the meshing of bodily processes with networks of signification and meaning, representation of sexuality in a patriarchal culture inevitably privileges male sexual desire. Thus in seeking to assert women's erotic desire, Hahn must engage with and challenge the dominant patriarchal system of signification and representation, while exploring new possibilities in language and the lyric form.

In her poem "Instead of Speech," Hahn employs a collage method to juxtapose patriarchal systems of signification with her persona's speeches from a feminist perspective. While watching a Noh play, the lyric speaker asserts her sense of exile from her heritage of Japanese culture whose patriarchal system forbids women to perform in Noh, in which all the female roles are played by men. Through collage juxtaposition, Hahn associates the exclusion of women in Noh with sexism in language and the speaker's everyday experience. This juxtaposition indicates that women's otherness defined by patriarchy negatively in relation to men is marked in the deep economy of culture and language:

> The reflection of Noh actors
> in the reflecting pool, the torches,
> the faces all turned in one direction
> make your heart throb:
> *this is home*. This is home the way a home
> will never admit you
> because you are by definition alien and female.

>> No matter what (bitchy, manipulative, fertile, on top)
>> you girl
>> are the vulnerable one by social
>> and biological inheritance.
>> At the moment.

>> *All women are streetwise*, she said
>> And, *the penis is the lynchpin*
>> *of linguistic systems*. Funny

>> the word penis.

. . . . . . . . . . . . . . . . . . .

> The actor's feet never left the ground
> as he slowly whirled across the wooden stage
> toward anything.

>> All summer you wore your husband's gym shorts and t-shirts.
>> *You wear that outside?* your sister asked.
>> A man on the stoop called: *too much meat for the*
>>     *street*. (*Earshot* 21)

Noh theater, which emerged during the fourteenth century, was regarded as the highest dramatic and poetic art in medieval Japan, and continues to hold high prestige today. Given the symbolic nature and cultural value of Noh, the prohibition of women from playing any parts in it is especially significant in the establishment and maintenance of gender hierarchy. Hahn juxtaposes the exclusion of women from Noh with fragmentary everyday speeches to suggest a correlation between the representation of gender difference in art and the ways in which women experience belittlement and humiliation in life.

This juxtaposition also suggests that the status of the female body, forbidden from the Noh theater, is produced by the networks of values, meanings, and significances that privilege the male body as phallic, bestowing power and authority on it. As Grosz states: "The phallus binarizes the differences between the sexes, dividing up a sexual-corporeal continuum into two mutually exclusive categories which in fact belie the multiplicity of bodies and body types" (*Bodies* 58).

While continuing to expose patriarchal values that shape the social, cultural, and personal, Hahn challenges the phallus as the organizing principle of gender and sexual differences, and undermines its primacy and privilege through the female lyric speaker in the second half of the poem. In contrast to the obscene sexual assault on a voluptuous woman in a subway poster, which asserts the power of the phallus over the female body, the female speaker articulates the possibility of her erotic desire for another woman:

> A woman with short blonde hair and white earrings
> entered the café.
> She wore an immaculate white t-shirt
> and you knew were you a lesbian and she were
> you would approach her
> and court her. (*Earshot* 22)

This assertion of the female lyric speaker's same-sex desire undermines the primacy of the phallus and its binarization of differences between male and female. The female speaker's gaze, like a caress, creates a sense of one woman's attraction to another woman's mystery and alterity, while her speech maintains a distance between self and other, which is signified through words such as "approach" and "court." A desire as such for a female other counters the violent male assault on a female body in the drawing on the subway poster. Rather than seeking to dominate or possess as the imposing penis in the drawing indicates, the speaker would "court" the desired other, suggesting an ethical relationship in which a distance between self and other is maintained, while the subject of the self and the alterity of the other are sustained.

In asserting her erotic desire for the other, the female speaker also articulates an alternative female identity and sexuality which are not subordinate to male domination or privilege. Moreover, this female erotic desire entails an ethical relationship which, according to Levinas, is embedded in eroticism. Levinas contends that in erotic desire, the alterity of the other is maintained, as is the subjectivity of the desiring subject. For Eros does not seek domination, knowledge, or fusion. "It is a relationship with alterity, with mystery." In this relationship with alterity, "one can no longer be able, the subject is still a subject through eros" (*TO* 88). By articulating erotic desire as such through the lyric I, Hahn intervenes in the patriarchal binary construction of gender and sexual differences which are inscribed in sexed bodies. Speaking of her sexuality and body as "a territory" for her poetry, Hahn says that investigation in this "territory" led to her "increasing awareness that women's bodies historically have not always belonged to them" ("Three Voices" 10). The female speaker's articulation of erotic desire is a way of reclaiming women's objectified body for male pleasure.

Hahn seeks to transfer female erotic desire into "metaphoric desire for political power" ("Memory" 69) by shifting the speaker's erotic gaze to her desire to express her rage on the Noh stage. Following her contemplation of same-sex love between women, the speaker returns to the moment of watching a Noh play:

There are only actors
yet so many female roles
so many women's masks it hurts.
I would like to climb the stage
in white tabi and silk
stretch my arms out —fingers together palms down —
and stamp.
Calling out: *nantoka nantoka soro*

like sorrow, sorrow sorrow (*Earshot* 22)

This desire to act as a Noh actress, like women's same-sex erotic desire, transgresses the boundaries that contain the female body in a subordinate position to male domination in a patriarchal social order.

In a large number of her poems Hahn seeks to reclaim women's bodies and their creativity by redefining women's otherness through an aesthetics that enhances both feminine and cultural differences. "Bon Odori," collected in her first volume, *Air Pocket* (1989), is a salient example. In this poem Hahn inscribes the otherness of women through her relationship with her Japanese American mother and grandmother, while reclaiming women's creativity and subjectivity, and rearticulating a femininity not defined by patriarchal laws. Like Chin, Hahn insists on incorporating her ethnic cultural heritage in the content and aesthetics of her poetry. Addressed to the speaker's mother, the poem begins with memories of her grandmother's dance kimonos in association with the annual Japanese festival for the dead, *Bon Odori*, which takes place in July. Its ceremony includes dancing and lighting paper lanterns for the deceased. Evoking the image of grandmother making paper lanterns, the speaker begins to challenge male artists' portrayal of feminine beauty at the service of male desire, by alluding to female figures produced by Utamaro Kitagawa, a renowned Japanese block-print artist who specialized in portraits of beautiful geishas of the "floating world":

> I do not see
> Utamaro's woman,
> paper in her teeth — not his
> woodcut, rather Cassatt's drypoint,
> *The Letter*: her head, black
> hair tied back, bent forward
> as she licks the envelope,
> exactly like you, mother. (*Air Pocket* 13)

Apart from rejecting male production of women's images, the speaker foregrounds women's creativity by comparing her grandmother and mother to the woman in a print by Mary Cassatt, the American impressionist painter who, under the influence of Japanese block prints, brought a new crispness, definition, and economy to etching and drypoint. In contrast to Utamaro's idealized women of the male gaze, the woman in Cassatt's *The Letter* refuses to be an object of male desire; she is portrayed as an individual whose interiority and subjectivity are signified through her provocative gesture of sealing an envelope. By identifying her grandmother and mother with the woman in *The Letter*, the speaker highlights their individual identities that undermine the stereotypical images of submissive, obedient Japanese women.

Further undermining male domination in cultural productions, the speaker identifies herself as one of the women who are part of a female tradition of writing and whose aesthetic sensibility evokes that of Japanese women's literature.[2]

> In winter we write
> about summer. We send letters: the silk
> the color of raw tuna, and its water pattern,
> tie-dyed shapes like fish eggs,
> will look well in the circle
> of dancers. The drummer
> is always so handsome! Sleeves
> and moths flutter and
> lanterns sway in the heat. The drummer,
> half naked, is in the center. (*Air Pocket* 13)

Significantly the female speaker alludes to women's epistolary writing — a genre of more private, individualized writing, available to women who do not have easy access to publication — as a practice of aesthetics, an act of imaginative creativity, and a gesture of friendship. Women who are creative subjects, Hahn suggests, are also sexual subjects. The metaphors the speaker employs to describe the colors of silk she imagines for a dance kimono subtly enhance her statements about the drummer being "always so handsome!" and "half naked," which express female erotic desire for the male body. In Japanese and Chinese, the character for *color* also means voluptuousness. Hahn incorporates this double meaning of "*color*" into her poem to articulate sensuousness and eroticism from a woman's point of view. Like Cassatt, she brings a gendered and cultural otherness into a male-dominated tradition of art, not to be assimilated into the dominant tradition by erasing sexual difference, but to disrupt the patriarchal production of gender identity. Thus women in her poem emerge as creative and sexual subjects.

Hahn further develops her collage method for engaging in intertextual dialogues and revisions in order to simultaneously undermine and rearticulate women's otherness produced by patriarchal cultures and discourses. In "The Izu Dancer," collected in her second volume, *Earshot* (1992), Hahn explores the aesthetic subtlety of Yasunari Kawabata's Japanese language and the gender ideology that underlies the visual construct of Chinese characters and the privilege of male sexuality in Kawabata's writing. Hahn's attention to the way language is used breaks away from the traditional view of language, which Levinas notes, regards language as simply the means for expressing thought and to "do the same work as that of thought: to know and to reveal being." Challenging this view of language, Levinas questions whether "language as *Said* has not been privileged, to the exclusion or minimizing of its dimension as *Saying*." He proposes an investigation of language that will bring out "from the *Saying*, an intrigue of meaning that is not reducible to the thematization and exposition of a *Said*." For Levinas, saying in the manner of everyday speech signifies something other than the themes and contents of the said. As such, saying is a language response that acknowledges the other. Thus "instead of forgetting" the other person in the "'enthusiasm' of eloquence," we approach him or her "in everyday language" ("Everyday Language" *OS* 141–42). Hahn seeks to enact this ethical relation with the other through an aesthetics implicated in the language act as an encounter with the other.

In addition to using everyday language in "The Izu Dancer" to approach the other, Hahn introduces into the poem an otherness through incorporation of Japanese language, which brings with it a new signifying mode. While exploring new possibilities of expressing sensibility in Japanese, Hahn investigates and challenges the construction of gender difference in the language and the narrative of Kawabata's short story, "The Dancing Girl of Izu," which she appropriates and revises in her poem.[3] This intertextual poem that crosses generic, linguistic, and cultural borders also signifies Hahn's otherness as an Eurasian American woman. For Hahn, Asian culture "is a source of identity, power and pleasure" ("Memory" 67). But like Chin, Hahn critiques patriarchy in Asian culture, even as she seeks enrichment from Asian cultures and literary traditions. Beginning with a summary of Kawabata's story, the poem immediately recreates the speaker's baffling experience of learning Japanese. Her struggle in learning the language seems to heighten her critical perspective on the sexism embedded in the language, and enhances her perception of the sensuousness of Kawabata's words:

> Though not a difficult text
> every few words I was stuck
> flipping through water radicals
> 水　氵　氺
> so I could resume the journey inside words
> I had begun as a child, as when Kawabata wrote

雨脚が杉の密林を白く染めながら

"while the shower bleached the cedars"

I did not know
I did not want to know Japanese
so much as a way back to, say, salt
and to him in his heaven.

. . . . . . . .

Yet from the fragrance of his lines I struggled to raise:
. . . . . . . . . . . . . . . . . . . . . . (*Earshot* 87)

With a young man as the protaganist, the story is told from his perspective and the sensuousness of Kawabata's language serves to articulate his desire. Although fascinated by "the fragrance of his lines," Hahn intervenes in Kawabata's repression of the female perspective.

Emulating the subtle voluptuousness of Kawabata's language of male desire, Hahn rewrites his narrative from the point of view of the girl with whom the student, Kawabata's protagonist, falls in love.

With closed eyes I imagine her thoughts:
*I swept my hair up off my back,*
*waded in from the heat of the road,*

. . . . . . . . . . .

*The air stung with a smell of iodine.*

. . . . . . . . . . .

*I wanted to lick the beads of sweat*
*from his temples.*
*The afternoon forecast a meeting,*
*clouds thickening offshore*
*but at fourteen my heart was not as willing*
*as my body. And too, I was afraid my body*
*looked funny.* (*Earshot* 88)

In contrast to Kawabata's expression of the student's desire for the girl, Hahn employs the subject position of the lyric I to reveal the girl's thought and her desire for the student. This imagined passage enacts Hahn's ethical response to the girl as an irreducible other whose alterity and subjectivity Hahn reclaims through the subject position of the lyric I, who expresses the girl's desire, which is absent in Kawabata's story. Morever, the sensuous everyday language in the girl's speech introduces a new vocabulary of female erotic desire in lyric poetry dominated by male consciousness and desire.

As she continues to examine Kawabata's writing, Hahn probes further into the relation between language and the female body. Just as the meaning of the female gender is signified in the visual structure of Chinese characters, the female body is treated as a spectacle, an object, or a readable sign:

Though in some respects the characters are astonishingly simple:

tree 木                       forest 森
woman 女                    mischief; noisy; assault 姦

. . . . . . . . . . . . . . . . . . . . . . . . . .

I persevered in my search for the fragrance of words
in this modest story — the only Kawabata story I could read.
Where did he unearth

不自然な程美しい黒髪が私の胸に触れそうになった。

("Her hair, so rich it seemed unreal, almost brushed against my
    chest.")
Where did I find the hands on my shoulders, sliding down my
    arms
then up under my t-shirt, into my bra,
squeezing my breasts, pinching my nipples so hard
I blinked to hold back tears.
He watched my expression as a meteorologist reads delicate
    instruments.

. . . . . . . . . . . . . . . . . . . . . . . . . .

(*Earshot* 89)

Interweaving lines from Kawabata and the speaker's fragmentary narrative of personal experience, Hahn suggests a correlation between the ways in which the female body is represented in language and the fact that it has become subordinate to male dominance and possessive desire. Unlike some Japanese American women writers' "reclamation of the body" which "is enabled by the subject's temporary positioning outside of the geographic boundaries of the United States," as Yamamoto argues (81), Hahn's reclamation of the racially marked female body is made possible through deployment of voice, language, and poetic form from a feminist subject position.

As she translates Kawabata's words and sentences about the student's feelings aroused by the girl, Hahn explores her own sexual desire through her persona. Although she is searching for a language to articulate her desire as effectively as Kawabata's "fragrance of words," the expressions she uses are everyday American idioms which contrast Kawabata's delicate, modest descriptions with bold expressions of female erotic passion:

> The student didn't know what to say
> to the little dancer, what would ease the calf-like movements
> that increased her charm — ease his own breath
> racing against his heart at the thought of her.
> If he read her a story,
> If she laughed or blushed but didn't run away
> that would mean something.

> The story is so clear I can dream his lines:
> *Stepping out of the waves*
> *I noticed a rash spread over my legs,*
> *the color of boiled lobster or genitals.*
> *It embarrassed her. She turned and ran away*
> *as if I had said something amiss.*
> *To kiss me there.*

> If I saw a red Volkswagen my heart would roll like a tsunami
> toward a man smoking a cigarette, leaning against the
>     chalkboard.
> Tall. Graying. In no time all lessons will be forgotten.
> But not a memory of no memory.
> Perhaps I did not want the language enough
> or wanted something else —
> —to leave a laundry-filled dormitory room
> and press my whole body against the professor's doorbell
> till he came downstairs and invited me inside.
> Cooked me dinner. Fucked in the guest room.
> Perhaps I didn't want any language. Any marriage. (*Earshot* 91)

This rebellious female student's sexual desire transgresses the conventional boundaries of sexual and gender relations in which the female's erotic desire is repressed, as shown in Kawabata's story. The girl dancer is subordinate to the development of the student, who is the desiring subject. Her desire remains buried, or rather erased, by Kawabata's portrayal of her coyness, modesty, and innocence. Hahn's persona offers an alternative female subjectivity and sexuality that undercuts the primacy of male desire and undermines the norm of female modesty. Moreover, the apparently erotic desire of Hahn's female persona is a desire for what cannot be satisfied by a sexual relationship, as is implied in her ambivalence about what she wants: "Perhaps I didn't want any language. Any marriage." Earlier in the poem, as she continues her "journey inside words" in search of a language for articulating female desire, Hahn's persona asserts her desire "to cross that fence / with the passion of leaving home, / the need for certain loss / that means constructing something for oneself —" (*Earshot* 90). This desire to leave the familiar, the domestic space to encounter the unknown signifies a transgression of conventional restrictions on the female body, sexuality, and subjectivity.

Intertextual revision with Kawabata's story enables Hahn to articulate from a different perspective the female desire for the other even as she draws on Kawabata's sensuous language and narrative strategy. In juxtaposition to the anticlimactic closure of Kawabata's story in which the student's intense erotic desire for the girl dancer disappears when he sees the girl naked, Hahn ends her poem with an anticlimactic incident, which has drastically different implications from Kawabata's anticlimax.

> When he saw her in the public bath the student was delighted
> the dancer was too young to consummate his
>
> fever                              熱
>
> He could sit beside her at dinner or the movies
> finally.
>         *
>
> A waitress pours me a warmcup and I look over
> to catch the back of a man's neck,
> his heavy black hair in a severe razor-cut style.
> I imagine he is B.D. Wong
> the incredibly handsome actor in *M. Butterfly*.
> His moist white cotton shirt

hangs a bit off his shoulders
and he holds a cup of cappuccino in one hand
and a slim hard-cover book in the other.
I imagine he turns around to ask for—
an ashtray
and ends up at my table
talking about contemporary poetry, mutual friends
and international affairs.
But as the man gathers his belongings he turns
and instead of the aristocratic profile and rakish glow
it's an older Italian man, moustached and serious.
But briefly that fragrance! (*Earshot* 92–93)

In Kawabata's story, the student's erotic desire vanishes at the sight of
the dancer's immature girlish body, and subsequently the girl's hair,
her shyness, and the movement of her body lose their enchanting
charm for the student, whose fantasy and sexual drive are bound up
with the corporeal significance produced through networks of mean-
ings and values. As Grosz points out, the immersion of bodily pro-
cesses into systems of meaning and signification is "intimately con-
nected to the structure of individual and collective fantasies and
significations." Kawabata's representation of the emergence, devel-
opment, and withdrawal of the student's erotic desire for the girl
dancer illustrates that "The domain of the sexual drives is doubly im-
plicated in representation and signification," to quote Grosz again
(*Bodies* 55). On the other hand, "The Dancing Girl of Izu" itself is part
of the networks of representation and signification which render the
emergence of erotic desire possible. In juxtaposition to Kawabata's
story, Hahn's articulation of female desire displaces the centrality of
male desire and its implications for gender relations. Moreover, by al-
luding to the Chinese actor in *M. Butterfly* and articulating her attrac-
tion to an Asian man's image through her persona, Hahn confronts
the difference of race in gender and sexual relations, subverting the
completely knowable racial stereotypes of Asian men as undesirable
"geeks" and "nerds" in mainstream American culture, where white
men are the privileged sign of desirability. Persisting in her "journey
inside words," Hahn creates an irresistibly attractive image of an
Asian man through a language of immaculate detail and sensuous am-
biance, which captures the other's alterity irreducible to any plasticity

of form, or transparency of meaning — alterity that summons, but remains ungraspable in "that fragrance" of a brief encounter.

This refined language, like the everyday language in her poem, enacts a mode of saying as a way of approaching the other. Hahn's use of language as a response to otherness entails what Levinas refers to as introducing "the new into a thought," rather than accelerating "the inward maturation of a reason common to all" (*TI* 219). Hahn's refashioning of a language of desire brings into American lyric poetry an otherness that disturbs and challenges established meanings and values of the gendered and raced body.

### Breaching Totality through Otherness

In disrupting gendered and raced constructions of identities by the dominant power, Hahn breaks the totality of patriarchy and racial hierarchy through the irreducible alterity of those who are categorized as the abject other. Her resistance to totalizing knowledge of gender and race produced by the dominant culture is often enacted through her strategy of multigeneric, intertextual collage, which situates the lyric I in a matrix of social and historical relations, and allows otherness to call into question the autonomy of the self and totality of knowledge or seemingly realistic representations of the other. This interventional recalcitrance of otherness is a salient aspect of Levinas's concept of alterity which renders thought inadequate and resists totality: "The breach of totality is not an operation of thought, obtained by a simple distinguishing of terms that evoke one another or at least line up opposite one another. The void that breaks the totality can be maintained against an inevitably totalizing and synoptic thought only if thought finds itself *faced* with an other refractory to categories" (*TI* 40). Hahn's articulation of otherness through female desire and his incorporation of Japanese and Chinese cultures have the effect of "an other refractory to categories" which undermines the totality of patriarchal gender ideology and resists Eurocentric cultural hegemony. Moreover, her insistence on responding to the otherness of Asian women also resists homogenizing feminist claims of sexual difference, which repress or erase the differences of race and class among women.

In her prose poem, "The Hemisphere: Kuchuk Hanem," collected in her third volume, *The Unbearable Heart* (1995), Hahn explores

further the disjunctive possibilities of collage for disrupting the pro-
duction of totalizing knowledge of the other, particularly women of
color, by interweaving fragmentary speeches and autobiographical
and fictional narratives with excerpts from Gustave Flaubert's
*Flaubert in Egypt* and Edward Said's *Orientalism*. While engaging in a
dialogic interaction of response, challenge, and critique, the inter-
locking disruptions of these fragments create tension, release, and
movement within the prose poem. Thus, even though the lyric I is
decentered and the voice pluralized, the poem is still emotionally
charged and the other maintains its alterity as resistance through the
elocutionary subject position of the "I."[4]

   Said's book illustrates that in constructing the Orient as the lesser,
subordinate other of the West, Orientalist discourses erase individ-
ual subjectivity, reducing the other to a homogeneous entity, as the
title of Hahn's poem — "The Hemisphere: Kuchuk Hanem" — indi-
cates. Within such a binary framework, the other defined as the op-
posite of the self-same is already "a part of totality encompassing the
same and the other," as Levinas says of the kind of self-other relation
in which the alterity of the other is absorbed by the same when the
other is only other relative to the self (*TI* 38). Represented as part of
the exotic world of the East, Kuchuk Hanem, the Egyptian dancer
and courtesan, becomes the embodiment of the East in Flaubert's
travel writing about Egypt. The power of Flaubert's nationality,
wealth, and gender, Said points out, allows him "not only to possess
Kuchuk Hanem physically but to speak for her and tell his readers in
what way she was typically 'Oriental'" (Said 6).

   Making use of the subject position of the lyric I, Hahn gives voice
to Hanem, allowing her to speak for herself and to talk back to
Flaubert. Hanem's speech renders it impossible for otherness to be
contained as a visible yet silent presence whose meaning is supposed
to be entirely graspable, and whose difference is reduced to a strange
and yet completely knowable spectacle. Levinas's emphasis on the
presence of the other in terms of speech — "The face speaks" (*TI*
66) — foregrounds the agency of the other in language. In her discus-
sion of Levinas's concept of the encounter with the face of the other,
Jill Robbins points out that "the figural transfer from vision to voice
is also an ethical transfer and an ethical exigency" (*Prodigal Son* 130).
Hahn's imagined speeches for Hanem perform "an ethical transfer,"
as such, from Kuchuk Hanem as a silenced Orientalized object of the

white male gaze in Flaubert's writing to an assertive subject as an irreducible other in her prose poem.

"The Hemisphere: Kuchuk Hanem" consists of two major counternarratives — one autobiographical, spoken in the voice of Hahn's persona, the other fictional, in the voice of Kuchuk Hanem — both of which respond to and subvert Flaubert's master narrative. Hahn begins the poem with a childhood memory of waking up from a nap, looking for her mother.

> I am four. It is a summer midafternoon, my nap finished. I cannot find her. I hear the water in the bathroom. Not from the faucet but occasional splashes. I hear something like the bar of soap fall in. I cannot find her.
>
> Flaubert's encounter, Flaubert's encounter, Flaubert's
> encounter — (*Heart* 45)

She strategically interrupts this narrative where her child persona cannot find her mother, by repeating the phrase, "Flaubert's encounter" — thus spotlighting the silencing of Hanem's voice by Flaubert's Orientalist discourse, while suggesting a correlation between the mother's actual and symbolic absence and Orientalism. When the girl-child finally finds her mother in the bathroom taking a bath and sees her naked body for the first time, Hahn again interrupts the narrative with a citation from Said's remarks about the silence of Hanem in Flaubert's book: "[S]he never spoke of herself, she never represented her emotions, presence, or history. [*Flaubert*] spoke for and represented her" ([Said 6]; *Heart* 45). Through resonances and contrasts of collage juxtaposition, the girl's search for her mother suggests an analogue to Hahn's search for the female other in her poem.[5] Interwoven in multiple narratives, Hanem's silence resonates with the child persona's memory of her mother's body, which Traise Yamamoto notes, "is unnarrated, marked by visuality" (255). Hahn's persona cannot recall if the mother said anything, or how she responded to her four-year-old daughter seeing her naked for the first time. This absence of the mother's words regarding her body echoes Hanem's silence, thus highlighting the absence of both the mother's and Hanem's subjectivity. The two major parallel narratives in the poem, then, could be understood as Hahn's attempt to enact an ethical transformation of the mother and Hanem from objectified mute figures to articulate subjects. Later in the poem, the mother emerges as "story-teller," "creator and healer" (*Heart* 60), while Hanem becomes an assertive, unconventional, and independent woman, speaking to the reader directly in the form of dramatic monologue.

Countering the essentializing tactics of Flaubert's discursive construct of Egypt and the "Orientals," Hanem's speech situates her encounter with the Frenchman in a specific historical moment and geographical location, foregrounding the interlocking of race, gender, and class in her identity: "*In 1850 a woman with skin the color of sand in the shade of Sphinx, midday, meant little and of course mine was seen more than veiled and I could earn a living 'dancing'*" (*Heart* 46).

Hanem's dramatic monologue also asserts an otherness that defies the conventions of social mores, and offers an alternative female subject position:

> *It's true when all is said and done, I am less a dancer than a whore. . . .*
> *That's what I am, a whore and alone. To be despised by the men*
> *because who else would let them come as they come but someone with*
> *vagrant morals. Despised by wives, mistresses, and fiancées for my*
> *abilities, independence, the peculiar attention that I receive. I am*
> *scorned by the religious. By the courts and by my parents. But I do not*
> *fear a man's departure. Know that.* (*Heart* 47)

By allowing Hanem to occupy an elocutionary subject position, Hahn makes it possible for the other to rearticulate her otherness. It is precisely by restoring Hanem's subjectivity through the possibilities of the monologue speaker that Hahn renders the articulation of her alterity possible. "To preserve the Other as Other," as Colin Davis says of a basic concept of Levinas's ethics of alterity, "it must not become an object of knowledge or experience," because as such what is encountered will immediately lose its alterity. Hence, Davis states that Levinas's ethics of alterity "requires a description and defense of subjectivity" (41). Transformed from a silent sexual object in Flaubert's book into an articulate, irreducible subject in Hahn's poem, Hanem is able to reject Flaubert's representation of her, and to undermine the authority and authenticity of visual realism in Flaubert's travel writing which produces Orientalist knowledge of the other.

Stressing the fact that within a binary system the self is defined by its other, Hanem indicates that her image and other exotic and inscrutable images of Egypt in Flaubert's narrative are part of the

networks of meaning and signification that construct the identities
of the Orient and the West as a power relation:

> *And I have made a name for myself that will, Flaubert boasts on his*
> *own behalf, not mine, that will cover the globe. Know that. That the*
> *image is not my own. My image does not entirely belong to me. And nei-*
> *ther does yours, master or slave. (Heart 47)*

> *When he writes about Egypt he will write what he has experienced: the*
> *adoration of the historical Cleopatra from boyhood lessons, Kuchuk*
> *Hanem — my cunt, my dance — the Nile, the squalor, a man slitting his*
> *belly and pulling his intestines . . . , people fucking animals which I'm*
> *told also happens in France but not in the cities. Because there are no*
> *animals. (Heart 47–48)*

While challenging Flaubert's Orientalist portrayal of herself and
Egypt, which reduces both to objects of his knowledge and his expe-
rience, Hanem calls into question French men's sexuality as the
norm. This disruption of Orientalist knowledge of the other is nec-
essary for the other to maintain its irreducible alterity.

The collage method Hahn employs also enables her to contest
racialized gender identity and sexuality through juxtaposition of frag-
mentary speeches by Hahn's persona with a passage from Flaubert's
book and with Hanem's monologue. Immediately following Hanem's
monologues, the juxtaposed fragments suggest that totalizing Orien-
talist knowledge of the other exoticizes and subjugates the othered
body for Western men's pleasure and domination:

> I knew what he wanted. He wanted to fuck me. He guessed I was
> 16. . . . Why would this Portuguese sailor come over to me and in
> his broken English point to the tatoo [sic] of a geisha as if I would
> identify with it. And I did a little.

> He wanted someone who did not resemble his mother or his
> friends' sisters or wives. The mistress he had dumped before
> departure. He wanted license. The kind available not even in
> one's own imagination — but in geographic departure.

> *"The morning we arrive in Egypt. . . we had scarcely set foot on*
> *shore when Max, the old lecher, got excited over a negress who was*
> *drawing water at a fountain. He is just as excited by the little negro*

boys. *By whom is he not excited? Or, rather, by* what?" [Flaubert, 43] (*Heart* 48)

Being defined as the other of whites in a binary totality, Asian women, the "negress," and "the little negro boys" have become objects of white men's lust. Their subjectivity and alterity are reduced to their racially marked bodies whose corporeal significances are produced by the networks of representation and signification that make the emergence and establishment of sexual drive possible. Hahn undercuts the objectification of the other by showing the limits of Flaubert's knowledge and experience through Hanem's speech which is juxtaposed with the above quote from Flaubert: "He will think that I am one thing, even as he learns about me. . . . Yet what he witnesses on tour and what I see daily are experienced differently" (*Heart* 48). By breaking the silence of Hanem, Hahn makes it possible for her to challenge Flaubert's representation of her otherness and to assert her alterity by revealing her interiority through monologues. Similar to David Mura's use of dramatic and interior monologues, Hahn's employment of Hanem's speeches as imagined by her is a strategy for revealing the other's interiority that is exterior to Orientalism.

However, Hahn raises questions about her use of Hanem's voice to assert a subversive otherness from a Western feminist position. She also questions her interest in the politics and aesthetics of women's erotic desire. These questions are directly related to the ethical relation between self and other:

> The female body as imperialists' colony is not a new symbol. Sexual impulse as revolutionary impulse? Do women depend upon the sexual metaphor for identity, an ironic figure of speech? Will I fall into the trap of writing from the imperialists' point of view? From a patriarchal one? How can we write erotica and not? What would an anti-imperialistic framework look like?
>
> .  .  .  .  .  .  .  .  .  .  .  .  .  .  .  .  .  .  .  .  .
>
> Can I speak for her? For the Turkish, Nubian, the — brown, black, blacker? (*Heart* 51)

In raising these questions, Hahn confronts the central concerns of her poem: What is the significance in asserting a female erotic desire? How to articulate female sexuality and erotic desire without falling into the trap of patriarchal or imperialist systems of thought and representation? By asking these questions, Hahn demonstrates an awareness of the other as other, and exploring a way of writing that does not silence, reduce, or violate the other as Flaubert's Orientalist text does. Her collage of citations from Said and Flaubert, and of fragmentary speeches from everyday life, indicates that to maintain the subjectivity and alterity of women, particularly women of color, in her writing, she must find an alternative language and a new poetic form to reclaim the female body from male possession and domination without reducing women's difference.

Hahn's strategy of using monologues to allow Hanem to speak is a form of response to the other as responsibility, which restores the Orientalized other's subjectivity and alterity by maintaining the distance between herself and Hanem, thus refusing to assimilate the other into her own consciousness or perspective. Left in her silence, Hahn's persona asserts, Kuchuk Hanem's "person" will continue to be "outlived" by her "name, talents, and shaved cunt" through Flaubert's narrative. "We remember her for the dance and the fuck. For the hemisphere created" (*Heart* 52). In responding to this silenced other as responsibility for the other, Hahn is compelled to break her silence in order to allow the other to speak. At the same time, she makes clear that Hanem's speech is imagined. "I trespass the boundaries of fiction and non-fiction," she writes. "But what would she [Hanem] have said? Could the words be translated?" (*Heart* 53, 52). In addition to resisting a fusion between herself and Hanem by indicating their separate subjectivity, Hahn calls into question the authenticity of realist representation, exposing the relation between power and representation: "Flaubert fucked her and wrote about her. His words. His worlds" (*Heart* 53). This interlocking between raced female body and privileged white male sexuality, between colonial, imperial power and the power of Flaubert's words, motivates Hahn's investigation of sexuality and desire, and compels her search for a language to express female eroticism outside the domination of patriarchy and imperialism.

### Words That Orbit the Body

Although she continues to explore a language and poetic form to articulate female erotic desire in her fourth book of poetry, *Mosquito and Ant*, Hahn's poems become less concerned with the repression of female desire in phallocentric writings, or with the objectification of the raced female other in Orientalist discourses. Rather, they focus on the traditions she has identified as a "female culture" and a "female aesthetic" in Chinese and Japanese women's writing ("Three Voices" 10).[6] The title of this volume refers to the unique style of "mosquito and ant" of *nu shu* ("female writing"), a written language created and developed by peasant women in Hunan Province, southern China, possibly during the Song Dynasty (900–1279) or earlier (some argue over a millennium ago) when the majority of women were denied an education. Through this language, which consists of some 7,000 characters, women were able to correspond with one another, exchanging feelings and thoughts, offering much needed support and advice, and protesting against gender inequality in a male-dominant society. With the development of this language, a women's subculture and writing tradition also emerged. Those who grew to be close friends through correspondences, including epistolary verses, became what was called "sworn sisters." Many wrote verses and songs which were sung in a call-response style when women got together to work in groups. Books of *nu shu* became so precious to these women that it was a custom to burn a woman's books on her death so that she might have them in her afterlife.[7] Chinese women's subculture and writing tradition inform the language, style, and subject matter of Hahn's *Mosquito and Ant*. In addition, Hahn incorporates in this volume feminist theoretical writings and Japanese women's writings, particularly *zuihitsu*, a genre of diary-like essay that combines observation with reflection developed from the model of *The Pillow Book*, part diary, part essay, and part miscellany written in the early eleventh century by Sei Shōnagon, a contemporary of Murasaki Shikibu, who is the author of *The Tale of Genji*.[8]

As she continues to explore a female culture, aesthetics, and desire, two kinds of relationships among women — the mother-daughter relationship and intimate friendship — become predominant in Hahn's fourth volume. While these relationships provide the framework for Hahn to explore a poetics alternative to that of the Eurocentric, male-dominant canon of American poetry, feminist writings that critique the repression of what Irigaray calls "the genealogy of the woman" (*Sexes* 3) underlie the centrality of relationships among women in *Mosquito and Ant*, and shape its structure and thematic concerns. In *Sexes and Genealogies*, Irigaray argues that "the patriarchal regime has made impossible" "the love between mother and daughter," which "has been transformed into the woman's obligation to devote herself to the cult of the children of her legal husband and to the husband himself" (2). Adrienne Rich in *Of Woman Born: Motherhood as Experience and Institution* also notes a similar transfer in the mother-daughter relationship resulting from "institutionalized heterosexuality and institutionalized motherhood" which "demand that the girl-child transfer those first feelings of dependency, eroticism, mutuality, from her first woman to a man, if she is to become what is defined as a 'normal' woman — that is, a woman whose most intense psychic and physical energies are directed towards men" (218–19). Their emotions, desire, and sexuality regulated by patriarchy, women become subordinate to men even in their intimate relationships with them which demands their renunciation of their intimacy with other women.

Confined by their roles of institutionalized motherhood or wifehood in male-dominant heterosexual relationships, women's creativity is repressed. So is their otherness because it is defined within the patriarchal system of the same. Irigaray urges women "to refuse to submit to" the role of the mother as "a desubjectivized social role," which contains them "in the ghetto of a single function." She argues that in order to claim creativity in art, politics, language, and all realms of human ingenuity, which has been forbidden to women for centuries, women must "take back this maternal creative dimension that is our birthright as women" (*Sexes* 18). In seeking to reject "a desubjectivized social role" and to reimagine their female identity, Irigaray contends, women also need to "find, rediscover, invent the words, the sentences that speak of" women's bodies and of the bond between women, and to realize that "another relation to sexual pleasure is available apart from the phallic model" (*Sexes* 18, 20). These tasks are embedded in Hahn's *nu shu* poems. Hahn finds in Chinese and Japanese women's writings an alternative to the phallic model.

*Mosquito and Ant* could be said to be a poetic evocation of what Irigaray calls the "genealogy of the woman." One of the poems in this collection, "Responding to Light," incorporates quotes from Irigaray's essay, "Body Against Body: In Relation to the Mother," included in *Sexes and Genealogies*. While citations from Irigaray's essay generate the poem, the gist of Irigaray's ideas of the relations among women's body, desire, and language in this essay inform all the poems in *Mosquito and Ant*. In many poems, Hahn explores the mother-daughter bond, which ramifies into the bond among women, as the term *mother* takes on numerous meanings. *Mosquito and Ant* opens with "Razor," which is about a daughter's attachment to and love for her mother. The speaker begins the poem with the statement, "I want to return to the moment / father and I brought the canister of mother's ashes / to the temple in some odd shopping bag" (*Mosquito* 13). This is the moment when the speaker is overwhelmed by her grief over her mother's death. Her whole body "shook without pause" as she wept quietly,

> and tears and mucus covered my face and
> sleeves because father did not know
> I needed the handkerchief
> mother had pressed a week earlier.
> At times the loss felt like an organ
> one could excise with a razor. (*Mosquito* 13)

Such pain speaks of the intensity and depth of the daughter's love for and attachment to the mother. As Hélène Cixous and Catherine Clément write in *The Newly Born Woman*, "Weeping is like an intimate celebration" (35). The speaker's return to this moment of uncontrollable weeping is in a way a return to rediscover the mother-daughter bond, the bond between women. Several poems echo this return in various ways. "I want to go where the hysteric resides," the speaker begins in "Translating Ancient Lines Into the Vernacular" (*Mosquito* 41). Contrary to Freud's definition of hysteria in terms of repression of improper female heterosexual desire, Grosz argues, "hysteria can be seen as the woman's rebellion against and rejection of the requirements of femininity. . . . It is a refusal rather than a repression of heterosexuality, and an attempt to return nostalgically to the preoedipal, homosexual desire for the mother" (*Subversions* 134). In articulating her intent to "go where the hysteric resides," Hahn's persona asserts a rebellious desire to return to her relation to her mother and to her own bodily pleasure, which refuse to be subservient to men's satisfaction. In another poem, "Orchid Root," the speaker articulates the necessity to return to the female body and female relations unmediated by patriarchy through an aesthetic identification with the tradition of Chinese women's writing: "I need to return to the Chinese women poets," the speaker declares, wishing she could run "to the sisters who know / how to instruct the senses" (*Mosquito* 57).

For Hahn, to return to women's own bodies and their relations, including the mother-daughter bond, in her poetry involves finding the language to rearticulate the female body and subjectivity which have been repressed in phallocentric discourses. In "Tissue," for instance, the speaker says she wants to return to the moment when she sees her mother's "face become radiant," when she feels the touch of her lips and the security of her hand. But the mother has become alienated from the daughter because of patriarchal discourses and of the mother's symbolic and actual death:

Mother, you have been exiled

by narrative and death so long
I forgot your heartbeat
until I leaned against my daughter's tiny chest,
heard the beat the baby mistakes for the whole world.
The heart inside the body the way the baby
was inside this body. (*Mosquito* 72)

In returning to those moments, Hahn is reconnecting to the mother's body through words that will "translate the bond between our body, her body, the body of our daughter," as Irigaray asserts (*Sexes* 19). In her poems Hahn reimagines mothers as women not subjugated to male domination, and invents women as mothers with desire, passion, and zest for life.

Seeking to rediscover the female subjectivity and difference outside the patriarchal social order, Hahn explores a new poetics for articulating female desire, especially the mother's desire, which as Irigaray notes, "the law of the father" prohibits. "The maternal function underlies the social order as well as the order of desire," Irigaray points out, "but it is always restricted to the dimension of need" (*Sexes* 11, 10–11). The social role of the mother domesticates women's erotic desire into the maternal function in subordination to the patriarchal social order, in which the woman loses her subjectivity and her alterity. Thus to assert a female erotic desire is to resist social impositions, posing a challenge to the patriarchal regime. And to do so with the support of other women is doubly subversive to the social order and discourses that privilege male desire. Continuing the tradition of correspondences among Chinese women who wrote in *nu shu*, Hahn has made a series of epistolary poems addressed to "L."

The speaker of these poems is a mother and middle-aged, who is "looking for clues / on how to stay a woman, not / a middle-aged woman," as she says in "Wax," subtitled "Initial Correspondence to L . . .," the first poem of the series (*Mosquito* 17). Turning to L for advice, the speaker intimates her erotic desire:

> And what I want at some moment
> in my forties
> is not an affair —
> that would rip my breast open —
> I would like to wrap my arms around a guy
> (I guess a guy)
> for a lengthy kiss.
> Standing up. In the dark.
> Pulse at the boiling point
> one recalls
> from those irretrievable initial encounters.
> L, send me advice quick. (*Mosquito* 18)

The significance of the speaker's erotic desire becomes clearer in another epistolary poem, "Kafka's Erection," addressed to L, in which the speaker offers L advice on what to say to her former lover and how to behave with her current one. But when talking about herself, the speaker refers to her body in terms of its nursing and reproductive functions: "With two children my own longing often / feels alien — / the breast for nursing, the genitals / for birth." In contrast to the passion and vitality of her erotic desire asserted in her first letter, the speaker now is almost lifeless in her role of the mother. As her coming-of-age daughters are becoming more aware of their bodies, she feels "I am more *the older woman* each day" (*Mosquito* 22). Within this context, the speaker's articulation of her erotic desire that emphasizes her bodily sensation has important implications. It enacts a search for a language to speak of the female body as a feminist task to "give life back to that mother" who "lives within us and among us," as Irigaray writes, but who "was immolated at the birth of our culture." In asserting her erotic desire, the speaker performs the feminist tasks which Irigaray delineates: "We must refuse to allow her [mother's] desire to be swallowed up in the law of the father. We must give her the right to pleasure, to sexual experience, to passion, give her back the right to speak, or even to shriek and rage aloud" (*Sexes*

18). This interlocking of motherhood and sexual desire, of the sexed body and language, collapses the hierarchical binary in which women are identified with the body, and men with the mind. In all the epistolary poems addressed to L, the speaker almost always refers to their creative activities along with their desire. By reclaiming the female body, desire, and creativity of the woman as mother in resistance to her socially imposed role of motherhood, Hahn reinstates the woman as an irreducible subject and other through the subject position of the lyric I and the particularized identity of the speaker of the dramatic monologue.

The challenges Hahn confronts in speaking of the female body involves developing a poetics and aesthetics that articulate a female erotic desire outside the "framework of a phallocratic economy" in which, Irigaray contends, women are "unable to live their affects, their sexuality" (*Sexes* 20). One of the strategies Hahn employs is emulating Chinese women's correspondences in *nu shu* in her epistolary poems to establish an intimate friendship among women, which provides a framework outside the phallocentric social order for women to develop and express affections, even passionate erotic feelings, for one another. This same-sex love between women, though not necessarily a manifestation of lesbianism, poses a challenge to binarized gender and sexual identities which privilege male desire and heterosexuality. Hahn subtly suggests that this same-sex affection between women disturbs the heterosexual phallocentric economy, by revealing in the speaker's letter to L her husband's unease about her relationship with L, while showing the speaker's fondness and attachment to L:

> My husband wants to know why
> I carry your poems around with me.
> As if a cashmere scarf. Or an air tank.
>
> . . . . . . . . . . . .
>
> I scribbled a ten-page letter to you months ago.
> It is folded on my nightstand among bills and bracelets.
> And Kafka. (*Mosquito* 22)

In contrast to her intimacy with L, the speaker feels alienated from her husband, who tells her what to do and what not to do, without any awareness of or interest in her needs or her desire, as another poem, "Jam," subtitled "on events in between correspondence to L," reveals. The husband spends his evenings watching the news and reading newspapers and spy thrillers. When the speaker says to him: "Remember how / the wind blew spray / off the crests of waves? How / some nights our footprints / were phosphorescent?" he says, "What?" Meanwhile, when the speaker reads about the Daoist "Immortal Sisters" who adopted students and were considered "*travelers / from another dimension*," she experiences a transmutation of her existence: "my fingertips tingle / as if catching breath. / My blood quickens as if to rip tide" (*Mosquito* 32). In contrast to her husband's indifferent, nonresponsive response, women's writing invigorates and empowers Hahn's female speaker. As the speaker says in another poem, "The Downpour," subtitled "a zuihitsu after Sei Shōnagon": "the power of women's poetry inspires me like an older sister lending me a lipstick" (*Mosquito* 45). Like her friendship with L, women's culture and writing enable the speaker, a mother and a middle-aged woman, to live her affective life and to articulate her desire and creativity.

The capacity of the lyric form enables Hahn to employ lyricism, narrative, and dramatic monologue to explore the possibilities of a same-sex love relationship which undermines the primacy of heterosexuality and the privilege of the phallic model. "Note on Thematic Redundancy in Women's Verse, No. Two" expresses the female speaker's passion for another married woman:

Neither cognac nor tea will stall
what a run through the blizzard
suggests: by the corner pay phone
the heart throbs publically.

.   .   .   .   .   .   .   .

I listen to the answering machine
answer for him
and though he is listening
I do not leave a message
about lilies. (*Mosquito* 37)

Although this relationship is not necessarily what might be called "lesbian," its intensity and its exclusively feminine aspect — "I do not leave a message / about lilies" to the husband "though he is listening" — is no less subversive to male dominance and privilege in a heterosexual relationship.

In addition to its subversive transgression of heterosexuality regulated by patriarchy, an ethics of alterity is embedded in the female speaker's impassioned relationship with a female other. To correspond passionately with the other as an equal subject suggests an ethical response to alterity. The speaker in "The Intelligentsia of the Chin Dynasty Desire Desire" says, when she first began to sort out her thoughts about L, she realized that "To correspond / with pulse and impulse" was to desire desire (*Mosquito* 71). Desire as articulated here is not the need to obtain what one lacks, or the need for fusion with the other. Rather it is desire for the unknowable otherness. "I mistook my desire to merge / for simple algebra / when that need is really *cosmic*," says the speaker in "Zinc," another epistolary poem apparently addressed to L (*Mosquito* 42). As Levinas contends, "Desire is desire for the absolute other." Rather than hunger for material satisfaction, "metaphysics desires the other beyond satisfaction, where no gesture by the body to diminish the aspiration is possible." A desire as such "without satisfaction," he adds, is desire which "precisely *understands* [*entend*] the remoteness, the alterity, and the exteriority of the other" (*TI* 34). The mode of correspondence in Hahn's poems makes it possible for the lyric speaker to express her desire for the other, while allowing the other to keep her distance and to maintain her alterity.

For the speaker, as for Hahn, moreover, this desire without satisfaction is necessary to the vitality for living as a woman and for writing poetry. Throughout the series of epistolary poems addressed to L, the monologue speaker exposes her vulnerability, revealing her desire for L, but all the while maintaining a distance between them, which renders L's exteriority unassimilable and their mutual subjugation impossible. Hahn's strategy of using only one speaker for all the dramatic monologues addressed to L, and occasionally allowing the speaker to make references to L's remarks, helps render L intriguing, mysterious, and unknowable. For example, in "The Tumbler," the speaker expresses her love for L explicitly, but L's love for her remains ambivalent:

i.

I call you
to hear your voice:

.   .   .   .   .   .   .

I call to hear you
tell me you love me
though you say so to everyone.
There.

. . . . . . . . . . .

iii.
You say you are curious
about what my new poems are "about."
I write this:
I've hardly eaten
for a week
and realize I need the hunger pangs
to match the longing for some thing — maybe
to sleep in your basement again,
maybe for that kid lingering on the corner,

. . . . . . . . . . . . . . .

Most likely the nicotine itself.
Even the second-hand smoke. (*Mosquito* 33–34)

In addition to establishing and maintaining a distance between them, the ambivalence of L's feelings for the speaker seems to serve the function of compelling the speaker to find various ways to express her feelings for L.

The speaker's uncertainty about the nature of L's love for her seems to spark her imagination and nourish her desire, leading her to find words which can articulate her love and erotic desire. In "A Boat Down the River of Yellow Silt," the speaker expresses her love for L by telling her how she will eat the persimmons L has given her:

I will eat the one you tended yourself:
slice it open and lick the dark halves
that nourish its oval pit — I will
suck out these plump tongues of fruit
that speak for you. (*Mosquito* 60)

The sensualness in the speaker's description of eating the persimmon is reminiscent of that in Li-Young Lee's poem, "Persimmons." But the sensuality in Hahn's poem is clearly identified as a woman's caress offered to a female friend, asserting love and pleasure in ways that break away from the phallocentric model.

Like Lee's corporeal aesthetics, Hahn's use of "words that orbit the body" (*Mosquito* 55) asserts an ethical relationship with the other. In rendering her lyric speaker vulnerable in her attraction to the other, Hahn breaks away from the primacy and autonomy of the lyric subject's consciousness which reduces the other to its object of desire or knowledge. The bodily language and erotic desire in Hahn's poems, however, insist on articulating a "feminine sexuality" that accentuates women's difference as an ethical and political commitment. Compelled to discover new ways of articulating love between women, and reclaiming the female body and desire, Hahn constantly evokes the writing traditions of Chinese women for inspiration. Alluding to the poems by one of the Seven Immortal Sisters of Daoism, Hahn in "'Guard the Jade Pass'" enacts her search for bodily oriented words:[9]

> Imagine words with a dimension
> not unlike the light and dark regions
> of the moon. The back of planets. The crators [*sic*].
> Words that orbit the body
> like a plea granted. (*Mosquito* 55)

Hahn's allusion to Chinese women's writing at once pays homage to and recreates a tradition of female eroticism and aesthetics. As she writes in "Orchid Root," "I need to return to the Chinese women poets. / The flat language / . . . / The words weighted in object / as much as flight" (*Mosquito* 57). In the same poem, Hahn reveals that while writing to one another "to protest the man's inattention," Chinese women "fall in love" consequently, "as the honeysuckle climbs the fence / from one garden to the next / its fragrance on the draft beneath the door" (*Mosquito* 58). Expressions like these reinvent words for articulating a female subject's desire for the other without becoming subjugated to the other, or seeking to possess, or asserting power over the other. This desire is similar to what Levinas calls "eros" which "differs from possession and power. . . . It is neither a struggle, nor a fusion, nor a knowledge." Levinas stresses that eros has an "exceptional place among relationships. It is a relationship with alterity, with mystery." In this relationship, even though "one can no longer be able, the subject is still a subject through eros," and "the *I* survives in it" (*TO* 88–89). Both the desiring I and the desired other maintain their respective subjectivity in Hahn's poems through aesthetics and "words that orbit the body."

Inspired by Chinese women's *nu shu* writings, Hahn finds a language and mode of correspondence to articulate a female same-sex eroticism for connection, empowerment, and stimulation, and eventually social and cultural transformation. Emulating the style of *nu shu* in her title poem, "Mosquito and Ant," Hahn celebrates the mother-daughter bond and the love between women: "This correspondence blossoms like sea anemone / ingesting the krill of our hearts" (*Mosquito* 29).

But to make this correspondence possible and this passion alive among women, Hahn, like the Chinese women who invented *nu shu*, must invent a new mode of writing.

iv.
I want my letters to resemble
tiny ants scrawled across this page.

.   .   .   .   .   .   .   .   .   .   .

and their strategy is simple:
the shortest distance between two points
is tenacity not seduction.

I want my letters to imitate
mosquitoes as they loop
around the earlobe with their noise:
the impossible task of slapping one
across its erratically slow travel.
Those spiderlike legs. The sheaths of wings.
The body that transports disease.
I wonder if a straight man can read such lines. (*Mosquito* 29–30)

This *nu shu* style of writing performs a search for a language, which according to Irigaray's conception of a new way of using words in women's writing, "accompanies that bodily experience, clothing it in words that do not erase the body but speak the body" (*Sexes* 19).

In her poems which speak the female body and desire, Hahn repositions the female subject and unsettles hierarchical binaries of gender, race, and sexuality. "[I]t is the other" who "resist[s] the system," as Levinas states (*TI* 40). Rather than suggesting a gender essence, Hahn's insistence on searching for a feminine aesthetics to articulate women's experience, desire, and creativity seeks more than resistance to patriarchy. It aims to imagine the feminine otherwise than what has been prescribed or deemed possible within a patriarchal system or a Eurocentric culture. In so doing, her poems embody a cultural transformation for the sake of social justice in their enactment of an aesthetics and ethics of alterity.

# CHAPTER FIVE

*Timothy Liu*

EACH OF US HARBORING WHAT THE OTHER LACKED

In his foreword to Timothy Liu's first book of poetry, *Vox Angelica* (1992), Richard Howard speaks of Liu's work as "a shocking poetry," noting that "the shock is not of recognition but of estrangement." For Howard, the extraordinary strangeness of Liu's poetry lies in the fact that it "makes an unfamiliar claim upon us, the claim of apostasy" (x). I would add that the astounding otherness of Liu's poetry may result from other unfamiliar claims it makes upon us — the shattering of the Freudian myth of the family romance, the intermingling of homoeroticism and sentiments of Christianity, and the mixing of the spiritual with the corporeal, of the religious with the profane, rendering Asian American homosexuality visible and the "unspeakable desire" provocative.

In articulating homoerotic desire, Liu also confronts the socially constructed debased otherness of homosexuality, which has led to violence and hatred directed at gay men. In poems such as "Against Nature," collected in his fourth volume, *Hard Evidence* (2001), Liu raises questions about human nature by juxtaposing images of love and beauty with those of hatred and ugliness: "Eight dollars for a dozen roses sold / on Christopher and Grove where another / fag was hunted down last night by some / fraternity boys who took their turns / with a pocket knife" (*Evidence* 74). This social construct of gay men's otherness and its effect contrast the alterity of the other, which gives rise to desire, including homoerotic desire, in Liu's poetry. More often than not, homoerotic desire in Liu's poems, like metaphysical desire, seeks the unfamiliar, the unknowable otherness of the other. As the speaker in "A Valentine" says, "each of us / harbor[s] what the other lacked: a wilderness" (*Goodnight* 27). Liu's exploration of this wilderness and its impact on "each of us" seems to have contributed to the surprising effect of estrangement that his poetry produces.

The shock of estrangement produced by Liu's poems, in part, is related to the confessions in them that are aimed to move and challenge by revealing the vulnerability of his personae, while retaining their irreducible otherness. For Liu, writing poetry is a way of confronting repressed rage, shame, guilt, and "The grief of a lifetime. Of lifetimes." Exploring those concealed areas of private lives that "remain under pressure," Liu asserts, is like "clean[ing] out the active volcanos." But he emphasizes that this exploration "is the business of poetry, a dangerous trade" ("Redemption" in Tabios 106). What is at stake, for Liu, is how to make the complexity and intensity of personal experience accessible to the reader without turning poetry into mere confession, and how to articulate a larger human desire through homoerotic desire without reiterating heterosexual norms and racial stereotypes constructed within phallocentric closure. Speaking of what he hopes to achieve in his poetry, Liu says, "I want soul in it!" Believing that he must use "a language that will not shield one from emotional experience but rather make it more available," Liu has stayed away from "experimental or avant garde writing," which for him, "is merely pyrotechnic" ("Redemption" in Tabios 70). While searching for a language to deal with repressed emotions, Liu was inspired by Sylvia Plath's volume, *Ariel* ("Redemption" in Tabios 105). Many of Liu's poems, especially those collected in his first two volumes, *Vox Angelica* (1992) and *Burnt Offerings* (1995), are autobiographical and confessional. Yet rather than being self-indulgent, his poems are concerned with the human conditions of suffering, loss, and mortality, while articulating homoerotic desire, exploring homosexuality, and confronting AIDS.

Through a lyric I who is Chinese American and openly gay, Liu introduces a marginalized otherness — Asian American and gay men — into lyric poetry along with themes which are considered universal. But rather than assimilating the otherness of ethnicity or homosexuality through a discourse of universality, Liu disturbs the white, heterosexual content of the universal, and unsettles the binary of gender identity formulated within a phallocentric economy. In articulating homosexual desire, Liu develops a poetics that radically challenges the definitions of the holy and the profane, blending homosexual encounter with religious experience and relating eroticism to the absolute otherness of death. Facing the uncertainty of the future and inevitability of unknowable death in a relationship with an other over whom the lyric I assumes no domination, the subject can claim no self-sufficiency or autonomy of consciousness. In fact, the subject loses its mastery as subject in a relationship with the other because, Levinas contends, the future cannot be controlled by consciousness and the prospect of death leaves the subject no initiative (*TO* 74, 81). The intricate relations between the spiritual and the corporeal, between the sacred and the sacrilegious, between present and future, between eroticism and mortality are embedded in the self-other relationship Liu explores in his poems. In dealing with these themes and experiences, Liu makes visible a particular aspect of social injustice regarding the otherness of gay men through an aesthetic and ethics of alterity.

### Denaturalizing Heterosexuality as the Norm

Being Asian and queer, Liu confronts a double otherness of social constructs. In the afterword to an anthology, *Take Out: Queer Writing from Asian Pacific America*, which he coedited, Liu mentions that he feels "conflicted" being Asian and queer. To explain his feelings, Liu quotes from Dan Bacalzo, a poet included in the anthology: "My body / is not the type you normally find in mainstream gay magazine ads" (Afterword 506). These remarks suggest that the conflict Liu and other Asian American gay men feel is associated with the invisibility of the racially marked Asian male body, which is feminized in colonialist and Orientalist discourses and in phallocentric mainstream American culture, where white images are the privileged normative signifiers of masculinity, desirability, and power. Nguyen, in his discussion of Jessica Hagedorn's *Dogeaters*, points out, "The Filipino queer subject as embodied in the transvestite is not equivalent to a modern, Western conception of a queer subject that often sees itself as the normative or universal model for gay liberation" (127). The intersections of race, gender, and sexuality are more often than not an integral part of Asian American gay men's experience. But racial or ethnic identity in Liu's poems is not as central as homosexual identity and experience.[1] Although Liu's poems do not directly engage with the Asian American experience or ethnic identity issues, their autobiographical references and homoeroticism intervene in significant ways in Asian American men's feminized, emasculated stereotypes.

Such gendered racial identity and raced sexuality of the Asian American male is an effect of racialized power relations in which Asian Americans are contained in a feminized position equated with the subordinate, disfranchised social status of women. In response to such impositions, some Asian American writers and critics, particularly the editors of *Aiiieeeee!*, protest against the emasculation of the Asian American male, proposing a cultural nationalist project which, as David Eng, among others, points out is "an untenable solution for the redress," "with its doctrine of compulsory heterosexuality and cultural authenticity." Eng further notes that the *Aiiieeeee!* editors' rhetoric "mirrors at once the dominant heterosexist and racist structures through which the Asian American male is historically feminized and rendered self-hating in the first place." Moreover, Eng contends that with a focus solely on heterosexual relationships between white men and Asian women as a manifestation of racial problems, "the figure of the Asian American homosexual [is] entirely banished." What is more troubling, Eng adds, is that "Asian American cultural nationalism posits a slippery equation of homosexuality instead of virulent homophobia with white racist agendas" (21). Liu's homoerotic poetry not only inscribes Asian American homosexuality in American culture and Asian American identity, it also undermines the privileging of heterosexuality as the norm — a privileged category that represses or erases differences in sexuality, and even engenders fear of otherness, mobilizing hatred of the other into violence against homosexuals.

Thus, in writing about homosexual desire, Liu, like Li-Young Lee, David Mura, Marilyn Chin, and Kimiko Hahn, confronts two kinds of otherness at once — the socially constructed otherness of the abject other in a hierarchical, binary scheme, and the irreducible, unassimilable otherness of the other. In his book, *Gaiety Transfigured: Gay Self-Representation in American Literature*, David Bergman states that "[t]he most significant term" which defines homosexual men's identity and subjectivity is "otherness," which is "categorical, perhaps even ontological." For "The otherness of the homosexual is not merely a heightening of the separateness which is a central feature of the ego structure of the heterosexual male, [it is] a separateness created by the hard and fixed boundaries heterosexual males erect both to protect their egos from the dangers of castration and to further their identifications with their fathers." The family structured by gendered binarism enhances the homosexual's sense of his "unlikeness" (30). Furthermore, defined within a binary totality, homosexuality is condemned in relation to a range of normative categories, as Bergman contends: "Indeed, heterosexual discourse calculated and labeled the homosexual with all the permutations of otherness. He was *not* Christian, *not* natural, *not* manly, *not* a woman, *not* of the heterosexual's country or region or continent, *not* human, *not* animal, *not* even to be named" (31). In fact, homosexuality was condemned as "the devilish and unnatural sin," a "crime that sinks a man to below the basest epithet," as Bergman quotes from an anonymous editor's "preface to the proceeding of the trial against Lord Castlehaven for various sexual offenses" in 1699 (Bergman 32). Rejecting "the stigma" that marks "their otherness," Bergman notes, many homosexuals "transform otherness from a mark of shame into the very sign of their superiority" (34).

In this transformation, "ethnographic account" has been a "particularly favored" form for some gay writers to express homosexuality as one of multiple variations of sexuality. Bergman adds that "no literary form was more congenial to gay writers of the nineteenth and early twentieth centuries than the ethnographic study, and it was in ethnographic discourse that homosexual writers often found the terms for their own attacks on heterosexuality" (35). Acceptance of same-sex relationships in other cultures, Bergman suggests, enables gay writers to represent homosexuality as natural. He states that "the most important effect of gay ethnography is its assertion of the naturalness of homosexuality" (35). But inversion as such that naturalizes homosexuality through ethnography tends to confine its debunking of heterosexuality as the norm to ethnic cultures outside of mainstream America.

Liu's articulation of homosexuality in his poetry suggests an alternative strategy for undermining heterosexuality as the privileged norm, and for subverting Asian American male stereotypes. Liu's poems disrupt both gender and sexual norms constructed within a phallocentric economy. Judith Butler in *Gender Trouble: Feminism and the Subversion of Identity* points out that gender operates as a regulatory construct that privileges heterosexuality. She argues, "Gender is the repeated stylization of the body, a set of repeated acts within a highly rigid regulatory frame that congeal over time to produce the appearance of substance, of a natural sort of being." Like gender,

Butler adds, heterosexuality is naturalized by the deployment of its expressions as its "results" (*Gender* 33). Liu's autobiographical and homoerotic poems challenge the primacy of heterosexuality naturalized through narratives on themes such as marriage, reproduction, and the Oedipal family romance, which are part of the regulatory discourses on gender.

Judith Roof's insights into the functions of the narrative in naturalizing gender ideologies highlight the importance of narrative in interpellating gendered subjects, and indicate the possibilities of subverting the ideologies through narratives. Roof argues that "Narrative's dynamic enacts ideology and narrative's constant production proliferates that ideology continually and naturally, as if it were simply a fact of life and sense itself" (xvii). Governed by a heterosexual ideology, Roof points out, Freud's story of sexual development produces heterosexuality as a norm that is "completely natural" and "inevitable" (xxi). Liu undercuts the primacy of heterosexuality through autobiographical poems about his relationship with his parents. The mother and father figures in Freud's formulation of the heterosexual norm are symbolic figures representing gendered binaries of the patriarchal family unit.

In several poems about the family, Liu unsettles this tidy arrangement of gendered male-dominant relations which regulate the child's sexuality and shape his or her gendered subjectivity. The opening lines of the poem "Mama" immediately raise questions about the conventions of the mother figure, the family, and marriage:

> If I had known this burden on my tongue,
> would I have refused the first syllable
> she taught me in the garden? *Ma. Ma.*
> It would take me years to make any new
> distinctions: *milk, truck, book, clock,*
> facets to a glass house I was trapped
> inside, until one day, that great stone
> of marriage fell from my mother's hand.
> Such freedom gave me grief to visit
> her poorly lit efficiency across town (*Angelica* 25)

As the poem progresses, we learn that the mother has been incarcerated in a mental hospital, named after the Good Samaritan in the Bible. The poem unfolds by free association with names and words, and their implications, which help the speaker sum up his relationship with his mother:

> *Mama*, the debt incurred from just one word.
> Locked up for twenty years, only syllables now
> for what we left unspoken: *rage, shame, guilt,*
> everything you taught me from the start. (*Angelica* 26)

In several poems Liu explores this deeply wounded bond with his mother in connection to his homoerotic desire.

Rather than suggesting that his homosexuality is biologically determined, or negating it, Liu explores the possible role of his fear of his mother in shaping his sexual orientation. He explores the formation of his homosexuality through his deeply wounded relationship with his mother in a prose poem, "Canker," which reveals that he was sexually abused by his neurotic mother when he was a baby. In his foreword to *Vox Angelica*, Richard Howard refers to the "alienated maternal bond" in Liu's poems as "an acknowledged bondage to what we have learned to call the Devouring Mother" (x). But given the fact that the mother suffers from schizophrenia and has to be confined to a mental hospital, such a generalizing label of "the Devouring Mother" erases her suffering and reduces her to a universalized category. Liu's portrayal of his mother in "Canker" is more sympathetic, revealing her vulnerability and helplessness, which resists the reductive label of "the Devouring Mother." Rather than attempting to define his mother, Liu's poem confronts both their sufferings by allowing the mother's voice into the poem. Thus Liu explores the otherness of his homosexuality without repressing the otherness and subjectivity of his mother:

> *Your father lies. Please God, don't hurt your mother. You were*
> *always so difficult, crying, crying. I couldn't shut you up. You*
> *didn't want my milk. Only your father. How could I live*
> *with myself?*

> After we cried, I put out the light. I left her in that room. I
> closed the door behind me.

> Tonight my roses bloom beside her bed, working their thorns
> into her lips, the words I never knew how to say:

> *Mother, nothing heals completely as long as I stay alive.* (*Angelica* 42)

Despite the unspeakable pain his mother has inflicted upon him, the speaker still feels love and tenderness for his mother. By letting the mother speak, Liu makes it possible for her to maintain her subjectivity in the poem.

Significantly, Liu incorporates both his parents' voices in the poem, which help piece together a narrative of the family romance that undermines patriarchal authority in the binary paradigm of the parents' gender roles. The poem consists of a collage of fragmentary memories and voices. By juxtaposing narratives with reflections, Liu is able to move back and forth between the past and the present, revealing the lingering effects of his damaged childhood on him.

> The wound would not heal for days. But that was nothing
> compared to my mother who ran her mouth all over my body.
>
> . . . . . . . . . . . . . . . . . . . . .
>
> I still can hear her voice that day in junior high when I was
> called out of class. She said to me in the backseat,
>
> *Love me, let me die,*
>
> her head bobbing in my lap, floating in its pool of chemicals.
> The woman who couldn't get in to clean drove us to the
> emergency room.
>
> *Let me die.*
>
> That's all I heard when I broke into her bedroom, the pills
> scattered on the floor like a broken necklace.
>
> She lived. That night there was a canker in the back of my
> throat. I couldn't eat for days. My father opened cans of a
> protein drink he'd brought home from the hospital.
>
> *Drink this. Now sleep. Good.*
>
> That was the first time I remember being held. I told my father
> at the end of our trip. I told him about the men who came
> into my life. The pain that made me feel alive. (*Angelica* 39–41)

In contrast to the unstable, disruptive, and demanding mother, Liu's father appears in the poem as a tender, caring parent who comforts him in ways that his mother never did or could. In fact, Liu feels violated by his mother — "My mother entered me with a kiss" — and threatened by her physical presence: "I wanted her in the earth, her body contained" (*Angelica* 41). This portrayal of the son's relationship with his parents undercuts the "completely natural" and "inevitable" heterosexual norm in Freud's master narrative of the "family romance," which Judith Butler would call a "regulatory ideal" of "normative frameworks of compulsory heterosexuality that operate through the naturalization and reification of heterosexist norms" (*Bodies* 22, 93).

By disrupting the production of gender and heterosexual norms in the Freudian model of the family romance, Liu denaturalizes heterosexuality as the privileged norm. In her book, *Queer Theory: An Introduction*, Annamarie Jagose notes the theoretical challenges Judith Butler's work poses to gender and sexual identity construction: "By persistently denaturalising gender and sexuality, Butler problematises many of the cherished assumptions of gay liberation and lesbian feminism, including their appeals to commonality and collectivity" (85). Such assumptions of commonality and collectivity would erase the significant differences of race and class; it would also obscure the naturalizing functions of the regulatory ideal of normative gender and sexual identities, thus repressing the particularity of otherness in the name of a totalizing category of the other. Liu's exploration of his homosexuality in his autobiographical poems subverts naturalized gender identity and sexuality, and breaks away from ethnographical presentations of ideal homosexuality in literature which Bergman discusses. In an interview with Eileen Tabios, Liu says that it is possible that having an abusive mother who terrified him has had an influence on his sexuality. He adds, "I did wonder why it was that the intimacy and safety I could feel was with my father and not my mother. I also wonder why that was the first thing I felt in my sexual intimacy with men: finally to be safe, that I'm finally *home*" ("Redemption" 73). However, Liu's portrayal of his intimate and secure relationship with his father does not naturalize or idealize homosexuality. Rather, it destabilizes the normative model of gender identities which privilege heterosexuality, thus claiming a homosexual subjectivity outside the binary construct of the Freudian family romance, without assuming an opposite totalizing account of homosexuality.

The lyric I in Liu's poems, as in the other poets' work discussed so far, has the characteristics of Levinas's concept of the subject in terms of the subject's vulnerability, sensibility, and responsibility in relation to the other. Like the other poets, Liu turns to the other, especially the suffering, neglected other, with attention, affection, and love. "Men Without," collected in Liu's second volume, *Burnt Offerings*, asserts a homosexual subjectivity through the speaker who offers love to men who are vulnerable, inadequate, and tender toward others:

> My father is a coward, and I have grown
> to love the man who took my hand, afraid
> of leaving my side or asking the head nurse
>
> for a blanket even while I lay shivering
> on a gurney with an IV in my arm.
> Helpless and restrained, I saw a father
>
> who made no move to stop an incensed mother
> . . . . . . . . . . . . . . . . .
>                                      I love
> men who still wear uniforms sewn with care
> by women expert with needle and thread.
>
> . . . . . . . . . . . . . . . . .
>                                I love men
>
> who do not raise their voices in a crowd
> even when they are moving in the wrong
> direction – men who were never loved, I love. (*Offerings* 53)

Although the speaker asserts a Whitmanesque love, he does not claim to be an encompassing self like Whitman's persona. Whitman's claim of the oneness of the self and others seems to repress the otherness of the other, as Robert Martin has noted in the expanded edition of his book, *The Homosexual Tradition in American Poetry*: "Whitman's conceit was that his self was the world's self, that he and the world were one." But Whitman's all-encompassing claim to oneness, Martin points out, is "grounded in an insensitivity to history and a blindness to race," as his poem "Ethiopia" demonstrates. Whitman's concept and celebration of the self, therefore, "offer no way of explaining the source, or agent, of that claim" (266). Rather than seeking oneness with the world or others, Liu's persona maintains the proximity of others in proffering his love for them, thus making it impossible for the self to ignore or to assimilate the other.

Moreover, Liu's articulation of a homosexual subjectivity does not claim masculinity as a primary component of his identity or his bonding with other men, as Whitman's self does.[2] Whitman's assertion of same-sex love is characterized by the masculine-versus-feminine binary of the phallocentric heterosexual model of gender construct. According to Byrne Fone, Whitman deliberately produces a masculine image and language in his assertion of the self as part of his project of transforming American literature. Fone notes that in a letter to Emerson, Whitman "characterizes the literature he hopes to displace as one 'without manhood or power' in which only 'geldings' are depicted." Fone contends that Whitman's intention to use "man's words" to "express manly friendship" is motivated by the predominant stereotype of "the effeminate homosexual," whose "weak and effeminate," "depraved and feeble" images "accord with the developing medical and legal model of the homosexual as sexually enervated, aberrant, and mentally damaged" (21). To counter prejudice as such against homosexual men, Fone argues, "Whitman wants to recover for American literature a masculinized, virilized, anti-aristocratic, democratic style that he defines within an aesthetics of homoeroticized male existence" (22).

This privileging of the masculine over the feminine reproduces what Butler calls the regulatory ideal of normative gender identities which naturalize heterosexist norms and phallocentric power. Whitman's democratic style of masculine aesthetics is thus still trapped in the framework of phallocentrism which underlies the unmanly stereotypes of gay men and of Jewish, African, and Asian men in racist, Orientalist discourses produced against different social and historical backgrounds. In his book *Nationalism and Sexuality: Respectability and Abnormal Sexuality in Modern Europe*, George Mosse provides abundant examples to illustrate that the idealization of manliness as a heterosexual norm, which was used to condemn homosexuality as abnormal and effeminate in nineteenth-century Europe, soon became identified with German national identity. Consequently, manliness and virility were found to be lacking in "inferior races" such as Blacks and Jews, as well as in homosexual males (36). Asians and Pacific Islanders also fell into the "inferior" category, marked by their supposed lack of masculinity. In 1899, Theodore Roosevelt justified U.S. imperialist intervention in the Philippines, Puerto Rico, and Cuba on the basis that European Americans were of a "stronger and more manful race" than the native people of these territories (Roosevelt 13:328).[3] As David Eng, among others, has noted, the effeminate image of Asian men corresponds to Asians' racial position in the nation-state of the United States. Hence to articulate a homosexual and racial identity in terms of manliness is to be caught in a circularity of the phallocentric construct of gender and sexual norms.

Liu breaks away from Whitman's model of masculine aesthetics in his assertion of a homosexual subjectivity.[4] As a result, his poems call into question the structural stasis of sexual binarisms, thus opening up more possibilities for investigating the conditions for the formation of homosexual subjects, and for articulating homosexuality beyond the opposing frameworks of social constructivism versus essentialism. By refusing to privilege masculinity, and by subverting heterosexuality as the norm, Liu also undermines the *Aiiieeeee!* editors' condemnation of Asian homosexuality, which the editors equate with white racists' construction of Asians' gendered racial stereotypes in American popular culture. From the subject position of the lyric I, Liu's assertion of homosexual love for men, including those who were "never loved," repositions the Asian American male subject who has been effeminized and unsexed as Asian Americans. Given the context of Asian American male stereotypes, Liu's assertion of homoerotic desire, like the investigation and articulation of desires in the poems by Li-Young Lee, Marilyn Chin, David Mura, and Kimiko Hahn, is subversive and transformative of Asian Americans' raced gender identities and gendered racial subject positions. But his poetic treatment of the difference of homosexuality broadens the issues of otherness in Asian American poetry and enriches its poetics of alterity.

### The Wilderness Inside of Us

In most of the poems collected in his four volumes, *Vox Angelica* (1992), *Burnt Offerings* (1995), *Say Goodnight* (1998), and *Hard Evidence* (2001), Liu expresses a homoerotic desire which collapses binary paradigms such as body versus soul, femininity versus masculinity, and domination versus subordination. His exploration of homoeroticism, moreover, accomplishes more than a subversive destabilization of subject positions of gender, race, and sexuality. Liu's articulation of homoerotic desire transgresses the boundaries of the holy and the profane, insisting on mixing images of Christianity with those of homosexuality, and sometimes, explicitly homosexual acts. To understand the implications and effects of such transgressions beyond the familiar rhetoric of queer theories to which Jagose has referred, I draw from Georges Bataille's definition of eroticism, Judith Butler's theory of "performativity," and Levinas's idea of the relations between erotic profanation and alterity in my reading of Liu's poems in this and the next section.

Bataille defines eroticism as a multifaceted experience, at once corporeal and spiritual, transgressive and religious. "Knowledge of eroticism or of religion," Bataille writes, "demands an equal and contradictory personal experience of prohibitions and transgressions" (35–36). Bataille emphasizes the paradoxical relation between eroticism and transgression: "The inner experience of eroticism demands from the subject a sensitiveness to the anguish at the heart of the taboo no less great than the desire which leads him to infringe it. This is religious sensibility, and it always links desire closely with terror, intense pleasure and anguish" (38–39). For Bataille, prohibition is the condition that gives rise to eroticism, which transgresses prohibition and derives pleasure in large measure from the experience of "sinfulness." He asserts that "the greater the anguish . . . the stronger the realisation of exceeding the bounds and the greater the accompanying rush of joy" (145). Thus the awareness of taboo and transgression is part of the experience of eroticism. Prohibition generates profanation.

The paradoxes in Bataille's formulation of the erotic can be further understood in the light of Butler's theory of performativity, which calls for a rethinking of power / law and normative heterosexist discourses not simply as repressive of homosexuality, but as "constitutive constraints" which are "the very condition of performativity" (Bodies 93, 94–95). Butler emphasizes that "performativity cannot be understood outside of a process of iterability, a regularized and constrained repetition of norms. . . . This iterability implies that performance is not a singular act or event, but a ritualized production, a ritual reiterated under and through constraint, under and through the force of prohibition and taboo, with the threat of ostracism and even death controlling and compelling the shape of the production" (Bodies 95). For Butler, "constraint" is "the very condition of performativity. Performativity is neither free play nor theatrical self-presentation; nor can it be simply equated with performance. Moreover, constraint is not necessarily that which sets a limit to performativity; constraint is, rather, that which impels and sustains performativity" (Bodies

94–95). This notion of performativity suggests that prohibitions generate and shape sexuality, including unsanctioned sexuality. Seeking to draw out the implications of this relation between performativity and prohibitions, Butler raises the question, "how can regulation itself be constructed as a productive or generative constraint on sexuality?" (*Bodies* 95). The answer to this question is embedded in part in Bataille's formulation of eroticism in terms of its paradox of prohibition and transgression as a necessary twin condition for the pleasure of erotic experience.

Levinas's concept of eroticism and profanation adds a new dimension to both Bataille's and Butler's perspectives, though it is formulated within a heterosexual framework. For Levinas, an erotic relationship is a relationship with alterity that is unknowable through reason. He argues that "Eros, strong as death, will furnish us with the basis of an analysis of this relationship with mystery — provided it is set forth in terms entirely different from those of the Platonism that is a world of light" (*TO* 76). The mystery of the other remains hidden even when it is portrayed in the "most brutal materiality, in the most shameless or the most prosaic appearance of the feminine." Thus Levinas contends: "Profanation is not a negation of mystery, but one of the possible relationships with it" (*TO* 86). Rather than generated by prohibitions or constraints, transgression or profanation for Levinas is motivated by erotic desire for the unknowable other. "Voluptuosity, as profanation, discovers the hidden as hidden" because "the discovered does not lose its mystery in the discovery, the hidden is not disclosed." He adds that, "To discover here means to violate, rather than to disclose a secret." In other words, profanation violates what is concealed, and its violation only reveals what remains hidden. As Levinas emphasizes, "Profanation, the revelation of the hidden as hidden, constitutes a model of being irreducible to intentionality" (*TI* 260). Levinas's ideas of the relation of erotic desire and profanation to alterity provide an additional useful perspective for our understanding of Liu's poems.

Liu's poems of homoeroticism not only offer a site for exploring the possibilities of regulation or prohibition as a generative constraint on transgressive sexuality, they also reveal the relation of eroticism and profanation to alterity. In a number of poems, Liu interweaves images from the Bible in his articulation of homosexuality. These images serve as symbolic constraints which indicate prohibitions that provide the condition for the transgression of homosexuality to be asserted. In "Passion," for instance, the allusion to Christ is one of a cluster of images which iterate the normative regulations for sanctioned and unsanctioned sexuality. This poem consists of a collage of juxtaposed images, through which a sense of taboo is produced. Liu organizes the lines in such a way that all the images are strung together into one single passage, hence the structure of the poem suggests both constraint and deceptive surface which are embedded in the images at the beginning of the poem. The poem begins with a beautiful, tranquil scene of a midafternoon when flowers are blooming brilliantly in the garden, "bees darting / in and out of the miniature roses," and two children are playing "in a maze of bronze trees," while their mother is "walking among the Erté statues" in a gallery and "turning the little price tags over." To further enhance this scene of peace, leisure, and niceties, Liu directs the reader's gaze to another pleasant sight: "in a bistro across the street," an old man is "stirring a cup of double espresso" while "reciting Rumi" and "contemplating the passion of Christ" (*Angelica* 6). Such seamless peacefulness on the surface enhances the gulf beneath revealed by the voices and contrasting images. A little more than one third into the poem, disturbing images intersected by fragmentary voices begin to emerge:

> a musician in a Brooklyn flat
> burning down his studio
> all the needles pushing red
> a lifetime of tape unravelling
> *for ye have the poor with you always*
> *but me ye have not always*
> a child selling plastic roses
> tiny charges running through the stem
> *I would love to kiss you*
> the scent of women wrapped in mink
> *the price of kissing is your life*
> lap dogs trailing behind on long leashes
> *now my loving is running toward my life*
> *shouting*, one of woman, another of Christ:
> a man with two tattoos on his biceps
> bashing a fag on Christopher Street (*Angelica* 6–7)

In contrast to the peaceful and delightful images, the musician burning down his studio and a child selling plastic roses begin to introduce chaos and ugliness into the poem, followed by images of violence and death. As the title "Passion" suggests, some of the italicized lines allude to Christ's crucifixion. The sentence, *"for ye have the poor with you always/but me ye have not always"* is spoken by Jesus, alluding to his impending death on the cross.[5] This statement resonates with the reference to death from AIDS later in the poem. In association with homosexuality and Jesus's crucifixion, the statements about kissing — *"I would love to kiss you"* and *"the price of kissing is your life"* — also take on double meanings, alluding to Judas's betrayal of Jesus by kissing and to kissing between gay men, the price of which is not only physical violence against them, but also possibly death from AIDS. The biblical allusion in the closing lines adds to the shocking effect of Liu's collage juxtaposition:

> a trick in Hollywood dying from AIDS
> making his way to the Avenue of the Stars
> to sink his palms in pavement
> *Eloi, Eloi, lama sabacthani*
> the children home in time for supper. (*Angelica* 7)

Through collage, Liu brings into sharp focus the contrast between what would be condemned as sinful or worshiped as sacred. The implied prostitution and homosexuality in the image of "a trick in Hollywood dying from AIDS" is juxtaposed with the image of conjugal heterosexuality, sanctioned by marriage and the church, embodied by family and children. This juxtaposition foregrounds both the regulatory images of normative heterosexuality and the transgression of fornication and homosexuality. Liu's incorporation of biblical allusions in the poem produces a shocking effect which is not exactly what Howard refers to as "the claim of apostasy" (x). Rather, the shock here is produced by Liu's insistence on relating homosexuality to the passion of Christ. This implied relation produces a profoundly subversive and disconcerting effect by collapsing homosexuality with Christianity and the white middle class, disrupting the social construct of homosexual otherness against which Christianity and the white middle-class family are set up as regulatory standards for morality and heterosexuality.

Moreover, the apparent profanation of the holy seems to be more than a transgression of taboos. It appears to be a search for the "hidden," a violation of the unknowable — God and death. The juxtaposition of "a trick in Hollywood dying from AIDS" with Jesus's words on the cross — "*Eloi, Eloi, lama sabacthani*" (Father, Father, why have you forsaken me?) — enhances the sense of transgression with regard to sexuality, which, as Bataille notes, "is religious sensibility" and "always links desire closely with terror, intense pleasure and anguish" (39). Immediately following the image of "a trick in Hollywood dying from AIDS," Liu's insertion of those words from the Bible may also express longing for divine salvation, even as those words indicate a moment of doubt about God. The profanation in the poem, then, may suggest "the revelation of the hidden as hidden," constituting "a model of being irreducible to intentionality," as Levinas contends (*TI* 260).

This aspect of profanation in erotic desire which constitutes the desiring subject's relation to alterity characterizes the lyric I's relationship with the other in Liu's poems. While serving to enhance the awareness of transgressions, religious images sometimes evoke a yearning for the unattainable in other poems. Liu's meshing of homoerotic desire with religious sensibility suggests more than the effect of creating the experience of torture and pleasure. Its profanation of the holy establishes a possible relationship with the mystery of the absolute other beyond intentionality, a relationship with alterity through a love relationship with a human other. As Levinas states in *Time and The Other*, "Profanation is not a negation of mystery, but one of the possible relationships with it." For Levinas, an erotic love relationship is a relationship with alterity, in which the mystery of the other remains an enigma. "It is a relationship with what always slips away," Levinas emphasizes. "The relationship does not *ipso facto* neutralize alterity but preserves it. The pathos of voluptuousness lies in the fact of being two. The other as other is not here an object that becomes ours or becomes us; to the contrary, it withdraws into its mystery" (*TO* 86). The other in a homosexual love relationship in Liu's poem remains remote, separate from the self.

This ethical distance not only preserves the alterity of the other, but also sustains the subject's desire for the other as shown in Liu's other poems such as "A Valentine." The lyric I's assertion of homoerotic desire relates the corporeal to the metaphysical, as the speaker asks: "Was your touch mere tease or prelude/to some obstinate paradise that I could not/enter?" The quest for this inaccessible "paradise," the speaker suggests, underlies his writing of poetry and his desire for the other:

> Perhaps I alone must smear these
> petty reveries across the page, the dawn's
> diaphanous wings now plummeting into some
> far corner unfathomed by the waves slow
> susurrus — that flaming shirt stripped off your back
> a salt-stained flag still floating on the bilge
> where the clang of weights refined your body
> into something the world could love, each of us
> harboring what the other lacked: a wilderness. (*Goodnight* 27)

Like Levinas's concept of alterity, this "wilderness" attracts, entices, but remains resolutely other. Yet, to sustain this wilderness in "each of us" and our erotic desire for each other, a distance between self and other must be maintained, as Liu suggests in another poem, "Sunday." When two lovers sat down "to bowls of cold cereal" in the morning, each "would notice the blades of a ceiling fan/spinning at the bottom of their spoons," "yet no one / ever mentioned it, neither looking up/nor into each other's eyes for fear/of feeding the hunger that held them there" (*Offerings* 38). "Desire is desire for the absolutely other," Levinas states (*TI* 34). This concept of the relation between desire and otherness resonates in Liu's emphasis on "a wilderness" that each of the lovers harbored, but the other lacked — a wilderness that generated and sustained the lovers' desire.

Situated in the context of a gendered and raced heterosexual norm binarized by the phallus, Liu's insistence on the subjectivity and alterity of the other as the basis of love and desire offers an alternative mode of articulating homosexuality without reinforcing the phallocentric model, or reversing the primacy of one gender, sexuality, or race over another. Asian American critics such as David Eng and Richard Fung insist on confronting racial hierarchy while investigating homosexuality within power relations. Eng argues that whiteness, like heterosexuality, "has functioned largely as a regulatory standard hitherto invisible within the field of the visible and unremarked in the protocols of social discourse." He adds: "In their 'ideal' form, heterosexuality and whiteness maintain their compulsory power by remaining veiled and undisclosed." Hence, Eng states that heterosexuality and whiteness "work in collusion, drawing their discursive force in and through their smooth alignment" (142).

On a similar note Fung, in his article "Looking for My Penis: The Eroticized Asian in Gay Video Porn" provides examples of smooth alignment between whiteness and normative sexuality as such in sociology discourses and American popular culture. Furthermore, Fung calls critical attention to the reiteration of the primacy of phallocentric sexuality and white supremacy in the representation of homosexuality. He notes that in "commercial gay sexual representation, . . . the images of men and male beauty are still of *white* men and *white* male beauty. These are the standards against which we compare both ourselves and often our brothers — Asian, black, native, and Latino" (149). Fung further notes that performance of homosexuality in gay pornographic videos often reflects racial hierarchy in its privileging of white men's image, desire, and pleasure. Asian men are represented as "mysterious" and "exotic," and the roles they play are passive and subordinate. Narratives organized on the primacy of phallic power and pleasure tend to assign Asian men "the role of bottom" (152–53). The persistent "house boy" role Asian men are assigned in the drama of homosexuality, Fung contends, actually acts out "the mythologized geisha or 'the good wife'" fantasies of white men about Asian women (156). He argues, "Self-conscious 'Oriental' signifiers are part and parcel of a colonial fantasy . . . that empowers one kind of gay man over another" (157).

Liu's poems such as "The Size of It" and "Power," in a way, reflect the problems Eng and Fung have discussed. In "The Size of It," the speaker confesses his feelings of inferiority because of his small penis, which has become a racial marker for Asian males. As the speaker says, "I began equating Asian with inadequate, unable / to compete with others in the locker room" (*Offerings* 11). In "Power," Liu at once reiterates and contests the values and signification of the phallus. Referring to various kinds of surgery men undergo to restore penises damaged by an accident or disease, the speaker says ironically:

How else restore their dignity? — phallic
    disabilities our nation's silent
        agony. But what of men

who want a couple of extra inches
    for their own self-esteem, standing outside
      a clinic in Toronto

among boutiques, no sample large enough
    to estimate what constitutes
      an "average" endowment?

Some say it's a power thing. Pure power.
    An impulse not to be resisted – (*Goodnight* 80–81)

From women's perspective, however, the penis can be an instrument of violence and oppression to be resisted. As in the case of "a manicurist from Ecuador," who had been abused sexually by her husband until she could not endure the torture anymore. So she "'Attacked/ the instrument of her torture'" by cutting it off — a rebellious act which is "'An impulse that she could not resist.'" The poem ends with an ironic statement, "'A world in which the biggest knife wins'" (*Goodnight* 81–82). By undermining the phallic power through mocking tone and references to everyday life situations, Liu subverts the equation of manhood, masculinity, and power with the penis.

Rather than focusing on exposing what Eng and Fung refer to as racial positions or what Butler calls "*racializing* interpellation" (*Bodies* 18), most of Liu's poems contest the regulatory standards of racial hierarchy, phallocentrism, and heterosexual norms by refusing to mark the body with race or position it in binarized power relations. Although his autobiographical and confessional poems reveal his Chinese background, race or ethnicity in Liu's poems is not central to his articulation of homoerotic desire. In "Two Men on a Bench Watching the Light Die Down," for instance, Liu moves from the corporeal to the metaphysical, connecting erotic desire to human mortality. The poem begins with a description of two gay men's attraction to the "shirtless men bronzed by the sun" passing by on rollerblades, which is implicitly juxtaposed with the approach of night, signifying impending death. Then the poem ends by suggesting that an erotic relationship is a relationship with the unknown future, which withholds both birth and death: "To undress those men is to hasten/what stirs inside our bones — an ocean within/that spills into this world from dark to dark" (*Goodnight* 60). The inevitability of death associated with a homosexual relationship is implicated in the title of the poem. While this association evokes gay men's predicament related to AIDS, it foregrounds the metaphysical dimension of homoerotic desire outside the hierarchical binary power structures of race and gender. The racially unmarked body in Liu's poems also rejects the exotic mystery of Orientalist otherness which Fung exposes and critiques. While making Asian American homosexuality visible without racializing the eroticized bodies, or privileging masculinity over femininity, Liu's poems offer an alternative mode of articulating homoerotic desire that at once undermines and transforms binarized identities of race, gender, and sexuality constructed in power relations.

## Desire, Alterity, and Death

Homoerotic desire in Liu's poems establishes a relationship with the other, through which the subject enters into a relationship with the unknowable future and death. Although in a few poems about AIDS, Liu confronts death as a reality, in most of his poems death follows eroticism like a shadow, rendering homoerotic desire a complex experience, rather than a mere confession of transgression. While poems such as "Volunteers at the AIDS Foundation," "Last Christmas," and "The Quilt," collected in *Vox Angelica*, deal with grief and horror at countless deaths from AIDS, "Elegy," collected in *Say Goodnight*, asserts Liu's rage at silence about AIDS. But in most poems, death seems to be inevitably related to eroticism. In "Highway 6," for instance, Liu describes two "shirtless men" "cruising down Commercial Street, hand in hand, / as if death were merely some erotic aftertaste" (*Offerings* 14). In "Wellfleet," he juxtaposes images of lovers "wading back to shore / with ankles garlanded in ropes of kelp" at the beach with images of "sandwiches / on sterile trays [being] wheeled past rooms / for the sick," and waves "heav[ing] up wakes of trash" while "shrieking / gulls circl[e] above those watery graves" (*Offerings* 15). Liu equates erotic desire with the fear of death in "I Came," in which the occasion of a sexual encounter is compared to the moment of the lovers' dying (*Offerings* 44). Such interweaving of erotic desire with death in Liu's poems can be better understood in terms of Bataille's and Levinas's respective ideas of eroticism.

In his study on the relationship between eroticism and death, Bataille writes: "Eroticism opens the way to death. Death opens the way to the denial of our individual lives." He asks, "Without doing

violence to our inner selves, are we able to bear a negation that car-
ries us to the farthest bounds of possibilities?" (24). For Bataille,
eroticism as transgression indicates "a conscious refusal to limit our-
selves within our individual personalities." But eroticism entails
much more than a transgression. He contends that "we achieve the
power to look death in the face and to perceive in death the pathway
into unknowable and incomprehensible continuity — that path is the
secret of eroticism and eroticism alone can reveal it" (24). However,
Bataille does not provide theoretical explanations for this entangled
relationship between eroticism and death.

Levinas's notions of eroticism and death advance the logic in
Bataille's statements, and offer a different perspective on death and
its relation to eroticism. For Levinas, the erotic relationship is a rela-
tionship with the other, and it is also a relationship with the future.
"The other is the future," Levinas writes. "The very relationship with
the other is the relationship with the future" (*TO* 77). Both the other
and the future bear the characteristics of alterity in relation to the
subject. "The future is what is in no way grasped" (*TO* 76). Levinas in-
sists on understanding the relationship with the other "in terms that
contrast strongly with the relationships that describe light." Quoting
a phrase — "Eros, strong as death" — from the "Song of Songs" (Bible
8 : 6), he emphasizes that the subject's relationship with the other is
one with "mystery," which is not knowable through consciousness
(*TO* 76). Like the unknowable other and future, death is beyond the
subject's mastery. "What is important about the approach of death,"
Levinas stresses, "is that at a certain moment we are no longer *able to
be able*. . . . It is exactly thus that the subject loses its very mastery as
a subject" (*TO* 74). He further notes: "The strangeness of the future of
death does not leave the subject any initiative. There is an abyss be-
tween the present and death, between the ego and the alterity of mys-
tery" (*TO* 81). Thus in facing death, the subject is in relationship with
"an unassumable mystery," with "the eventuality of the *wholly other*,
of the future." It is a relationship "with what remains absolutely out-
side" (*TO* 35). Our relationship with death, then, is a relationship with
time, the future, and an absolute alterity. This relationship is estab-
lished in our encounter with the other. As Levinas states: "Relation-
ship with the future, the presence of the future in the present, seems
all the same accomplished in the face-to-face with the Other. The sit-
uation of the face-to-face would be the very accomplishment of time;

the encroachment of the present on the future is not the feat of the subject alone, but the intersubjective relationship" (*TO* 79). This view of the subject's complex relationship with the other, the future, and death helps explain Bataille's contention that "Eroticism opens the way to death," and we "perceive in death the pathway into unknowable and incomprehensible continuity" (*Erotism* 24), a contention which describes the characteristics of Liu's homoerotic poems.

In "The Tree That Knowledge Is," Liu employs biblical allusions to relate erotic desire to human transgression in the Garden of Eden and to human mortality. The opening line highlights death as the punishment of the primal sin in the Garden. The speaker's statements about his unwillingness to die for love or knowledge foreground erotic desire as the singlemost important impulse forcing him to confront the inevitability of death:

> I do not want to die. Not for love.
> Nor a vision of that tree I cannot
> recollect, shining in the darkness
> with cherubim and a flaming sword.
> All my life that still small voice
> of God coiled up inside my body.
> The lopped-off branch that guilt is
> is not death. Nor life. But the lust
> that flowers at the end of it. (*Angelica* 5)

Fear of death or awareness of prohibition fail to prevent the speaker's transgression. In fact, guilt invigorates his erotic desire. Even so the speaker is not free from his anguish about death or God's chastising voice. Homoerotic transgression in this and Liu's other poems precisely "opens the way to death," as Bataille says of eroticism.

In the second poem, "A View of the Garden," of a sequence poem, "Naked," the speaker relates his homosexuality to the experience of confronting death's inevitability and nearness:

> What had been forbidden
> transformed us: a mouth-shaped abyss
> opened all around us, the sky
> framing absence where a voice had been,
> *the voice of God*, you said –
>
> What reawakens is but a muted cry
> to the choirs that shook those bowers

where we had slept. No singing now,
only that endless ticking
from a clock we cannot silence. (*Offerings* 58)

With their transgression of a homosexual relationship, the speaker and his lover enter into a relationship with death which is "not a pure nothingness," as Levinas contends, "but an unassumable mystery and, in this sense, the eventuality of the event at the point of making an irruption within the Sameness of immanence" (*TO* 35). This irruption of death perceived as "a mouth-shaped abyss / opened all around us" takes place in these two lovers' relationship with God, whose withdrawal signifies not a negation of divinity, but the absence of an unknowable presence. The secession of the divine and the lovers' violation of a prohibition are accompanied by a sort of face-to-face encounter with the image of death, an unknowable abyss that threatens to swallow up the lovers. It is worth noting that the speaker emphasizes the effect of their sexual transgression on them: "What had been forbidden / transformed us." Their transformation is implied in their anxiety and fear—"What reawakens is but a muted cry/to the choirs"—and in their sense of helplessness while facing the eventuality of death, an inevitable future that is completely out of their control—"that endless ticking / from a clock we cannot silence." In its relationship with death, the absolute other, the subject is inadequate, unable. This inadequacy of the subject undermines the autonomy of the self, while highlighting the role of the other in constituting the subject and in establishing the subject's relation with the future and the unknowable.

Situated in a relationship with the other, the lyric I in Liu's poems neither assumes mastery over the transitory world, nor seeks to conquer death through his creative mind as the Wordsworthian lyric I does. The fundamental difference between Liu's lyric I and the lyric I in traditional Romantic lyric poetry results from a new conception of the self and its relationship with the other, the world, and human mortality. The self in Liu's poems is not defined in terms of a thinking subject grounded on the supremacy of self-consciousness, which defines the world and others as the object of its knowledge, and conquers death through the creative power of the mind. Rather than self-sufficient in its imagination or creative mind, Liu's lyric speaker is always bound in a relationship with an other — a relationship in which a relation to future and death is implicated. Levinas emphasizes,

"The future is what is in no way grasped" in the subject's relationship to death (*TO* 76). This logic introduces a new way of thinking about time "not as a degradation of eternity, but as the relationship to *that* which [is] unassimilable, absolutely other" (*TO* 32). The resolute alterity of death, like that of the future, which cannot be deciphered by thought, breaks the subject's solipsism and undermines its mastery of the world and the other through rational knowledge, thus calling into question "the unlimitedness of light and the impossibility for anything to be on the outside," as Levinas says of the traditional philosophy of idealism (*TO* 65). The "outside" of unknowable death and future cannot be mastered by the subject's intentionality.

In Liu's poems, erotic desire binds the lyric I to the alterity of the other, bringing the lyric speaker a keener awareness of death's inevitability and the self's vulnerability. In pursuing his erotic desire, Liu's poems suggest, the subject is closer to death and further from God. As the speaker in "The Tree that Knowledge Is" states, "I do not want to die," but the "lust" that banishes him from God and eternal life flourishes despite his fear of death and awareness of God's supposed prohibition. This conflict enhances the intensity of erotic desire, and accentuates the experience of torment, apprehension, and pleasure in the act of transgression, revealing a subject indulging in his erotic desire, while staring into the face of death with terror. In addition to heightening both prohibition and transgression, Liu's insistence on relating homosexuality to Christianity also helps move his persona's or characters' erotic desire to something beyond the personal and the corporeal.

Speaking of a draft version of "The Road to Seder" collected in *Burnt Offerings*, Liu reveals that his association of divinity with a human lover suggests a larger desire, a hunger that cannot be satisfied by the material. The "you" in the first line of this draft is at once a human other and God as the absolute other. "I also wanted the 'Beloved' to be God — the ultimate Beloved," says Liu. "The poem pleads, *Lord have mercy on the souls that thirst*! I wanted the reference to God to show that there was a much larger issue here than just a dumb love affair — that there was a larger hunger" ("Redemption" in Tabios 103). The "larger hunger" in Liu's poems seems to intensify with the desiring subject's awareness of approaching death. In "Forty-Percent Chance of Rain," the speaker wonders if it is "fear of dying alone that moves" him and his lover "toward each other in this room," where petals are "falling on a Bible marked in red"(*Offerings* 18). Apart from juxtaposing images which resonate the transitoriness of life, Liu relies on the syntax of a complex sentence to produce the effect of an ephemeral, fleeting moment:

> Only static hiss from a local station
> comforts us, singing off in a still small voice
> that echoes in our bones, a moon now painting
> the side of a broken bed where our faces
> grow too heavy for us to lift, and the room
> we share starts sinking into the ground. (*Offerings* 18)

Framed within a single sentence, the fleeting life we share appears to be especially evanescent, and our deaths particularly close and inevitable.

Liu explores further the relationship between erotic desire and the phenomenon of death in "Two Men on a Swing Watching Their Shadows Lengthen," while foregrounding the transitoriness of life. The poem begins with a description of a garden with budding grape vines and a newly painted arbor. The serenity of this scene is quickly disturbed by "Another robin crashed into the earth,/its carcass scattered by the blades/of a reconditioned mower." The instant death of the bird affects the couple on a swing:

> The swing
> slows. You touch my knee, and I hear
> the brass weights of a grandfather clock
> steadily falling in that cottage where
> we met, . . .
>                   Is life nothing more
> than two men on a swing watching
> their shadows lengthen? (*Goodnight* 19)

The event of death forces the speaker to confront his own mortality and the meaning of life. Rather than offering any answer to the question he asks, the speaker is preoccupied with the passage of time and the transiency of life:

> No more music
> stirs in that room, only a window
> overlooking a yard with a birdbath

filling up with snow. Touch me again
even while an ant on a rotten stump
struggles to carry a petal underground. (*Goodnight* 19)

In response to their impending death as suggested by the surrounding images of winter, the speaker desires the other. His response to mortality in terms of erotic desire seems to be a search for the unknowable. "The seeking of the caress," Levinas contends, "constitutes its essence by the fact that the caress does not know what it seeks." He adds, "It is like a game with something slipping away, . . . not with what can become ours or us, but with something other, always other, always inaccessible, and always still to come [*à venir*]. The caress is the anticipation of this pure future [*avenir*], without content. It is made up of this increase of hunger, of ever richer promises, opening new perspectives onto the ungraspable. It feeds on countless hungers" (*TO* 89). In Liu's poem, the speaker's seeking of the caress can be understood as an attempt to grasp what always slips away — something "always inaccessible, and always still to come" — something like death which feeds insatiable hunger.

To show that there is a larger hunger embedded in erotic desire, Liu explores the possibilities of imagery without personal narrative in "White Moths."[6] The image of white moths in this poem is reminiscent of the white moth — an image of death — in Robert Frost's poem, "Directive." But rather than an object of the lyric I's meditation on death as in Frost's poem, the white moths in Liu's poem are a phenomenon of life, whose death is portrayed as an event that foreshadows the deaths of the men in the park:

White Moths


      espaliered
to a radiator grille
or hurled
     from the glass cave
of a child's mason jar

into the garden spider's web –
a slow dance
     of paralytic

stings, death's handiwork

spun out of silk, cradled
by the wind –
               and the bodies
warm to touch in the rising

drone of dusk still flutter
among
          the bronzed backs
of men in the park –
                              pale wings
fanning a glitter of dust. (*Offerings* 42)

Liu introduces time into this imagist poem by depicting the white moths' death as an event, whose temporality accentuates the multiplicity of time. In other words, the temporality of the white moths' dying coincides with the temporality of the men's love making in the park, but this instant of time does not contain the diachronic life passages of either the moths or the men. In fact the moment in which the white moths are fluttering "among / the bronzed backs / of men in the park" is what Levinas calls "the temporality of time where diachrony precisely describes the relationship with what remains absolutely outside"— the past of the moths and the men, the future, and the eventuality of the men's deaths. By juxtaposing the image of the moths' "bodies / warm to touch" with "the bronzed backs / of men in the park," Liu suggests a parallel between the moths' struggle in the moment of death and men's desire in anticipation of death. With the last word "dust" in the closing line — "pale wings / fanning a glitter of dust"— echoing the inevitability of the men's death, the poem again links homoerotic desire to death, which remains outside this temporality of moths and men.

Thus death in Liu's poems remains a phenomenon, an event, and an absolute other, rather than knowledge to be grasped, or a fear to be overcome by the subject. The proximity and unknowability of death in Liu's homoerotic poems have a generative effect on the subject's sexual transgression. But death, like the other, or future, maintains its irreducible alterity. Its eventuality and yet ungraspable mystery outside the subject's temporality and knowledge suggest a new way of thinking of time "as the relationship to *that* which . . . would not allow itself to be assimilated by experience; or to *that* which — of itself infinite — would not allow itself to be comprehended," as Levinas proposes. By binding time to the alterity of the other, Levinas makes it possible to allow time to signify multiplicity, the always "noncoincidence, but also the *always* of the *relationship*" (*TO* 32). This insistence on the irreducible, unknowable aspects of otherness of not only homosexuals, but also each individual subject, characterizes Liu's poems, whose autobiographical narratives move beyond mere personal confession. As the speaker in "In Fear" suggests, his poems confront what it means to be a gay man in facing the fear of the other, the "brick // that flies through the glass / with a magic-markered // message not to be ignored —" (*Evidence* 72). Being the target of violence, hostility, and terror, how then should Liu, who is in fear of the fear of otherness, respond to the message sent with the brick? He could choose to hide his sexual orientation, or not to write about topics related to gay men. But Liu, like other Asian American poets, insists on asserting his otherness, while responding to the otherness of the other as mystery. In articulating same-sex love and homoerotic desire, Liu's poems about the human condition of love, loss, suffering, and mortality are an ethical response to homophobic hatred. His treatment of erotic desire and human mortality, like that of Li-Young Lee, transforms the content of universality with an unsettling, unknowable otherness.

# CHAPTER SIX

*John Yau*

THE I OF CHANGES, THE DESTROYING I, THE ITS OF THE I

John Yau's poetry is characterized by a poetics of resistance from the position of the other. "I, who was and is one of *Them*, do not want to become one of *Us*," states Yau in his essay, "Between the Forest and Its Trees" (1994 "Trees" 43).[1] In an earlier version of the same essay, Yau writes: "I am interested in what lies beyond reason, what is irreducible. Not the theme, not the subject. . . . Why not begin with music, its meaning? The music of the voices of the boys you do not want to hear again, . . . . The young woman's silence, which continues. Why not begin with words whose music disturbs, music whose words disturb?" (1993 "Trees" 187–88). Yau's poetics is grounded in his belief in "Writing as an attempt to hear the Other, the Others," and "as a form of attention and responsibility" (1994 "Trees" 41).

In his *Talisman* interview with Edward Foster, Yau deplores the "aesthetics of the assimilated" and asserts his interest in "resistance," particularly in "artists whose work resists assimilation into the accepted discourses" (Foster 37). One of the "accepted discourses," Yau suggests, is to be found in the autobiographical lyric poems of Robert Lowell and Frank O'Hara, which are marked by "subjective excesses" of the poet-I and the centrality of the poet's own life (Foster 45). Yau says in another interview that "almost from the beginning I wanted to get away from that 'I,'" which seemed to be "something privileged" (Tabios *Black Lightning* 386). In trying to avoid the solipsism of the poet-I as the lyric I in his poetry, Yau explores new ways of using language to disrupt the self-enclosure and self-sufficiency of the traditional lyric I. He says to Foster: "I don't want to write in a language that comes from an 'I,' from an interior subjectivity, I want something that comes from out there, from . . . that I who doesn't know who the 'I' is" (Foster 46).

The I in Yau's poems is multiple and heterogenous, trapped in the syntactic enclosure of language, and bound up with the other(s) and with its socially constructed identities, but uncontainable and elusive in its otherness. This I is unassimilable and disturbing because of its otherness: "I am an indigestible vapor rising from the dictionary / you sweep under your embroidered pillow," says the speaker in "Peter Lorre Records His Favorite Walt Whitman Poem For Posterity" (*Poems* 60). But this I subverts its foreign otherness constructed by Hollywood, and insists on being part of a pluralistic America as envisioned by Whitman. Speaking as Peter Lorre, who plays the role of Mr. Moto — a Japanese spy working for the United States and its allies in several Hollywood films — and evoking Whitman as his favorite poet, the I in Yau's poem enacts its subjective agency for resistance, change, and intervention. Yau articulates multiple aspects and possibilities of the first-person singular through the speaker in "830 Fireplace Road (2)," one of the poems created as "Variations on a sentence by Jackson Pollock" — "When I am *in* my painting, I'm not aware of what I'm doing" (*Poems* 12): "I have no fear of because, / no fear of destroying the I. / . . . / The I of changes, the destroying I, / the its of the I" (*Poems* 13–14). These lines suggest that even though the I and its images, attributes, and functions can be destroyed, the I remains the agency of this destruction and its subsequent changes. In his poems, Yau seeks to dismantle the Cartesian I, the authoritative and self-indulgent lyric I, without eliding the subjectivity of the poet-I, or the lyric speaker. For Yau, transforming the ways in which language is used in traditional models of lyric poetry is necessary for reconceptualizing the lyric I and reinventing lyric poetry.

## A Poetics of Resistance

In his poems, Yau breaks away from the conventions of Wordsworthian inward-turning lyric poetry by exploring the various possibilities of language, including those of syntax and sound, for establishing an ethical relationship between self and other. His poetics of resistance entails a complex task of subverting the discursive conventions that construct the solipsistic, authoritative lyric I, undermining the naturalized racial stereotypes of Asians in American popular culture, and rearticulating the "I," including the I as other, through a new poetic language oriented toward the other. As Yau says in an interview with Edward Foster, "Maybe I'm trying to figure out a way to get beyond the location of simply my life and see if something can happen out there instead of saying this is what happened here. So I try to find ways to find out there, in words" (Foster 49).

The premise of this task, for Yau, entails breaking away from self-enclosure and the authority of the lyric I and opening up the poetic space to the oppressed and excluded voices of the other. He investigates the ways in which language constructs identities, especially the possibilities of agency in language for asserting a multiple, incomplete, and unstable self, who signifies an unsettling otherness. In his essay, "Between the Forest and Its Trees," which could be read as a manifesto of his poetics, Yau articulates the central ideas underlying his poems. He begins by contesting the self-sufficiency of the Cartesian self grounded in the primacy of consciousness as the defining principle of the subject. "How does the 'I' begin?" Yau asks. "Where the 'I' begins is in a sentence, obeying the rules of language, its illusion of order," he contends. "To continue to repeat the structures of language as it is used (abused) is to continue to oppress and be oppressed" (1993 "Trees" 185). This concept of the I constructed in language challenges the equation of the author with the I in a text, while calling attention to the oppressive aspect of syntax and discursive conventions, thus suggesting the necessity for disrupting conventional ways of using language in poetry.

Yau highlights a correlation between the assumption of universal meanings in the visible observed by the lyric I/eye, and the apparently natural language used as a transparent medium for communicating the lyric I's/eye's insights. He writes: "I do not believe in the lyric I — the single modulating voice that names — writing in a language that is transparent, a window overlooking a world in which we are all present. It is not a world that includes me. It does not speak for me or to me. . . . It has Modern written all over it" (1993 "Trees" 186). Even though Yau rejects this Modernist convention of the lyric I and its autonomous, authoritative self, he does not believe in the autonomy of the text or words as a viable alternative, either.

In trying to break away from conventional modes of poetic language, Yau seems to share some Language poets' notions and practices. Charles Bernstein, for instance, considers grammatical rules and syntactic order too limited and restrictive. Seeking to make "the structures of meaning in language more tangible and in that way allowing for the maximum resonance for the medium," Bernstein states that Language poets "see the medium of writing . . . as maximally open in vocabulary, forms, shapes, phoneme/morpheme/phrase/sentence order, etc., so that possible areas covered, ranges of things depicted, suggested, critiqued, considered, etc., have an outer limit (asymptotic) of what can be thought, what can (might) be" ("Semblance" 15–16). On a similar note, Bruce Andrews deplores writings based on the assumption of language and imagery as transparent media through which reality is represented and meaning is produced and understood. "One mode of writing tips its hat to assumptions of reference, representation, transparency, clarity, description, reproduction, positivism. Words are mere windows, substitutes, proper names, haloed or subjugated by the things to which they seem to point." However, he contends that dominant ideologies and apparently fixed meanings can be "blown apart" and "be opposed by . . . a political writing practice that unveils, demystifies the creation and sharing of meaning," and "problematizes the ideological nature of any apparent coherence between signified and referent, between signified & signifier" ("Writing Social Work" 133, 135). Even though Yau shares these Language poets' beliefs and practices to a certain extent, he differs in significant ways from them in his insistence on the impact of the author's racial identity and subject positions on the text. For some Language poets, the death of the author is a crucial part of their subversive writing.[2] Bruce Andrews, for instance, writes: "Author dies, writing begins. The subject loses authority, disappears, is *unmade* into a network of relationships, stretching indefinitely" ("Code Words" 54). Even though Yau, like Andrews, questions the authorial authority, such celebration of the disappearance of the writing subject for him is politically disabling and theoretically inadequate for those who have been marginalized and excluded as the other. As he states: "Nor do I subscribe to the death of the author, that there is no self that is writing, that there is no self that is trying to speak in words, and through words. That seems another way to silence the Other, to keep them from speaking and writing" (1993 "Trees" 186). In her provocative discussion of Yau's poems, Dorothy Joan Wang points out that Yau deconstructs a traditional lyric I, a subject that "has been cast by some white critics as generic postmodern erasure of the subject" ("Undercover Asian" 152–53). Transforming the lyric I, rather than getting rid of it, constitutes a crucial part of Yau's poetics of resistance.

For Yau, writing poetry entails attention to the other and allowing the silent or silenced other to be heard. Although the I is constrained by the structure of language, it is a site where agency for resistance, intervention, and alterity of the other is possible. Emile Benveniste's discussion of subjectivity in language can shed light on the importance of the subjective agency in Yau's poetics of resistance and otherness. In "Subjectivity in Language," Benveniste writes:

> *I* refers to the act of individual discourse in which it is pronounced, and by this it designates the speaker. . . . Language is accordingly the possibility of subjectivity because it always contains the linguistic forms appropriate to the expression of subjectivity. . . . In some way language puts forth 'empty' forms which each speaker, in the exercise of discourse, appropriates to himself and which he relates to his "person," at the same time defining himself as *I* and a partner as *you*. The instance of discourse is thus constitutive of all the coordinates that define the subject. (730–31)

If language renders subjectivity possible, discourse constitutes a discrete subject and its relationship with others. These intricate relations among language, discourse, and subjectivity make both oppression and resistance possible for the self and the other in language.

The constitutive relation among language, discourse, and subjectivity which Benveniste delineates is a point of departure for Yau's poetics of resistance. Yau seems to suggest that for his writing to be "an attempt to hear the Other, the Others," and to be a form of attention to and responsibility for the other, he must assert an alternative mode of subjectivity which breaks away from the Cartesian self. Yau articulates the underlying principles for an alternative model of the subject in "Between the Forest and Its Trees": "I believe there is a self made up of many selves, incomplete and fragmented. None of them knows the whole story, not even the one who is speaking, the one who is in this sentence" (1993 "Trees" 186). Yau's rejection of the Cartesian self, however, does not result in a simple replacement of the unitary self with a fragmented self. Rather it establishes a relationship between self and other whose alterity cannot be deciphered or reduced to a common measure or to a variation of the sameness of self. Thus to acknowledge the multiplicity and incompleteness of the self, to recognize how the self as subject is produced in language, and to question the totality of knowledge are necessary conditions for challenging the sufficiency of consciousness, for resisting self-enclosure, and for responding to the other. Yau states that in writing poems which begin and end "in the worlds and words that make up this world," he must not be afraid of speaking (writing) out of the pieces, the fragments, the mishearing of voices that you manage to hear, to pay attention to, to utter, even as they sometimes refute you, disgust you, show you something you might not have known, wanted to know, can know" (1993 "Trees" 187). For Yau, to hear the other, to recognize the irreducible alterity of the other is to inscribe the impossibility of speaking for the other, to utter the vulnerability and insufficiency of the self.

Yau articulates an ethical self-other relationship registered in language and enacted in discourse, which resonates with Levinas's ethics. For Levinas, ethics occurs when the ego or the Same is called into question by alterity in the encounter between self and other, in which I loses mastery over the irreducible otherness of the other. Simon Critchley has summarized this ethics succinctly. "Ethics, for Levinas, is critique; it is the critical *mise en question* of the liberty, spontaneity, and cognitive emprise of the ego that seeks to reduce all otherness to itself. The ethical is therefore the location of a point of alterity, or what Levinas also calls 'exteriority' (*extériorité*), that cannot be reduced to the Same" (5). An ethics as such is embedded in Yau's poetics of resistance, in his insistence on writing as a form of attention to and responsibility for the other, and as an opening of the self toward alterity as an ethical event in language. Departing from self-consciousness as the subject matter of the lyric, and from an autonomous, authoritative I as the organizing principle of lyric poetry, Yau's poems seek to hear the voices and silence of the other.

### Meeting the Other through Saying

Yau explores various possibilities of using language as "saying" to establish an ethical relation with the other. His early poems, such as the prose-poem series "Angel Atrapado," illustrate Yau's departure from conventional lyric speech that establishes the centrality, singularity, and authority of the lyric I. According to Yau, the title "Angel Atrapado/Entrapped Angel" is inspired by a group of paintings he saw in Venezuela. He wanted the series to be "poems made up of voices, male and female, authority and anti-authority, all kinds. All of them would speak, which suggests at the very least that the 'I' is multiple."[3] Rather than multiple versions of the same I, Yau's poems articulate plural, different subjects who refuse to speak in a "single modulating voice" of an authoritative lyric I.

Several poems in this series dramatize the process of I trying to escape various kinds of entrapment. "I don't want to live inside my head, I want to live out of my body, live out of what my body wants," says the speaker in "Angel Atrapado II" (*Edificio* 155). This I trapped in the self's mind and body can be self-enclosed, manipulated, or erased: "I lived on the outside shelf, a jar facing the world of the handlers and the handled. I was a handle, something to grasp and lift and wash away." Thus "I don't want to live there anymore, but here in the flannel soot I am breathing." How does one, then, move from this position, trapped in a binarized world of "the handlers and the handled," to a different one? In other words, how can the I break out of its self-enclosure, and escape the confinement of a particular category of identity inscribed on the body, in order to inhabit multiple positions and meet the other? As the speaker says: "In and among and in. Inside of but outside. Outside out there, and inside in here. How then to meet, make mesh and emerge." Yau suggests that these new possibilities for the self have to be initiated in a language that disrupts the predictable order of narrative and syntax, and in images that make their meanings opaque, rather than illuminating them: "Every because is a catapult waiting for a snowflake to drop. The night is ferment and departure. My fingers are trembling as they unbutton the broken windows between us" (*Edificio* 156). Even though the speaker is trying to reach the other who is nearby, the distance between them remains.

Yau's innovative use of language and surrealist images in this poem, as in others, undermines the autonomy and authority of the traditional lyric I who names, perceives, and deciphers the world and the other. The impossible images and irrational statements of the I in Yau's poem resist transparency and bring representation into crisis, indicating a problematic correlation between intelligibility and mimetic representation. Levinas's insights into the implications underlying this correlation can further our understanding of the significance of unsettling surrealist images and ambiguous language in Yau's poems. "To be intelligible is to be represented and hence to be a priori," Levinas writes. "To reduce a reality to its content thought is to reduce it to the same." Levinas suggests that what is intelligible and representable is already reduced to an object of thought. He argues: "To represent is not to reduce a past fact to an actual image but to reduce to the instantaneousness of thought everything that seems independent of it; it is in this that representation is constitutive" (*TI* 127). Yau's imagery and language expose the oppressive potential of naturalized, seemingly realistic representation, while resisting epiphany of the visionary moment of the lyric I/eye, thus indicating the irreducibility of the world and the other to the lyric speaker's thought or vision.

For Yau, how imagery, language, and voice are used in poetry are matters of ethics and politics, as well as aesthetics. Who is speaking and whose voice is heard in poetry are among the central issues Yau explores. One of his strategies for breaking away from the traditional lyric I as "the single modulating voice that names" is constantly shifting the pronouns in one poem. In "Angel Atrapado III," for example, the multiple pronouns the speaker refers to have the effect of simultaneously decentering the I and introducing into the poem others who resist becoming the object of knowledge or observation of the I/eye:

> We did not know how to dance when we met. . . . I sent you a dance mat and a prayer mat, each woven from the fiery hair of children who pretended to be angels. . . .

> A voice, neither yours nor mine, was heard between where we were sitting and where we were dying.

> I tried to tell him where to begin, but he would not listen. I tried to tell him he had to follow the sequence or the order would be wrong. I tried to tell him this was how the sentences we were in would be written. (*Edificio* 157)

None of the multiple subjects — "we," "I," "you," "children," and "he" — occupies a dominant or subordinate position in relation to one another. And, there is an unknowable "voice" between "yours" and "mine," heard, but not recognized. Thus a world of multiplicity, mystery, and heterogeneity emerges. In this world, the I fails to grasp the enigmatic, or master the different, or dominate over others.

Unidentifiable with the poet-I, or any stable, singular identities, the I in Yau's "Angel Atrapado" series operates as an empty subject position from where multiple subjects can speak as an I, and from different perspectives. Thus, the I in these poems is sometimes speaking as one who resists syntactic closure, one who breaks away from the traditional lyric I, and one who is the other. The speaker in the opening lines of "Angel Atrapado XI," for instance, asserts his otherness in terms of his apparently strange difference: "I eat rice with two wooden sticks. / I beat lice with burning wicks" (*Edificio* 173). These statements do not define exactly who the "I" is, but they allude to an odd Asian identity. The oddity of this identity, the poem suggests, is produced to match the name assigned to the identity. In fact, these statements seem to be made by someone who is "speaking to the name he is called by others." The third passage of the poem suggests that the I wants to escape the identity attached to his or her body by changing his or her appearance. Even though "I" tried to get rid of "my" identity by wearing "my" parents' clothes on different occasions, "I was still there, still inside what I didn't want to be inside of, flagrant flesh and its musty cling" (*Edificio* 173). This passage and the opening lines raise questions about the identity of the I — not so much about who the I is, as about how and why the body of the I seems to have become a fixed basis for defining its racialized (yellow) identity, as suggested by "its musty cling." The speech of "I" in this poem might allude to Yau's own experience of being Chinese American, but the lack of autobiographical details renders the I an empty signifier or a subject position which can be occupied by any one who identifies with it. The issues raised in this poem, then, are rendered larger than those concerning an autobiographical I. While Yau refuses to make his personal experience of being the child of immigrant parents from China the central subject matter of his poetry, he doesn't want to ignore that experience, either (Foster 48–49). His employment of a multiple I, which refuses to be identical with the autobiographical poet-I, enables him to investigate the relationship between subjectivity and identity, particularly the racialized identity of Asian Americans, which is at once personal and collective.

The constant shifting of pronouns and their destabilized identities in Yau's poems establish a dialogic self-other relationship which breaks away from the reductive and hierarchical relations embedded in binary identity construction. This dialogic relationship between self and other is characterized by Yau's use of nonrepresentational language and narrative, which resists turning speech into "the single modulating voice that names" (1993 "Trees" 186) or into the kind of discourse which Levinas calls "internal discourse." While discussing the ways in which language can be used to reduce and assimilate otherness, Levinas contends: "Language can be constructed as internal discourse and can always be equated with the gathering of alterity into the unity of presence by the *I* of the intentional *I think*." Thus the entry of the other into this assimilative representational language of intentionality marks "the key moment of re-presentation and vision as the essence of thought!" (*EN* 162–63). To resist this mode of using language as "internal discourse" that reduces the other to the object of "my" vision or "my" thought, Levinas proposes a dialogic mode of speech as an alternative: "I call upon him. I do not just think that he is, I speak to him. He is my *partner* within a relation that was only to have made him present to me" (*EN* 7). Speech as such, Levinas argues, is a condition for an intersubjective relationship with the other through saying oriented toward the other. "The point is to see the function of language not as subordinate to the *consciousness* we have of the presence of the other, or of his proximity, or of our community with him, but as a condition of that conscious realization" (*EN* 6). Speech as attention to the other and as a way of establishing an ethical relationship with the other informs Yau's innovative use of language in his poems.

Yau's employment of language as fragmentary speech seeks to engage the other as an interlocutor whose presence and voice not only refuse to subordinate to the consciousness of I, but also affect, or even transform, the I. In "Angel Atrapado XVI," the speaker watches and listens to the other whose gesture and words resist defining his or her identity:

> I was watching you dance before the mirror, drying your hair
> and arching your back. I was listening to you point the words
> toward me, their arrowheads dipped in the motions of your
> mouth. I began hearing you whisper: My tongue is a turtle, its
> head locked inside the words I place around my name. I am the
> seasons inside my body, windy days proceeding towards the
> northern dust. I was born during either the Feast of Chickens
> or the Festival of Dragon Dung. (*Edificio* 183)

By switching the pronoun from *you* to *I*, Yau allows the other to be the speaking subject, unlocking his/her tongue "locked inside the words" placed around his/her "name." The other's statements about himself or herself through the elocutionary I at once reveal and conceal his or her otherness — "I am the seasons inside my body. . . . I was born during either the Feast of Chickens or the Festival of Dragon Dung." These references evoke and make fun of the Chinese zodiac signs, thus rendering the speaker's apparently Chinese identity subversive and elusive, resisting homogenous racial and ethnic stereotypes. While the elusiveness of the other renders alterity irreducible to thought or representation, proximity as "the sense of the sensibility" (*OB* 19) establishes what Levinas calls the "sociality" between self and other (*EN* 164) in Yau's poem: "We are each other's fireplace, something to stand in front of and get warm, something to take us away from where we are singing" (*Edificio* 183). This relationship between us who are each's other is a bond, one which according to Levinas is "not reducible to the representation of the other, but to his invocation, and in which invocation is not preceded by an understanding" (*EN* 7).

Levinas's emphasis on proximity as "the sense of the sensibility," not intentionality, highlights the condition for an ethical relation between self and other, which gives rise to saying as approach to the other. In other words, saying establishes a relationship with the other "whose monadic inwardness eludes my gaze and my control" (*EN* 71). This relation between proximity and saying is operative in Yau's poems such as the "Angel Atrapado" series in which the bond between you and I is not the result of my knowledge of the other, but is rather an "invocation" of the other, an expression of my acknowledgment of the other in meeting the other. The meeting between self and other is grounded in what Levinas calls "the event of language" (*EN* 6), one that entails the ethical movement "from the Same to the Other, without suppressing the difference" (*EN* 63). Response to the other in language as an "event," rather than knowledge inaugurates an ethical self-other relationship in which the self is open to the impact of the other. Yau enacts a self-other relationship as such in language through the speaker in his poem, who says, "We were beginning to learn if the right words could tempt us away from our bodies" (*Edificio* 184). Yau suggests that a self-other relationship in which each maintains its subjectivity and alterity through language can result in new discoveries which lead us away from sameness to otherness, rather than returning to the same.

In his "Angel Atrapado" poems, Yau insists on paying attention to the other by replacing conventional self-centered interior monologues of self-reflection with dialogues between I and You. Levinas points out a correlation between self-enclosure and the mode of discourse characterized by "Reflection [which] gives us only the narrative of a personal adventure, a private soul, incessantly returning to itself, even when it seems to flee itself" (*EN* 11). To disrupt this incessant returning of a private soul to itself, Yau lets the I in his poems constantly invoke the other as an interlocutor, whose presence compels the self to respond to the other through speech. As the speaker says to the addressee in "Angel Atrapado VIII": "I want to see you swimming between the pages of a book, all the words in profile. I want to hear you talk about the oracular menaces infiltrating the daily rust" (*Edificio* 167). Yau uses expressive assertions to invoke the other as an "attempt to hear the Other," and as "a form of attention and responsibility" (1994 "Trees" 41) that enacts an ethical relation with the other through speech, which refuses to assimilate the other as an object of consciousness or representation.

The surrealist images and nonrepresentational language Yau employs serve as an expressive performance of opening the self to the other for the other:

All the air is mine as this body, my body, is yours to twist off
its locks. Drink from it and be thirsty. All this snow is mine,
wash in it, and I will come and greet you with my tongue of
bright glass, dry the bones you are hiding beneath your skin.
(*Edificio* 181)

This saying as turning toward the other in passivity involves exiling the subject from self-enclosure in consciousness as the home of the autonomous self. Rather than seeking to absorb the other into the self-same, Yau uses expressive speech as a form of attention to and responsibility for the other.

A self-other relationship established through saying, Yau suggests, opens new possibilities for writing poetry. As the last sentence of "Angel Atrapado XV" suggests: "Or maybe the words we bring to the air outside our mouths leads [*sic*] us away from here, toward rooms and clouds that have yet to open" (*Edificio* 182). Yau's verbal performance explores not only "what lies beyond reason, what is irreducible," but also how to open the poetic space for the excluded or repressed other. As the title of his eleventh book of poetry, *Edificio Sayonara*, suggests, in breaking away from literary establishment and the syntactic enclosure of language which, like an edifice, can contain, constrain, and exclude the other, he must open the established poetic space and discourse to marginalized and excluded otherness. These implications are embedded in the title of the Spanish word *edificio* (edifice) and the Japanese expression *sayonara* (bye-bye).

### Mimicry of the Abject Other

While the prose poems in his "Angel Atrapado" series are textually bound verbal performance, the poems in Yau's "Genghis Chan: Private Eye" series situate the verbal performance in the context of Asian Americans' stereotypes produced and circulated in American popular culture. Yau's "Genghis Chan" poems produce a complex identity of the self as other, one who exposes and critiques the constructed otherness of the abject other, while articulating an elusive, unknowable alterity of the other. Given this complexity of the I, who is at once a mimicry of racial stereotypes and an irreducible other, Yau's employment of postmodern aesthetics of multiplicity, fragmentation, and indeterminacy, as well as surrealist images and performative language, are particularly effective in problematizing representation, enacting social critique, and encountering otherness. Combining investigation of language with interrogation of identity construction, Yau undermines the representation of Asian Americans in American popular culture, exposing not only the effects, but also the naturalizing tactics, of racial stereotyping. At the same time, Yau explores the relations between language and the subject, between the lyric I and the racially marked self, mostly through parody, which at once alludes to and demolishes racial stereotypes. It is precisely through culturally specific parody that postmodern aesthetics of multiplicity, fragmentation, and indeterminacy in Yau's "Genghis Chan" poems become situated in the social and historical conditions of the raced subject. The combination of postmodern, surrealist aesthetics and a Levinasian ethics of alterity renders Yau's parody of the social construct of the other particularly provocative and subversive.

Yau's parody in his "Genghis Chan: Private Eye" series critiques and disrupts what it mimics. The title "Genghis Chan: Private Eye" is itself a complex parody. "Genghis Chan" simultaneously evokes two

opposing stereotypes of Asian immigrants and Asian Americans —
the yellow peril associated with Genghis Khan and the model minor-
ity epitomized by Charlie Chan. Genghis Khan, the historical figure
of conquest, has been associated with the fictional character Fu Man-
chu, the yellow peril incarnate in Hollywood films which was in-
spired by thirteen novels by Sax Rohmer. The apparently opposing
fictional character, Charlie Chan, a Chinese American detective from
Hawaii, was played by three white men (Warner Oland, Sidney Toler,
and Roland Winters) in forty-eight Hollywood films adapted from
five Charlie Chan novels by Earl Derr Biggers.[4] In collapsing these
two names and stereotypes together, Yau highlights the apparent
contradictions in the racial stereotypes of Asian Americans, while
indicating that the yellow peril can be contained by turning it into a
subordinate model minority image through representational tactics.
Gary Y. Okihiro's insight further complicates the relationship be-
tween these two stereotypes. Rather than "denoting opposite repre-
sentations along a single line," Okihiro argues that the yellow peril
and the model minority "in fact form a circular relationship that
moves in either direction." Even though "model minority mitigates
the alleged danger of the yellow peril," if taken too far it "can become
the yellow peril" in a reversed direction. "In either swing along the
arc," the model minority serves to maintain "white supremacy" (142).
Yau's use of the hybrid name, "Genghis Chan," though it evokes both
stereotypes and their intricate interrelationships, refuses to corre-
spond to the exact names and their identities.

In contrast to such stereotypical public figures as those suggested
in the title, the subtitle, "Private Eye," suggests a private self/I that re-
sists its socially constructed identities of race and gender. The allusion
in the subtitle to Charlie Chan's profession as a detective — "Private
Eye" — puns on the lyric I whose utterance is supposed to be private,
overheard by the reader, and whose transcendence is supposed to be
the virtue of lyric poetry. However, Yau's use of the racially marked
name, Genghis Chan, situates the speaker's private speech in a specific
social, historical, and cultural context which shapes the speaker's
subjectivity and identity. Resonating with interrogation and confes-
sion, the private eye/I in Yau's "Genghis Chan" series investigates the
interlockings of the public and the private, the collective and the per-
sonal in the formation of ethnic identity and subjectivity, while en-
hancing the tension between a stable social construct of racial identity

and the shifting, elusive identity of the private I. While locating the identities of the Chinese American I in their social, historical formations, Yau allows the racially marked, yet elusive, private I to undermine and move beyond those identities imposed by the dominant culture.

In his "Genghis Chan: Private Eye" poems, Yau explores the possibilities of articulating the ambivalence and complexity of the self that is at once a social construct and an elusive, private self. In the first poem of the "Genghis Chan" series, for instance, the speaker shows no immediate resemblance to the stereotypes to which the title alludes. Rather, the "I" reveals a self whose identity insinuates that of Charlie Chan, and yet refuses to be identical with him, thus remaining open to alternative identities. As is characteristic of *film noir*, the poem is set at night, apparently in the detective/speaker's office:

> I was floating through a cross section
> with my dusty wine glass, when she entered,
> a shivering bundle of shredded starlight.
> You don't need words to tell a story,
> a gesture will do. These days,
> we're all parasites looking for a body
> to cling to. I'm nothing more
> than riffraff splendor drifting past the runway.
> I always keep a supply of lamprey lipstick around,
> just in case. (*Silhouette* 189)

The I in this poem is unsettling because the speaker resists being identified according to any definitive race or gender codes which the reader expects to find — codes that are implicated in the name in the title. In other words, the I in this poem breaks down the correspondence between the name and its identity, or, between the signifier and its referent.

In "Genghis Chan: Private Eye" Yau disrupts the production of stereotypical Asian American identities by refusing to give any familiar racial codes for the reader to decode and encode simultaneously the speaker's identity and words. Rather than refashioning an image in opposition to the Hollywood versions of Charlie Chan, Yau questions naturalized identities of race and gender which assume a stable relationship between bodily differences and the essence of race and gender. The images of "I" and "she" in his poem have a sense of bodilessness that resists encoding the bodies with racial or gender markers, thus destabilizing a seemingly stable location of identity. The reader, then, is forced to rely on narrative and the speaker's statements to figure out who the speaker is and what is happening in the poem, but all these remain elusive because the narrative and language Yau employs are deliberately ambiguous. The encounter between I and she in the poem may allude to Genghis/Charlie Chan's meeting with one of the numerous female victims or clients on his job. But Yau gives no definitive clues to their identities or the story she tells.

Although the narrative of the poem remains vague and discontinuous, Yau achieves subversive effects precisely through ambivalent mimicry:

> It was late
> and we were getting jammed in deep.
> I was on the other side, staring at
> the snow covered moon pasted above the park.
> A foul lump started making promises in my voice. (*Silhouette* 189)

With the line break, Yau shifts the narrative from her story back to the encounter between I and she with an indication of the passing of time and development in their encounter. But he keeps the meaning of this development — "we were getting jammed in deep" — vague. In fact, the identity of "we" becomes even more ambivalent when the following lines shift the focus of the narrative from "we" to "I," whose obscure statements paradoxically shed light on his complex identity. The ambiguity of the speaker's position in terms of the temporal-spatial relationship — "I was on the other side, staring at / the snow covered moon pasted above the park" — may suggest that the I is a fictitious character, like a copy of Charlie Chan, whose existence is similar to the calendar photography of "the snow covered moon pasted above the park." Hence the I is "on the other side" of the reader's world, that is, in the fictional space of Charlie Chan novels and films. Therefore, "we were getting jammed in deep" may refer to the fact that both the actor/character and the audience/reader are ensnared in the narrative, while suggesting possibly a scene of intimacy between the detective and his female client, which Yau refers to as "that archetypal encounter of Private Eye (man) and potential client/victim (woman) seeking help."[5] On the other hand, the statement — "I was on the other side" — could also mean the opposite, that is, I was on the other side of the fictive world of Charlie Chan, emphasizing the fact that the I is not identical with Charlie Chan.

This ambivalence blurs the boundaries between fiction and reality regarding the identity of the I, suggesting that the I who was "staring at / the snow covered moon pasted above the park" may exist simultaneously in two places — the world where the reader lives and the world of fiction. In so doing, Yau draws the reader's attention to the naturalizing process of representation in constructing racial identity. By keeping the connection between Genghis Chan and the Hollywood Asian American stereotypes tenuous and ambivalent, Yau is able to undermine constantly these stereotypes through parody, while making use of elements of *film noir*. Detective story, ambivalent identity, and elusive reality, which characterize *film noir*'s narratives and themes, are congenial to Yau's exploration of identities in his "Genghis Chan" series. Thomas Schatz observes that *film noir* portrays a "bleaker vision of the world, which was more psychologically 'realistic' and yet more visually abstract" (113). The *noir* style of partial lighting, skewed visions, and oblique shadows contributes to creating a sense of hidden truths about characters and events. In a characteristic *film noir* such as *Citizen Kane*, Schatz notes, the *noir* style is incorporated into the narrative and the "style of storytelling" to address thematic issues such as "the tension between subjective and objective impressions of reality" and "the inability of anyone . . . to ever really 'know' another human being" (118). Similarly, in discussing women in *film noir*, Janey Place finds that in the world of *film noir*, nothing is stable, "nothing is dependable." The characters' identities are constantly "shifting and must be redefined at every turn" (41). Thus *noir* style, which provides the visual and psychological tone of the hardboiled detective film, also serves similar functions in Yau's "Genghis Chan" series, which deals with psychological and epistemological questions about identity and reality.

In "Genghis Chan: Private Eye IV," Yau parodies another aspect of racial identity politics by alluding to another night scene in which the Chinese American detective encounters a white female, evoking a major theme of romance in *film noir*. As Schatz notes, "romantic narration" is one of the characteristics of *film noir* (117). But in Yau's "Genghis Chan" poems, the possibility of a romantic relationship between the I and the she remains remote because of socially policed racial boundaries:

> Rusted pundit, throttled chin
>
> I was turned by a tendril adrift,
> pale freckled skin bathed
> in insect iridescence,
> lips sucked through a straw
>
> . . . . . . . . . .
>
> She was a farm of concrete
> cleanly poured, and I
> — the quarantined flash —
> was tilting above Newt Falls,
> its glossy stanzas of imitation snow
>
> Hours of sigh practice loomed ahead (*Silhouette* 192)

The unbridgeable gap between the forbidden white woman — "a farm of concrete / cleanly poured" — and the Chinese American I — "the quarantined flash" alludes to the implications of the absence of romance in Charlie Chan's relationships with all of his white female victims or clients. In keeping with the anti-miscegenation laws in several states of the United States and the taboo against showing intimate contact between whites and people of color, including kissing, on the screen, Earl Derr Biggers and Hollywood took special care to eliminate any possibility of romantic involvement between a Chinese man and a white woman. Portrayed as a portly middle-aged father of eleven children, who is perfectly content with his patriarchal position at home, Charlie Chan is established as a devoted family man, who is simply incapable of transgressing racial or sexual boundaries, thus posing no threat to white dominance in the social power structure based on gender and racial hierarchy. Speaking heavily accented artificial pidgin English with an archaic flavor, frequently quoting mostly fabricated Chinese sayings, Charlie Chan is a perfect image of the assimilated model minority who remains perpetually foreign. White women are completely safe with such a male image, for he has neither "sex appeal" nor interest in women. These attributes of Charlie Chan are naturalized as a fixed racial and cultural essence.[6] "We Chinese are different," Charlie Chan says to his white clients in the novel, *Behind that Curtain*. "Home is a sanctuary into which we retire, the father is high priest, the altar fires burn bright" (Biggers 67). Yau's parody denaturalizes Charlie Chan's desexualized, domesticated racial identity by exposing socially policed boundaries of raced bodies. Like Charlie Chan, Genghis Chan is a "rusted pundit," whose body is "quarantined" from white women. It seems that Yau uses the phrase "quarantined flash" to evoke simultaneously the word *flesh* — Charlie/Genghis Chan's racially marked and socially contained body — and to allude to the fact that Charlie/Genghis Chan's image and subject position are prescribed and maintained in Hollywood films. As the speaker in "Genghis Chan: Private Eye VI" asserts, "I am just another particle cloud gliding across the screen / . . . I am the owner of one pockmarked tongue" (*Silhouette* 194).

Yet, Genghis Chan is significantly different from the fictional and Hollywood Charlie Chan. As his name indicates, the yellow peril and model minority stereotypes are collated into him, and the tension between public and private selves ("Private Eye"/Private I) is embedded in the title of Yau's series. The multiple facets of Genghis Chan enable Yau to position the speaking subject differently. Sometimes, the I seems to be a white actor playing the role of Charlie Chan, sometimes the I seems to be a Chinese American, and other times, the I is speaking in a collective voice of Asian Americans. In "Genghis Chan: Private Eye VIII," for instance, the speaker is apparently speaking as one of the white actors who played the role of Charlie Chan:

> I plugged in the new image fertilizer
> and complained to my inaudible copy
>
> We did tour the best spots
> trying to attract basic signs of pity
>
> touched a disaster every now and then
> and remained ridiculous and understaffed (*Edificio* 73)

Yau employs surrealist images to foreground the commodified Chinese American stereotypes in American popular culture. By emphasizing that his "copy" — a Chinese American — is "inaudible" and yet accompanies him everywhere he goes ("We did tour the best spots"), the speaker is revealing the fact that the Chinese American he pretends to be is actually silenced. While talking about himself, this private eye/I is hearing the silence of the other.

As the speaker continues to unravel "thought's stunted projectiles," speaking at once as the detective and the private I, the reader learns about his feelings of inadequacy in pretending to be who he is not:

Now I am clamped to the desk
unraveling thought's stunted projectiles

Had I been as visible as a chameleon
I would have crossed my eyes

so as to look more like you
than your silver reflection

I would have hummed to the statue
inside your black eyes and black tongue

I would have memorized its song (*Edificio* 73)

The speaker confesses that his imitation of a Chinese American is no more than their "silver reflection" on the screen. Allowing the speaker to assume the identity of the actor of Charlie Chan and to speak of his private thoughts, Yau is able to subvert the Hollywood versions of Chinese Americans constructed through bodily images and a foreign accent naturalized as the inevitable racial and ethnic attributes. Yau's emphasis on the speaker's imitation of you and your "black eyes and black tongue" exposes the manipulated and fictitious nature of the Asian American identity, thus at once highlighting and destabilizing the corporeal as a site for naturalizing racial identities.

The menace of Yau's mimicry of Asian American stereotypes is produced through an ambivalent I that vacillates between a fictional and a real-life identity, and between public and private selves. This oscillation involves a shift from a fixed identity grounded in naturalized racial or ethnic attributes to an unstable identity constructed through language, narrative, and performance. Thus Yau's postmodernist parody is similar to the kind of subversive shift in identity construction which Judith Butler discusses. In *Gender Trouble: Feminism and the Subversion of Identity*, Butler argues that "the shift from an *epistemological* account of identity to one which locates the problematic within practices of *signification* permits an analysis that takes the epistemological mode itself as one possible and contingent signifying practice." "Further," Butler adds, "the question of *agency* is reformulated as a question of how signification and resignification work" (184). It is precisely through an alternative mode of signification that

Yau achieves agency for resistance and subversion — an agency which is foreclosed by an epistemological account of identity that insists on essence and authenticity.

The unstable identity of the I in Yau's poems also enables him to reposition the speaking subject who enacts the agency of resistance and intervention. Instead of speaking from the position of a white actor as the I in "Genghis Chan: Private Eye VIII" indicates, the speaker in "Genghis Chan: Private Eye III" is plural and apparently Asian American:

> We surfed out of the alley,
> the stories our parents told us
> trailing behind, like angry yellow toads
>
> You spoke first:
> One of my ancestral coupons
> composed the bulldozer anthem
> Perhaps she too was waiting
> for the bumper crop showers
> to subside, another dust mote picker
> in a long line of lovelorn imports
> Yes, I too was stymied by the animal of music
> and the shadow its breath sent through history (*Silhouette* 191)

Both "you" and "I" are burdened and haunted by their parents' stories, which suggest racial discrimination and hostile social environments for Asian Americans. Again, Yau relies on surrealist images to capture the speakers' emotional and psychological states ("the stories our parents told us / trailing behind, like angry yellow toads") and to refer to the impact of the social, economic, and political climate on Asian Americans ("Perhaps she too was waiting / for the bumper crop showers / to subside, another dust mote picker / in a long line of lovelorn imports"). U.S. relationships with Asian countries have always affected the lives and social status of Asian Americans since the nineteenth century.[7] Yau's use of abstract, compact images renders the meanings of his lines opaque, ambivalent, and yet more elastic and richer than conventional imagery or narrative. The lines spoken by "You" might refer to the impact of World War II, the Cold War, the Korean War, the Vietnam War, and the trade war on Asian Americans. The lines spoken by "I" in response to what "You" said — "Yes, I too was stymied by the animal of music / And the shadow its breath sent through history"— emphasize the lingering effect of history on Asian Americans, an effect that is also implied in the name "Genghis Chan."

However, what the I wanted to say in "Genghis Chan: Private Eye III" entails more than how histories and politics shaped Asian American experience and identities. As the speaker says:

> I wanted to tell you
> about the bank teller and the giant,
> the red moths hovering above their heads
>
> I wanted to tell you
> about the gizmo pit and the kinds of sludge
> I have cataloged during my investigation
>
> I wanted to tell you
> about how the sun
> dissolved all of this long ago
>
> leaving us in different rooms
>
> registered under different names (*Silhouette* 191)

There are extraordinary, fantastic, and heterogeneous things and people which resist identity labels, as the speaker suggests. Yet, all that is outlandish, marvelous, and uncanny of us and among us was divided and reduced to categories of names. Here Yau seems to be indirectly articulating through Genghis Chan his belief that the self is not "purely a social construct," just as it is neither a unified, "a fixed entity" like the Romantic I, nor a complete autonomy of the Modernist I.[8] This complexity of the self and its intricate relationships with white America and Asian America are played out in the "Genghis Chan: Private Eye" series.

In the "Genghis Chan" monologues, the complex self who is not "purely a social construct" operates as a site of resistance and subversion through confessional monologues. "I prefer rat back flames to diplomatic curls," says Genghis Chan in poem VI of the series. He continues: "I am the owner of one pockmarked tongue / I park it on the hedge between sure bets and bad business" (*Silhouette* 194). Unlike the humble, modest, and discreet Charlie Chan, Genghis Chan is deliberately unceremonious, rebellious, and even reckless. Similarly, switching from I to you in "Genghis Chan: Private Eye VII," Yau represents a self who is aggressive and uncompromising:

> You will speak to the driver of a blue horse
> You will grasp someone's tongue with your teeth and pull
>
> You will prefer the one that bleeds on the carpet
> to the one that drools on your sleeve. (*Silhouette* 195)

This private I contests the public Hollywood image of Charlie Chan who speaks non-standard English cautiously with a typical "Chinese" flavor, by using language with an innovative audacity. As the speaker says, "You will grasp someone's tongue with your teeth and pull." This violent gesture matches Yau's radical transgression of conventional poetic metaphors. For Yau, using language the way others have used or abused it is more than a form of conformity; it is a mode of oppression, and possibly a distortion of who the I is.

Breaking away from conventional ways of using words, for Yau, is a mode of resisting the "little boxes" of "the structures of language — the accepted narratives" (1994 "Trees" 38) — in order to articulate elusive, multiple selves and the self as Other. As he writes in his essay: "I am the Other. . . . You have your labels, their falsifying categories, but I have words. I — the I writes — will not be spoken for" (1994 "Trees" 40). The private/lyric "I," then, can be an enabling subject position, a site of resistance and intervention. The "I" who speaks in the "Genghis Chan" series mixes words in such a way that they at once parody and subvert Chinese American stereotypes. As the speaker in "Genghis Chan: Private Eye XX" asserts: "I posed / as a cookie / fortune smeller // . . . / I squeezed / the liars alive // I bent their bubbles / around air's broken coat" (*Edificio* 87). Yau's appropriation of the voice of the lyric/private I and his critical engagement with the social and cultural constructs of racial stereotypes through mimicry with a difference, not simply dismantles the authority of the Cartesian lyric I or disrupts the production of racial stereotypes; it gives voice to the silence and objectified other.

*Hearing the Other and Sounding Other*

Yau's appropriation of what seems to be pidgin English in some of his "Genghis Chan" poems marks the beginning of what becomes a more radical use of the musicality of language in his Language poems of the "Genghis Chan" series. In poems collected in his two later volumes, *Forbidden Entries* (1996) and *Borrowed Love Poems* (2002), the ethnically marked sound of nonsensical or disturbing words and phrases is a primary principle of composition. With this primacy of sound, Yau's poems are further removed from the conventions of lyric poetry characterized by individual voices and the lyric I/eye. As a result, speeches or dialogues are replaced by impersonal voices evoked by the sound patterns of language. Voice, narrative, and observation also give way to the music of language.

This turning toward the materiality of language is reminiscent of a similar turn in American Language poems. In his introduction to *Close Listening: Poetry and the Performed Word*, Charles Bernstein argues for the significance of nonsensical sound in poetry: "It is precisely because sound is an arational or nonlogical feature of language that it is so significant for poetry — for sound registers the sheer physicality of language, a physicality that must be the grounding of reason exactly insofar as it eludes rationality. Sound is language's flesh, its opacity as meaning marks its material embeddedness in the world of things. Sound brings writing back from its metaphysical and symbolic functions to where it is at home, in performance" (21). Although these attributes and functions of the physicality of language are salient characteristics of what might be called Yau's Language poems in the "Genghis Chan" series, Yau pushes the limits of the materiality of language further beyond the performance of words, beyond the opulence of language, and beyond the thingness of things to an unsettling otherness. The opacity of meaning in sound that resists logic or eludes reason serves to articulate the absolute alterity of the other in Yau's poems.

This unique function of the sound of language for signifying an unassimilable, uncontainable otherness is embedded in Levinas's emphasis on speech as the meeting ground between self and other, where the other cannot be grasped as an object of the self's intentionality. "Speech refuses vision," Levinas argues, because the speaker "is personally present in his speech, [but] absolutely exterior to every image he would leave." He adds, "This presence whose format exceeds the measure of the I is not reabsorbed into my vision" (*TI* 296). In other words, speech signifies the presence of the absent other whose alterity exceeds and remains outside of "my vision," and is irreducible to representation. Thus Levinas states: "In language exteriority is exercised, deployed, brought about" (*TI* 296). This possibility of language for exercising, deploying, and bringing out the exteriority/otherness of the other that cannot be absorbed into the same is precisely what Yau seeks in his poems.

Yau explores a radical mode of evoking otherness by deploying the sound patterns of words to replace speech in his Language poems. But since the sound patterns in Yau's "Genghis Chan" poems are ethnically marked, they also allude to the socially constructed, racialized ethnic identity of Chinese immigrants and Chinese Americans. Yau's Language poems, then, escape becoming socially detached, politically disabling experimental poems, even though there is no I to function as the subjective agency of the other. Rather than using words as free-floating signifiers, Yau employs Cantonese-sounding words as "an attempt to hear the Other, the Others," and "as a form of attention and responsibility," to quote him again (1994 "Trees" 41). As he asks, "Why not begin with words whose music disturbs, music whose words disturb?" (1993 "Trees" 188), the other-sounding music in Yau's poems insists on confronting social issues. "Genghis Chan: Private Eye XXIV," for example, breaks away from grammatical rules, syntactic order, and traditional poetic form, relying on sound as the organizing principle. The resulting sound patterns produce a disturbing music of the other, while the equally unsettling words at once allude to and resist Asian American stereotypes:

Grab some
Grub sum

Sub gum
machine stun

Treat pork
pig feet

On floor
all fours

Train cow
chow lane

Dice played
trade spice

Makes fist
first steps (*Entries* 102)

In her discussion of this poem, Marjorie Perloff notes Yau's allusion to Chinese stereotypes, but she finds Yau's version of stereotyping Chinese Americans reductive: "Here the clever puns and specific images refer to the oldest of 'Chinese' stereotypes: . . . the belligerent stance of the poor immigrant Chinese who must 'Grab some / Grub sum,' 'makes fist' and slave in factories ('machine stun') as his 'first steps' toward assimilation. Yau is calling attention to the lingering orientalism of U.S. culture, the labeling that continues to haunt Chinese-Americans. But his version of that labeling is itself guilty of reductionism" (Review of *Forbidden Entries* 40). Perloff continues to single out examples of Hollywood Orientalism in another of Yau's poems, "Bar Orient," arriving at the conclusion that the image of China in this poem "seems as out of date as it is one-dimensional" (40). Perloff's critique of Yau's reductionism misses the point of Yau's subversive parody that undermines precisely the assumption of authenticity in seemingly realistic representations of ethnic culture and identity in American popular culture. In his discussion of "Genghis Chan: Private Eye XXIV," Yunte Huang notes that Perloff's reading overlooks Yau's "play with pidginization." He contends, "Sound and spelling approximations between *grab* and *grub, sum* and *some, sum* and *sub* . . . are all characteristic of the kind of pidginization by which Oriental languages have been portrayed in American racist literature" (136). In fact, "what is involved in Yau's poems," Huang adds, "is an intentional play, a countermockery of the mockery of Charlie Chan, just as the title of the series, Genghis Chan, contains an explicit double irony" (136–37). In so doing, Huang argues, "Yau's work, especially, through ventriloquizing Imagism's ventriloquism and pidginizing racist literature's pidginization of Chinese, problematizes rather than foregrounds language's ties to racial identity" (137).

While Huang's perceptive reading of Yau's "Genghis Chan" poems calls critical attention to salient characteristics of Yau's strategy, there is still yet another linguistic feature worth noting.[9] In addition to a subversive double mockery that contests language's ties to racial identity, Yau uses sound patterns which resonate with Cantonese to articulate, with a sort of tongue-in-cheek humor, an otherness which resists explication and contaminates dominant standard Anglo

American English. Hence the music, rather than the meaning, of the words is crucial to the unsettling effect of these poems whose ambiguity cannot be explained away by deciphering the meanings of the words, images, or nonsensical phrases. "Genghis Chan: Private Eye XXIV," like the other Language poems in the series, is organized by the audible sounds of words, which not only undermine stereotypes through mockery, but also evoke a disturbing, unassimilable otherness. While the rhythm and rhymes of monosyllabic words may be a playful mockery of the pidginization of Chinese, producing a music similar to that of Cantonese, a dialect spoken by immigrants from Guangdong and Hong Kong, the meanings of the words do not correspond to either the ethnic identity or racial stereotypes the sound might evoke. Yau's play with the letters and sounds in couplets such as: "Grab some/Grub sum," "On floor / all fours," and "Train cow / chow lane" in Poem XXIV, and "Dimple sample / Rump stump, "Dump fun / Dim sum," "Strong song / Oolong" in Poem XXV (*Entries* 103), may allude to racial stereotypes of the Chinese through pidginization, but his use of actual Cantonese words *dim sum* (snacks often served at Sunday brunch in the United States), and the mandarin Chinese word *oolong* (a type of tea), and English phrases *on floor*, *train cow*, and *makes fist* in nonsensical couplets makes impossible the construction of either a racial identity or any definitive Chinese racial stereotypes. Thus the boundaries for constructing racial identities are at once evoked and blurred by Yau's deployment of bilingual words.

A comparison of Yau's Language poems in the "Genghis Chan" series with those written by white Americans who parody pidgin spoken by Chinese immigrants in popular poems or songs illustrates well the difference between stereotyping and anti-stereotyping. Elaine Kim in her groundbreaking book, *Asian American Literature: An Introduction to the Writings and Their Social Context* (1982), notes that "A mainstay of popular American culture, the comic Chinese dialect is characterized by high-pitched, sing-song tones, tortured syntax, the confounding of *l*'s and *r*'s, the proliferation of *ee*-endings, and the random omission of articles and auxiliary verbs. Bret Harte's poem 'Plain Language from Truthful James' — better known as 'The Heathen Chinee' (1870) — provided the model for writings in this vein, which for two decades were epidemic in American newspapers and journals" (12). As an example, Kim cites from Charles G. Leland's *Pidgin English*

*Sing Song* (1903), a collection of "songs and stories in the Chinese-American dialect," which "had remarkable success" (12). Like Bret Harte's "The Heathen Chinee," Leland's poem constructs a morally despicable Chinese American character with appalling habits, while parodying pidgin English, through narrative and conventional meter and rhyme:

Ping-wing he pie-man son.
He velly worst chilo alló Can'tón.
He steal he mother piclum mice,
And thlowee cat in bilin' rice.
Hab chow-chow up, and "Now," talk he,
"my wonda' where he meemow cat be?" (Leland 28 qtd. in Kim 12)

Nevertheless, Leland and others, according to Kim, claim that "their rendering of Chinese American dialect was accurate, however unlike it was to the actual pidgin English spoken by the Chinese of Hawaii and the Caribbean" (12–13). By insisting on the accuracy, or authenticity, of their rendering of Chinese American dialect, Leland and others attempt to naturalize their ideologically mediated construction of the Chinese American stereotype as the latter's fixed racial, ethnic identity. Their claim to authenticity not only presupposes that there is a racial and ethnic essence which their poems can accurately represent, it also assumes that Chinese and Chinese Americans, notwithstanding their inscrutability, are completely knowable to them. While their parodies represent Chinese Americans' unassimilable otherness which justifies their exclusion, they reduce this otherness to the opposite of the self-same in a binary paradigm, thus domesticating otherness by defining it according to a normative totality. As Levinas argues, "If the same would establish its identity by simple *opposition to the other*, it would already be a part of totality encompassing the same and the other" (*TI* 38). The debased, alien otherness of the Chinese constructed in American popular culture and literature is resolutely different from the otherness of the other, which is "not the simple reverse of identity, and is not formed out of resistance to the same, but is prior to every initiative, to all imperialism of the same" (*TI* 38–39). It is precisely the alterity of the other that Yau seeks to articulate in his poems.

Unlike Harte and Leland's parodies of Chinese pidgin English, Yau's use of Cantonese-sounding English refuses to construct racial meaning; instead it undermines the formation of such meaning by insisting on the primacy of sound, and eliminating narrative and the speaking subject in his "Genghis Chan" Language poems. While discussing the possibility of subverting naturalized identity through parody, Judith Butler argues that "Parody by itself is not subversive, and there must be a way to understand what makes certain kinds of parodic repetitions effectively disruptive, truly troubling, and which repetitions become domesticated and recirculated as instruments of cultural hegemony" (*Gender Trouble* 176–77). Robert G. Lee's discussion of the construction of Chinese racial stereotypes in nineteenth-century popular culture and literature reveals that the combination of pidginized Cantonese and nonsensical words was a characteristic strategy of parody in popular songs. Despite the nonstandard use of English the meaning of the lyrics can be easily understood because the racially marked speaker and his or her narrative serve as the locus of meaning. One of the examples Lee gives is the song "Hong Kong," which appeared in Nick Gardens's *Two Ring Circus Songster*:[10]

My Name is Sin Sin, come from China
In a bigee large shippee, commee long here;
Wind blow welly muchee, kick upee blubelly
Ship makee Chinaman feelee wellee queer.
Me fetchee longee a lillee gal nicee
She com longee to be my wife
Makee bigee swear to it all her life.

Me likee bow wow, wellee goodee chow-chow,
Me likee lillee gal, she likee me
Me fetchee Hong-Kong, whitee man comee long,
Takee lillee gal from a poor Chinee. (qtd. in R. Lee 37)

The parody of pidgin in this song has all the characteristics Elaine Kim has noted. Apart from turning the Chinese into a laughingstock, the exaggerated characteristics of mispronunciations and ungrammatical English highlight pidgin's deviation from standard English, which Chinese immigrants were supposed to be incapable of speaking because of their racial characteristics. The ethnically marked voice of the speaker corresponds with pidginized English, while the speaker's narrative serves to designate his ethnic identity and naturalize his racial subordination to the white male whose dominant power is asserted in his taking the Chinese man's fiancee away. The speaker's use of "me" instead of "I" for himself foregrounds the subjugated subjectivity and the lack of subjective agency for the racially marked speaker. Thus the language in this song is supposed to mirror the alien racial traits of the Chinese speaker and to justify his subordinate position and exclusion.

With this stabilized and naturalized correspondence between pidginized Cantonese and raced Chinese identity, the nonsensical words in these songs serve to reinforce racial hierarchy and exclusion of the Chinese from U.S. citizenship. According to Robert Lee, "a variety of pidgins and creoles were in use throughout the nineteenth-century American West. . . . The common use of pidgins and creoles threatened to subvert the hegemony of Anglo-American English-language-based culture and undermine its teleological myth of nationhood." The deployment of pidginized English and nonsense words in the construction of Chinese stereotypes in the popular songs reflects minstrelsy's response to the crisis of racial and cultural identities by reinforcing "the hegemonic power of standard English, setting the linguistic standard for participating in citizenship" (36). "Hong Kong" is one of the numerous examples of such reinforcement of racial and cultural boundaries in cultural productions. According to Lee, in this same poem, published under the title "Chinese Song" in Charles A. Loder's *Hilarity Songster* (1885), "the chorus is heavily inflected with nonsense words, making the meaning of the song itself incomprehensible" (37).

> Ki, Ki, Ki, Ching, Ching, Ching,
> Hung a rung, a chickel neckey
> Suppe, fatte hung
> Eno Posa keno Posey, keno John,
> Chinese manee goode manee from Hong Kong. (qtd. in R. Lee 37)

Even though the nonsensical words here render this chorus indecipherable, the chorus maintains the same characteristics of comical proliferation of *ee*-endings and repetition of deriding sounds which are attached to the alien Chineseness they simultaneously construct and essentialize. Being the chorus of the song, which typecasts both Sin Sin and Hong Kong as representatives of the Chinese, its incomprehensible words inflected with pidginized Cantonese sound reinforce the inscrutable alien identity of the Chinese stereotype represented as the racial other of white Americans. Paradoxically, the supposed inscrutability of the Chinese is made transparent, completely knowable as the essence of racial otherness.

The technical characteristics and their effects, as well as their underlying assumptions about the Chinese in those nineteenth-century popular songs, help shed light on the significant difference in John Yau's use of Cantonese-sounding words. As Levinas says, "The word that bears on the Other as a theme seems to contain the Other" (*TI* 195). While the otherness of pidginized Cantonese and English in the songs is constructed as an essence of the racial other to buttress racial hierarchy and Eurocentrism, the otherness of Yau's Language poems evokes the alterity of the other which resists definition or explication. Even though the sound patterns of the words in Yau's poems resonate with Cantonese, the words, unlike those in the songs cited above, are not pidginized Cantonese or English. Yau's pairing of couplets which are associated by sound patterns, rather than semantic meanings, creates an unsettling ambivalence that resists any coherent meaning the phrases seem to yield. This resistance indicates that while language can invoke the other, it "cannot encompass the other," as Levinas says (*EN* 32).

Moreover, the otherness Yau's language invokes is not contained within racial or geographical boundaries through racially marked characters or narratives. The other-sounding words in Yau's poems are mixed and juxtaposed with familiar English phrases as in "Genghis Chan: Private Eye XXVII" and other poems of the series:

> *Moo goo*
> Milk mush

> *Guy pan*
> Piss pot (*Entries* 105)

The juxtaposition of Cantonese "Moo goo" (French mushrooms) and "Guy pan" (chicken pancake) with English phrases of equally mundane words with equally humdrum sounds undermines the privilege of English, and subverts the hegemony of Anglo American English-language-based American culture. The importance of Yau's insistence on introducing Cantonese sounds into his poem can be understood in terms of Levinas's concept of the relationship between an ethical language and otherness. "The presence of the Other, or expression, source of all signification," Levinas argues, "is not contemplated as

an intelligible essence, but is heard as language, and thereby is effec-
tuated exteriorly" (*TI* 297). Like his use of nonsensical phrases, Yau's
refusal to translate the Cantonese maintains its disturbing otherness
which remains undomesticated, unassimilable.

In his two Language poems of the "Genghis Chan" series collected
in *Borrowed Love Poems*, Yau takes his resistance poetics a step fur-
ther in contaminating English. In "Genghis Chan: Private Eye XXX,"
Yau mixes Cantonese-sounding and English words in such a way that
no dominant standard English is set up as the norm against which
pidgin or Cantonese is shown to be its deviation or opposite other:

> shoo war
> torn talk
>
> ping towel
> pong toy
>
> salted sap
> yellow credit
>
> hubba doggo
> hubba patootie
>
> wig maw
> mustard tongue. (*Poems* 38)

Here the Cantonese-sounding words, as well as the Chinese and En-
glish words, have the same status in Yau's play with the letters and
words, which evokes otherness without defining it. The otherness in-
voked by words such as *shoo* (dish) and "ping pong," the onomato-
poeic Chinese pronunciation for table tennis, challenge the purity
and hegemony of Anglo American English, severing the naturalized
tie between language and racial identity, which characterizes the con-
struction of Asian American stereotypes. In fact, the American
phrase, *hubba hubba*, like the Chinese *ping pong*, is separated and
made fun of. Similarly, the phrase "wig maw" alludes to *wigwam*, the
name given to a kind of Native American dwelling, calling the au-
thority of naming into question by switching the letters from "wam"
to "maw." In association with "maw," the ending phrase "mustard
tongue," though it signifies a bodily organ, suggests the contamina-
tion of English (tongue) by Asians ("mustard" as a racial marker of
yellow). Through the agency of language, otherness in Yau's poems

penetrates the Anglo English American language, challenging its normative standard and resisting its oppression.

Yau's shift from the speaking subject to the language itself as a site for articulating a subversive otherness in his "Genghis Chan" poems suggests an alternative mode of resistance and intervention to the lyric mode grounded in the agency of the I. However, Yau shows no intention to eliminate the I in his poetry. He continues to explore the subversive possibilities of the interrogatory, confessional private I and the subjective agency for articulating otherness in poems such as the series of Peter Lorre's monologues: "Peter Lorre Improvises Mr. Moto's Monologue" and "Peter Lorre Dreams He Is the Third Reincarnation of a Geisha," collected in *Forbidden Entries*, and "Peter Lorre Reminisces about Being a Sidekick," "Peter Lorre Records His Favorite Walt Whitman Poem for Posterity," and "Peter Lorre Speaks to the Spirit of Edgar Allan Poe during a Séance," collected in *Borrowed Love Poems*. Just as he continues to push the limits of language in his Language poems, Yau further expands the range of lyric voices of a multiple I in poems such as "Self-Portrait with Max Beckmann," "I Was a Poet in the House of Frankenstein," and "Borrowed Love Poems" collected in his 2002 volume, *Borrowed Love Poems*. In both his Language and lyric poems, Yau has found a way of using language to get beyond the poet-I without ignoring his ethnic background, a language to hear the other and to let the other be heard. As Levinas contends: "Language is not enacted within a consciousness; it comes to me from the Other and reverberates in consciousness by putting it in question. This event is irreducible to consciousness, where everything comes about from within" (*TI* 204). Yau's insistence on using language as such in his poetry enables him to develop a poetics of resistance that enacts a politicized aesthetics as an ethical relationship with the other which transforms the authoritative, self-indulgent lyric I. "I own no I," says the speaker in "830 Fireplace Road (2)." "The image of the I has a life of its own, / its own making, making the image of I" (*Poems* 14). In dismantling the Cartesian I, however, the I in Yau's poems is indispensable: it is "The I of changes, the destroying I" that remakes "the its of the I."

# CHAPTER SEVEN

*Myung Mi Kim*

SPEAK AND IT IS SOUND IN TIME

In her fourth volume of poetry, *Commons* (2002), Myung Mi Kim raises a number of questions which underline the challenges and politics of a language-centered poetics that she has developed since her first volume, *Under Flag* (1991). "What *is* English now, in the face of mass global migrations, ecological degradations, shifts and upheavals in identifications of gender and labor? How can the diction(s), register(s), inflections(s) as well as varying affective stances that have and will continue to filter into 'English' be taken into account? What are the implications of writing at this moment, in precisely this 'America'? How to practice and make plural the written and spoken — grammars, syntaxes, textures, intonations" ("Pollen Fossil Record" *Commons* 110). While engaging with these questions in her poems, Kim investigates otherness in gendered and raced power relations, and in the encounters between nations, cultures, and languages. Writing about Korean Americans' experience of exile and diaspora resulting from imperialist conquest, transnational accumulation of capital, and migration of labor, Kim, like John Yau, is particularly interested in the ways in which English is "contaminated" by immigrants. Her rendering of English with "foreign" accents dislodges binary constructs of national and ethnic identities which assume essence, fixity, and hierarchy. Interweaving her investigation of language with an exploration of collective memory and history, Kim examines what she refers to as "the questions of translation between cultures and languages and in particular the kinds of resemblances and contaminations that inform how language(s) systematize and engender notions of power" (J. K. Lee 94).

Although Kim's poetics is radically different from that of the other Asian American poets discussed so far, her poems, like theirs, confront the political, cultural, and ethical questions of otherness. As a Korean American whose first-language ability remains at the third-grade level,[1] and as a writer who has "arrived at an uncanny familiarity with another language (and having Korean as a tenuous *and* fierce spectral language)" (J. K. Lee 102), Kim is particularly interested in immigrants' and colonized people's relationships with the dominant languages and their mother tongues. Her investigation of these relationships undermines the naturalization of language and its seemingly natural bond to identities of nation, race, and ethnic culture. As the fragmentary utterances in the title poem of her first volume *Under Flag* indicate: "What sound do we make, 'n', 'h', 'g' / Speak and it is sound in time"(13) — the English letters *n, h*, and *g* are romanized phonemes and are pronounced differently in Korean and other languages. Being a poet who is "attentive to acts of living between and among borders, interstices," Kim insists on "practicing questions of national narratives, transcultural narratives, narratives of cultural and political diasporas," or rather "*hybridizations* of human community" in her poems (J. K. Lee 102–103). For Kim, hybridization of national identity, language, and culture are inevitably related to power relations in the production of meaning and knowledge. Her poems produce "[s]ocial and psychic identifications that disrupt and (re)envision," and "throw into question conventions of codifying" ("Pollen Fossil Record" *Commons* 108). In developing a language-centered poetics of otherness, Kim seeks to "[c]ounter the potential totalizing power of language that serves the prevailing systems and demands of coherence" (*Commons* 110). Through a poetics as such, Kim enacts her sense of the poet's ethical responsibility.

A Levinasian ethics is embedded in Kim's radical experimentation with language and the poetic form, which executes her conviction of writing "as response and attention" (J. K. Lee 102). Kim's preoccupation with the way language is used to repress or release otherness demonstrates her conviction about the responsibility of the poet for the other. She regards "[p]oets as 'agents for the most arduous, most dangerous cause there is: to love the other, even before being loved'"[2] ("Pollen Fossil Record" *Commons* 109). The ethics of this love for the other is implicated in Kim's poetic renderings of the voices of the other(s), and in her attention to otherness repressed by patriarchal, colonial, and hegemonic discourses. For Kim, reinventing lyric poetry entails "prob[ing] the terms under which we denote, participate in, and speak of cultural and human practices." She suggests that making poetry as a form of critical inquiry, a political action, and as formal innovation that participates in and generates changes in cultural practices can "mobilize the notion of our responsibility to one another in social space" ("Pollen Fossil Record" *Commons* 111). While Kim shares with the other poets discussed so far many similarities in her conviction in the social responsibility of poetic innovations and in her exploration of otherness in her poetry, she differs significantly from them in resolutely situating her work in a transnational historical continuum of encounters between nations, cultures, and populations in the contexts of colonialism, imperialism, and capitalism.

## Countering the Potential Totalizing Power of Language

In her poems about Korean Americans' experience of diaspora and displacement collected in *Under Flag*, Kim explores the diasporic subjects' relationship to language, history, and U.S. citizenship. She employs what might be called a language of diaspora, whose other-sounding music transforms the prosodic structure of traditional English lyric, making the English language "shift," putting it "to flight," to borrow Gilles Deleuze and Claire Parnet's terms and concept (*Dialogues* 58). In their discussion of marginalized and subjugated peoples' relationship to the English language, Deleuze and Parnet maintain that it is precisely by being "a hegemonic, imperialistic language" that English "is all the more vulnerable to the subterranean workings of languages and dialects which undermine it from all sides and impose on it a play of vast corruptions and variations." This subversive and creative shift in a hegemonic language, they contend, also characterizes official American English: "The American language bases its despotic official pretensions, its majoritarian claim to hegemony, only on its extraordinary capacity for being twisted and shattered and for secretly putting itself in the service of minorities who work it from inside, . . . nibbling away at that hegemony as it extends itself" (*Dialogues* 58). To corrupt the hegemonic language from within is precisely Kim's strategy.

In fact, Kim materializes immigrants' experience of disjunctive time in terms of memory, desire, and sensibility registered in language. In the opening poem of *Under Flag*, "And Sing We," Kim uses displaced English words to enact Korean immigrants' fragmentary memories of home, including the "Um-pah, um-pah sensibility of the first grade teacher" and the sound from "feet firm on the pump organ's pedals," evoking the pumping of water into rice fields (14). At the same time, she explores the possibilities of what Deleuze and Félix Guattari call "the deterritorialization of language," opposing "a purely intensive usage of language to all symbolic or even significant or simply signifying usage of it" (*Kafka* 18, 19). By making "a purely intensive usage" of English, which resists unified symbolic meanings, Kim is able to oppose the "oppressive quality" of an official national language and to arrive at the kind of "perfect and unformed expression, a material intense expression" which Deleuze and Guattari refer to when speaking of the deterritorialization of Yiddish and German in Kafka's writings (*Kafka* 27, 25, 19). Kim's use of language as such breaks away from what Levinas calls "internal discourse" which absorbs alterity into "the unity of presence by the *I* of the intentional *I think*," to quote his words again (*EN* 162). The fragmentary utterances in Kim's poem articulate the immigrants' memories of home and sense of dislocation in a land where they can no longer trace their ancestry.

As she invents a new prosody in English to render the experience of diaspora visceral through verbal sound not identifiable with any single system of language, Kim allows immigrants to confront their feelings of exile and the process of their becoming. She employs what Deleuze and Guattari might call "deterritorialized sounds" (*Kafka* 26) to destabilize national and cultural identities:

Once we leave a place is it there

Prattle (heard, found, made) in kitchen

No longer clinking against the sides of the pot set to boil

Prattle displaced. Guard birds

That should have been near, all along

Prattle done trattle gone just how far

Do voices carry

What we might have explored, already discovered

Falling down falling down

Callback fallback whip whippoorwill

Not the one song to rivet us trundle rondo

Not a singular song trundle rondo

What once came to us whole

In this we are again about to do

In the times it takes to     dead dead dead la la la

Trundle rondo     for a long time it stood marker and marked

Mostly, we cross bridges we did not see being built (*Flag* 14–15)

With what used to be familiar noises of prattle in the kitchen displaced, "we" find the songs we hear no longer identifiable with a common nation, ancestry, or language, as we realize we are not the pioneers in the land where we live now. The singing of London Bridge (or perhaps some other structure) "falling down falling down" is interrupted by a different song with a disparate rhythm and cadence: "Callback fallback whip whippoorwill." Both are intersected by yet another song of a different music, "trundle rondo." This singular music, "trundle rondo," has become part of a heterogeneous assemblage of songs, in which each maintains its distinctiveness. These songs are markers of time, diaspora, and duration of memories, not traceable to a single source of nation or ethnicity. In her sensitive reading of this poem, Laura Hyun Yi Kang observes that while articulating the exile's longing of the homeland, Kim suggests "There is no innocent and permanent repatriation, only a repetition of fraught and yet temporary returns and expulsions that are mediated by language. . . . Any resettlement involves a transsubstantiation of both language and community" (235–36).

On a similar note, Joseph Jonghyun Jeon explores further immigrants' experience of dislocation, displacement, and assimilation by focusing on a close reading of the poem (130). Jeon offers a compelling examination of the ways in which Kim's use of language reduces "speech to the status of mere sound," and "orchestrat[es] the sound of words in order to call attention to" how "these sounds form a level of coherence distinct from the poem's semantic content." This deployment of language, Jeon contends, demonstrates a "primary concern of much of Kim's earlier poetry" about "how a non-native speaker of English might come to make the language her own so that she may be able to express the subtleties she wishes to convey" (133).

While I concur with both Kang's and Jeon's readings, I would add that the transubstantiation of language and community, and the process of learning and eventual mastery of English entail a mutual transformation of the languages and identities of both the Korean immigrant communities and the United States. As immigrants' cultural identities lose their traceable origins in a land where they can claim no "natural" bond through lineage, their otherness contaminates the dominant language and disturbs the cultural homogeneity of the U.S. nation-space. Refusing to be defined as the opposite of the norm by Orientalist discourse, or reduced to the Same by assimilationist ideology, the alterity of diasporic subjects in Kim's poems at once resists and intervenes in the dominant culture even as immigrants themselves are being transformed in the process of becoming.

Kim's poems also break away from linear, chronological time in expressing immigrants' experience of dislocation and becoming with regard to collective and individual identities. In her collage composition, time as duration of articulation and memory is intersected by national history and the history of colonialism and imperialism. Kim interweaves markings of time as geographical and cultural displacements through polyphonic articulation that resists any "regularizing, maintainable 'pattern'," to borrow Kim's own words ("Anacrusis" par. 2). Like the other-sounding English, the multidimensional time and disjunctive simultaneity in Kim's poetry open up the textual space not simply to the social, historical, and political, but also to the unutterable, the silenced, and the erased. In "Food, Shelter, Clothing," the speaking voices follow the trajectory of refugees' and immigrants' diaspora, while shifting from one historical moment to another. Using blank spaces on the page and fragmentary utterances, Kim creates a sense of disruption, isolation, and exile, which is intertwined with Korean history, including the Korean War, the Japanese invasion, and Korean resistance. This method enables Kim to bring into her poem a remarkable range of geographical locations and historical moments as well. Take, for example, the arrangement of these lines on one page, and their juxtaposition with the lines on the opposite page:

They had oared to cross the ocean

And where had they come to

These bearers of a homeland (*Flag* 22)

Leaving the rest of the page blank to suggest disruption of narrative and a shift in time and geographical location, Kim uses incomplete sentences on the opposite page to evoke two historical events—the landing of the amphibious tanks of U.S. military in South Korea on September 15, 1950, at the "same spot" where Japanese invading armies landed before. The arrival of the U.S. amphibious tanks marks a turning point of the Korean War and an unequal relationship between U.S. and South Korea; the landing of the Japanese invading armies in Korea led to the brutal colonization of Korea by Japan from 1910 to 1945. Although the U.S. military presence in Korea was motivated by purposes different from those of the Japanese military campaigns, it also brought massive destruction and countless deaths to Korea:

Those landing amphibious (under cover of night)

In a gangplank thud and amplification take

Spot of ground. Fended it might remain

Republic and anthem, spot and same spot

How little space they take up given the land's reach

All those whose feet had resounded

Smear fear tyranny of attack

Already the villages already the cities receding (*Flag* 23)

Resisting syntactic enclosure in her use of language that breaks open the poetic form produced and maintained by conventional prosodic structure or syntax, or by sequential development of argument, Kim is able to incorporate into the poem through a few fragmentary lines the aftermaths of both the Japanese invasion and the Korean war, as well as Koreans' struggle for freedom and democracy:

A face hauled away and a small flag of the country nearby

They were stripped

They were made to roll in one direction then the other

If they didn't do it right, they were kicked

An ambulance on which the words "blood bank car"

Had been written in blood (*Flag* 24)

Shifting from the geographical locations of Korean history in Korea to indeterminate time-spaces of Korean immigrants' experience of diaspora, Kim's use of language becomes further "deterritorialized," breaking further away from metaphoric or symbolic signification. Her lines become more fragmented as the utterances resist centrality of the self and the privilege of the lyric I/eye:

"In my country" preface to the immigrant's fallow

Field my country ash in water follow

Descent   slur   vowel

Stricken buoys

Span no tongue and mouth

Scripting, hand flat against the mouth (*Flag* 26)

With these departures in her use of language and form, Kim is able to investigate "what it means to find a connection between poetry and the world," as she says in an interview with Yedda Morrison (Y. Morrison 77). Finding this connection, for Kim, is not so much a matter of what to tell, but how to tell in her poetry. "Part of the meaning of being a historical subject," Kim says, "is to engage in *how* to tell. . . . How to refigure and reinvent and reoccupy the manner of telling" (Y. Morrison 80).

The last two pages of this poem illustrate well the ways in which Kim refigures, reinvents, and reoccupies the manner of telling Korean diaspora through radically fragmented utterances.

Up against bounty and figured human

      allaying surge

                neighboring

Geographical trodden shelter

Locate deciphering

        by force

As contour

Hurls

    ga ga ga ga (*Flag* 27)

Will be plain foil credo

Figures pervious arboretum

        ave      mella      ferro (*Flag* 28)

These scattered words and phrases, and the visual and aural effects they create translate the seemingly untranslatable experiences of violence and destruction, separation and loss, endurance and hope. Dislocated from its geographical origin and cultural, linguistic environment, the repetition of the first single and double consonant of Korean language *Hangul ga* becomes as incomprehensible as the displaced Latin words "ave    mella    ferro."

Kim's use of language in such a way so as to accentuate the sound patterns of words is similar to what Deleuze and Guattari call "pull[ing] from the language tonalities lacking in signification," thus "open[ing] the word onto unexpected internal intensities" (*Kafka* 22). Paradoxically, these internal intensities of the word in Kim's poem are brought out by her engagement with historical events of war, colonization, and diaspora, which are external, though not unconnected, to language and poetry. It is precisely through her engagement with the world and historical moments by pushing the limits or extremities of language that Kim finds new creative possibilities for articulating what seems impossible to articulate.

Speaking of the writings by Paul Celan and Theresa Hak Kyung Cha, Kim notes that the space where the "collaboration between the impossibility of utterance and finding the means by which to utter" is in "constant motion, and constant reshaping of itself" (Y. Morrison 81–82). She adds, "any poem is always on the cusp of coming into legibility — formally, psychically, politically. For me those works that keep re-invigorating that space of silence and erasure, the space of the seemingly untranslatable, are the ones in which you connect to a source of endurance and power" (Y. Morrison 82). The empty spaces left on the page, and the spaces among words, sentences, and images in this and other poems by Kim, are spaces which articulate silence and erasure resulting from massacre — "An ambulance on which the words 'blood bank car' / Had been written in blood"—and from oppression by patriarchy and colonization—"She could not talk without first looking at others' mouths (which language?) / (pushed into) crevice a bluegill might lodge in" (*Flag* 24, 21). These spaces also mark the seemingly untranslatable process in which this poem, "Food, Shelter, Clothing," is coming into legibility, moving from one fragmented image to another, from interrupted utterances to silence, from silence to utterances, as fragmentary evocations of home and national history give way to experiences of exile and diaspora. By reinvigorating those spaces, Kim connects to "a source of endurance and power" such as that found in the writings of Celan, Cha, Kafka, and Beckett, as well as in the collective memories of Koreans' resistance to Japanese invasion and colonization: "These men these women are throwing stones / These men these women chant and chant" (*Flag* 25).

In her other poems collected in *Under Flag*, such as "Body As One As History," "Demarcation," "These Fishing," and "From the Sea On to the Land," intonations and cadences of deterritorialized words, and fragments and deformations of sentences engage with historical moments of violence, destruction, and mass migration. Lyric utterances in these poems are intertwined with experiences of diaspora and moments in Korean history. Kim's disjunctive poetics denaturalizes national and ethnic identities, particularly Asian Americans' essentialized bodily and cultural differences which were used to justify their exclusion from U.S. citizenship and the nation-space. In another poem, "Into Such Assembly," for example, Kim employs collage juxtaposition to expose the contradictions in the process of being naturalized as U.S. citizens, and to articulate an alternative concept of belonging, which does not seek to erase difference or reduce otherness. While relating the acquisition and usage of English to state power in the process of disciplining and assimilating the "aliens," the first part of the poem simultaneously enacts and undermines the official procedure of naturalization:

Can you read and write English? Yes_____. No_____.
Write down the following sentences in English as I dictate them.
      There is a dog in the road.
      It is raining.
Do you renounce allegiance to any other country but this?
  (*Flag* 29)

In juxtaposition to this process of naturalization for U.S. citizenship, Kim introduces a passage of apparently Korean immigrants' nostalgic memories of home, including a line of Korean song in Korean:

> Cable car rides over swan flecked ponds
> Red lacquer chests in our slateblue house
> Chrysanthemums trailing bloom after bloom
> Ivory, russet, pale yellow petals crushed
> Between fingers, that green smell, if jade would smell
>
> . . . . . . . . . . . . . . . . .
>
> The other, the pine wet green side of the mountain
> Hides a lush clearing where we picnic and sing:
> Sunn-Bul-Sah, geep eun bahm ae (Flag 29)

However, the images of this home seem to be a nostalgic and typical Orientalist depiction of the East frozen in time and space. The line from a Korean song —Sunn-Bul-Sah, geep eun bahm ae ("Deep into the night at the Temple of Becoming the Buddha"[3])—highlights the nostalgic and popular Orientalist depiction of Korea isolated from history. In contrast to this Orientalist construct of Korea, Kim's references to Korea's colonization by Japan and to U.S. military and political interventions in Korea, as well as Koreans' protests against Japanese colonialism and American imperialism in the preceding poems, particularly the title poem, "Under Flag," indicate the impossibility for Korean immigrants to claim a stable, singular identity of nation or culture. Kim spotlights the ambivalence of Korean immigrants' national and cultural identities in the provocative ending lines of the first part of this poem:

> Neither, neither
>
>
> Who is mother tongue, who is father country? (Flag 29)

The double negative and the questions refuse binarized choice of either this or that category of national or cultural identification.

In the second part of this poem, Kim suggests that a binary, hierarchical scheme of an identity construct of the American self and the Oriental other is formulated and maintained in terms of geographical locations. Using collage to juxtapose different voices,

Kim at once reveals and subverts such reductive binary identity constructions:

> Do they have trees in Korea? Do the children eat out of
>   garbage cans?
>
> We had a dalmation
> We rode the train on weekends from Seoul to So-Sah where we
>   grew grapes
>
> We ate on the patio surrounded by dahlias
>
> Over there, ass is cheap — those girls live to make you happy
>
> Over there, we had a slateblue house with a flat roof where
> I made many snowmen, over there (*Flag* 30)

The emphasis on geographical locations for defining ethnic and national identities in these lines evokes the question raised in the opening poem of *Under Flag*, "And Sing We": "Once we leave a place is it there" (14). The juxtaposed questions and statements suggest a mode of identity construction out of historical contexts, but contained in an ethnically designated space fixed by geographical boundaries. Kim challenges spatially bounded and dichotomized identities by introducing in the same part of this poem a passage of instructions for how to pronounce certain English words: "No, 'th', 'th', put your tongue against the roof of your mouth, . . . that's better" (*Flag* 30). This passage reveals a power relation and identity formation in the immigrants' relationship to the English language, indicating a process of Korean immigrants' identity transformation through learning English, a process which destabilizes spatially defined identities of nation or culture.

Further exploring Korean immigrants' experience of exile, dislocation, and becoming other than what they used to be or are supposed to be, Kim raises questions about immigrants' relationships to their mother tongue and the official English. As the speaker asks in the closing lines of Part 2 of "Into Such Assembly":

> And with distance traveled, as part of it
>
> How often when it rains here does it rain there?
>
> One gives over to a language and then
>
> What was given, given over? (*Flag* 30)

These questions are central to Kim's exploration of the relations be-
tween diaspora and national, cultural identities. Rather than offering
any direct answers to the questions, Kim moves beyond Korean im-
migrants' experiences to suggest an alternative view of who "we" are
as historical subjects in Part Three of this poem.

Evoking the indiscriminate nature of the rain, Kim articulates an
inclusive vision of "our" identity that encompasses all of us across
ethnic, national, and geographical boundaries:

This rain eats into most anything

> And when we had been scattered over the face of earth
> We could not speak to one another

The creek rises, the rain-fed current rises

> Color given up, sap given up
> Weeds branches groves what they make as one

. . . . . . . . . . . . . . . . . . . . . . .

> What gives way losing gulch, mesa, peak, state, nation

Land, ocean dissolving
The continent and the peninsula, the peninsula and the
    continent
Of one piece sweeping

. . . . . . . . .

Each drop strewn into such assembly (*Flag* 31)

This "assembly" of us — all of us from all corners of the world — un-
dermines the insistence on a monolingual, uniform ethnic or na-
tional identity, and subverts the hierarchical binary constructs of
"us" over here and "them" over there, as alluded to in the first two
parts of the poem. In this assembly there is no hierarchy of race, cul-
ture, or nationality, no preordained binary social order, no estab-
lished center to which the new, the different must conform. Indeed,
this assembly consists of what Deleuze might call "differences within
multiplicities," which "replace schematic and crude oppositions"
(*Difference* 182). It is an assembly constituted by "an internal multi-
plicity" which is "non-localisable," thus having an "indetermination
[that] renders possible the manifestation of difference freed from all

subordination" (*Difference* 183). As the title "Into Such Assembly" suggests, Kim's poems of diaspora call into question naturalized singular, homogeneous, or hierarchical national and cultural identities.

Asserting an unassimilable otherness that suggests this internal multiplicity, Kim's poetry disrupts binary relations between majority and minority cultures. In so doing, her poetry carries out the task Palumbo-Liu proposes for minority discourse: "It is a specific task for minority discourse to ascertain the interpenetration of minor and dominant cultures, and to see that reconfiguration as a site of a politicized aesthetics" ("Universalisms" 202). Keenly aware of the agency of her poetics as a site of politicized aesthetics, Kim regards her writing of poems as a way of "circulat[ing] questions of national narratives, transcultural narratives, narratives of cultural and political diaspora, and concepts or perhaps more accurately, hybridizations, of human community" (Y. Morrison 84). Speaking as the other in the U.S. nation-space, bringing into English and American poetry an irreducible difference, Kim, like the other Asian American poets discussed so far, is transforming the once Eurocentric American poetry, while inscribing histories of other times and places across national borders. The hybrid prosody of Kim's poetry is the sound of history. As those lines from the opening poem of *Under Flag* state: "What sound do we make, 'n', 'h', 'g' / Speak and it is sound in time" (13). The "sound in time" in Kim's poetry is duration of memory, of history, and of the process of becoming, materialized in contaminated English.

---

### Sound in Time: Infidel Translation

In her second volume, *The Bounty*, Kim continues to interrogate the agency of utterance in a language that reflects the historical process of transcultural encounters, but with a focus on questions of translation. She investigates the "ideas of translation, translatability, transliteration, transcription" between Korean and English, including the sites where the authority of the romanization of Korean resides, and how translation of Korean might be entered into other than through a standard romanizing system (*Commons* 109, 110). While foregrounding the impossibility of "accurate" linguistic or cultural translation, Kim rehearses "listening," or rather "practicing sound and gesture between languages, between systems of writing" (*Commons* 110). Like Yau, she refuses to domesticate the otherness of a foreign language and culture, insisting on attending to the absolute alterity of the other embedded in the opacity, incompleteness, and heterogeneity of language and utterances. But she takes a different approach from Yau's in her exploration of the encounters between an Asian language and English even though she often relies on the irreducible sound of words for articulating an unassimilable otherness as Yau does. Pushing further her investigation into "the questions of translation between cultures and languages and in particular the kinds of resemblances and contaminations that inform how language(s) systematize and engender notions of power" (J. K. Lee 94), Kim seeks to develop a poetics that draws from "the recombinant energy created between languages (geopolitical economies, cultural representations, concepts of community)" (*Commons* 110). Kim's poetics draws from this recombinant energy, including phonemes, syllables, verbal sound patterns, not simply the sense-making, of languages.

Kim's attention to language in her enactment of transnational and transcultural encounters marks her departure from conventional translation that focuses on meaning. The assumption that meaning is transparent, stable, and containable in language underlies the naturalizing construction of the racialized other by the dominant culture which elides the mediation of power relations and historical contexts, as shown in the pidginized popular songs about Chinese immigrants discussed in the previous chapter. This assumption also informs the conventional practice of translations, travel writings, and ethnography. At issue are questions of the complicity of representation of the racial, sexual, and cultural other in maintaining domination of particular groups of peoples or nations over others. As Lydia Liu contends in her introduction to *Tokens of Exchange: The Problem of Translation in Global Circulations*, "we can no longer talk about translation as if it were purely linguistic or literary matters; nor can we continue to acquiesce to the material consequence of what anthropologists have termed 'cultural translation,' practiced for centuries by missionaries, ethnographers, travelers, and popular journalists in the West and subsequently adopted by scholars from other parts of the world" (1).

Although arising from colonial discourses, these problems of translation seem to be rooted in the metaphysical tradition of Western philosophy. In her study of translation in the colonial context, Tejaswini Niranjana points out that the idea of the unproblematic translatability of meaning, grounded in the assumption that "signified and signifier can be separated, informs the classical conception of philosophy as well as translation." She further notes that "Derrida has long contended that translatability as transfer of meaning is the very *thesis* of philosophy. The notion of the transcendental signified for him is a founding concept of Western metaphysics that '[takes] shape within the horizon of an absolutely pure, transparent, and unequivocal translatability'."[4] These assumptions underlying translation, Niranjana adds, also characterize Orientalist discourses. "The concept of translation that grounds Western metaphysics is the same one that presides over the beginnings of the discourse of Orientalism. Neither is prepared to acknowledge, in its humanism and universalism, the heterogeneity that contaminates 'pure meaning' from the start, occluding also the project of translation" (55).

Given these intricate relations among language, philosophy, and ethics, Levinas's emphasis on the importance of the expressive aspect of language, and his critique of the primacy of reason for the Cartesian self and intentionality, can provide a theoretical perspective for understanding alternative translation strategies, which Kim employs. Speaking of the necessary correlation between absolute alterity of the other and illegibility, Levinas writes, "The face [of the other] is present in its refusal to be contained. In this sense it cannot be comprehended, that is, encompassed" (Levinas *TI* 194). Resistance to containment, then, is refusal to be comprehended as the object of knowledge, or to be absorbed into the same by the dominant. This logic underlies Kim's poetics of fragmentation, and aesthetics of opacity, which signify the irreducible alterity of otherness and inscribe the insufficiency of logic, thought, and representation. Levinas suggests that resistance to objectification by representation, or refusal to be assimilated by totalizing systems of thought, comes from language as saying, as expression and articulation of the other. "Speech proceeds from absolute difference," argues Levinas (*TI* 194). "The presence of the Other, . . . is not contemplated as an intelligible essence, but is heard as language," to quote Levinas again (*TI* 297). Rather than simply a system of signs for inscribing meaning, transmitting information, or representing reality, language for Levinas can break homogeneous oneness and resists totality. "Absolute difference, inconceivable in terms of formal logic, is established only by language. Language accomplishes a relation between terms that breaks up the unity of a genus. . . . Language is perhaps to be defined as the very power to break the continuity of being or of history" (*TI* 195). In Kim's poetry, language enacts precisely resistance and rupture as such.

In addition, Kim attempts something further in her use of language to explore "how the polyglot, porous, transcultural presence alerts and alters what is around it" (*Commons* 110). The irreducible alterity of the other, for Kim as for other Asian American poets, also has the agency of intervention in bringing change in the hegemonic language and dominant culture. Her exploration of various aspects of language in the encounters between different peoples and cultures offers an alternative mode of cultural translation that emphasizes a mutually transformative process of major and minor languages, while transcribing a marginalized "foreign" language, culture, and history in her poems.

In the opening poem of *The Bounty*, "Primer," Kim enacts the encounters between Korean and English. While situating these encounters in the contexts of colonialism and imperialism, she probes into the process of translation between languages, transcribing what occurs in the traversal. Kim introduces the orthophonic Korean alphabet known as *Hangul*, developed in 1443, as the epigram of the poem:[5]

1443

—to represent 14 single and 5 double consonants, Hangul starts
with five basic symbols, which are shaped to suggest the
articulators pronouncing them. For example, a small square
depicts a closed mouth pronouncing /m/.

This is the study book. (*Bounty* 11)

Corresponding to the title and the epigram, the sections of "Primer" are organized according to the order of the fourteen consonants in *Hangul* transcribed in roman letters, with the exception of the opening section, which consists of fragmentary phrases:

templates scored

        seven tributaries splay infection

finally not even the wrenching apart

        onion applied as poultice

crossing rivers' arms

rivers in veins

inverted bowls steeped plates

slothful plain to harden with rust
(*Bounty* 13)

While phrases such as "seven tributaries splay infection" and "onion applied as poultice" evoke elements of Korean history and culture, these fragmented lines at once interrogate and perform the possibilities for sense-making which resists syntactic closure and grammatical rules. Compelling the reader to utter, these phrases, though semantically and logically independent of one another, are connected by consonants through which the lines move by repetition with variation, and by resonance and contrast. For instance, the second line picks up the "s" sound and repeats the "p" sound in the first line, while introducing a new consonant, *f*, which is repeated in the third line. The fourth line echoes and foregrounds the *n*, *p*, and *s* consonants, while relaying the "s" sound to the end of the line, thus setting up the ending consonant pattern for the remaining lines. Similarly, the rest of the lines in this section move through repetition with variation of existing consonants, and through introduction of new consonants to be reiterated. This pattern of relations among the consonants emulates that of the consonants in *Hangul* — a pattern which recurs with new elements in the rest of "Primer."

The second section of "Primer" transcribes the first single and double consonant of *Hangul* through the roman letter *g*. By insisting on using the order of *Hangul* consonants in transcribing the sounds in English, Kim explores the possibilities of a poetic language that is "beyond what is systematically Korean and English — a language called into service to hold the space created out of the conversation between the two locations — a language that necessarily sets in motion questions around resemblance, contamination, boundary," as she says of her attention to and interrogation of language (J. K. Lee 94–95). In this "g" section, the method for transcribing consonants is neither completely English or Korean, but resembles both. The broken lines and spaces between phrases or linguistic units seem to visually reflect the relation between the two languages and their unfixed locations or boundaries:

[g]

dwell a longer somnolent

*g* is for girl  *g* is for glove  distinguish decipher

*g* is for golden  first grind

sickness alter hunger  glower scour remnant

gumbling ransom  bran poison

must custom  ear left

roam willow stick  pen hearing (*Bounty* 15)

As the transcribing continues, the Korean consonant and its romanization, *g*, disappears. But the alliterative sound pattern of the passage remains. Despite its radical departure from the conventional English lyric mode, this passage of fragmentary phrases and word groups is held together by a prosody that emulates the music of Korean, thus making English behave like Korean, "an English shaped by a Korean" (J. K. Lee 94). As the ending phrase, "pen hearing," suggests, the disappearance of the "g" sound gives prominence to the "m" sound and eventually to the sound of "n"—the consonant next to *g* in *Hangul*, and the organizing, or rather the generative, consonant of the next section of "Primer."

In addition to challenging the hegemony of English by setting in motion the contamination of English by Korean, Kim extends what she calls "practicing and gesture between languages, between systems of writing" (*Commons* 110) to the making of history. Beginning with section "[d]", for instance, Kim interweaves into her rehearsal of "resemblance, contamination, boundary" between languages, fragments of Korean national history, including the history of colonialism, imperialism, and patriarchy, which shape documentation of official history, construction of identity, and production of knowledge. Thus Kim's exploration of language entails the interrogation of documented history and the evocation of undocumented histories of exploitation, oppression, violence, and resistance. Take, for example, these lines:

in that reading

between diligence and document . . . they will be found

to be unobjectionable and of good service, easy to

control from their long habit of obedience . . .

carrier      printed      through what has been written (*Bounty* 17)

The intricate relations between the exploitation and subjugation of a particular group of people filter through the rehearsal of the consonant *d*, the preceding consonant *n*, and the subsequent consonants *r/l* in the *Hangul* alphabet. The lines are thus generated, not simply by sound associations, but also by evocation of history and by an unrelenting inquiry of power relations embedded in the circulation of knowledge through written language. So too are the words, materials, and succession of each section.

Following the *Hangul* alphabetic order of consonants, and responding to issues of exploitation and subjugation raised in section "[d]," lines in section "[r] [l]" reiterate a specific mode of exploiting and exporting Korean labor:

group of twelve group of six and another six

the boats Manchuria, Doric, Siberia

indigenous weed

so there were seventy five of us working fourteen hours a day

water and rice water and rice

parcel partial      study 1, study 2, study 3 (*Bounty* 18)

This study of language, then, is also a study in the making of history, or rather what Kim calls "markings of time — not to report, or narrate, or categorize — rather, what is the poem's potential for registering a correspondence between speed of perception and word, for allowing a complex nexus of variables, temperings, and modulations to take place at the instant of writing" ("Anacrusis" par. 7). By breaking away from chronological time in reportage or narrative, and by resisting categorical selection, Kim employs collage juxtaposition capable of a complex nexus of variables which enacts echoes, correspondences, disruptions, and contestations among the heterogeneous materials — images, voices, utterances, verbal sounds, and historical references.

In fact, Kim's use of the *Hangul* alphabet in "Primer" works as a complex nexus of variables between, as well as within, the sections. While echoing the references to subjugation, exploitation, and labor in the rice fields ("water and rice water and rice") in section "[r] [l]," section "[b]" ushers in another location and time, and further expands on the variations of the markings of time, particularly the collective history of Korea:

[b]

Let us look at the barn let us imagine the night life across beams

Refractory desire scurry rats

Suggestion of fur, suggestion of black

Plow baler disc tiller        grain planted among refuse

Come to the crossing and the river

The place of the rocks washed smooth

A hundred killed and pushed in

Grass on the banks grown back

Water that is the hundred dead (*Bounty* 20)

The desolate images of the countryside and their suggestion of the aftermath of colonization or war supplement the references to Japan's imperialism and colonization of Korea in the preceding sections. Using space to indicate distance and the passage of time, Kim shifts the last part of this section to a different location and time to evoke the massacre of Koreans. The consonant *b* of the *Hangul* alphabet is transcribed through words which participate in articulating collective memory, and inscribing Korean history, including what might become forgotten history. The contrast of the numerous *d* consonants in the lines above and below the one that translates the *b* consonant of *Hangul* highlights the implied warning against the amnesia of history: "A hundred killed and pushed in / Grass on the banks grown back / Water that is the hundred dead." Thus Kim's language-centered lyric is capable of keeping history alive, particularly the history of the colonized, the silenced, or displaced.

At once rehearsing and moving away from a purely phonetic and semantically or syntactically based method for translating single and double consonants of *Hangul* — "*g* is for girl   *g* is for glove   distinguish decipher" — Kim further develops her poetics of fragmentation which resists syntactic enclosure, breaks down categorical order, and disrupts chronological time or linear narrative. The subsequent freedom enables Kim to establish a complex nexus of variables within a much wider range than what is possible in conventional poetic forms. While the fourteen sections of "Primer" proceed according to the alphabetic order of the fourteen *Hangul* consonants, each section operates within a network of resonances and disruptions, correspondences and contrasts among the visual, aural, semantic, narrative, lyrical, and historical elements of all the sections of the poem.

With this method of complex recurrences and variables, section "[s]" probes further into Korean national history. Proceeding through fragment and increment, Kim integrates the consonant *s* into allusions to Japanese imperialism and the colonization of Korea. At the same time, she creates a new prosody different from that in the other sections by juxtaposing single lines on the left with multiple lines on the right:

[s]


Up tore the heavy rooted corn

                                        When brute force
                                        And spirit of plunder
Roamer in the filtering *w*


From the first months of one year

                                        of breaking many solemn
                                        treaties since 1636

Each floor is to be levelled          nor to single out
                                        the teachers in the schools

who treat our people
and civilization as

Begun and prolong

a nation of savages

The crooked ships

Three Items of Agreement

The Four Thousand Two
Hundred
and Fifty Second Year of the
Kingdom of Korea, Third
Month (*Bounty* 21)

Rather than using individual voices, Kim relies on semantic evocations and memories of collective history to set up a sort of correspondence between the lines on the right and left. Responding to and resonating with the brute force used to tear up the "heavy rooted corn" in the opening line, the lines on the right extend the application of brute force to colonial plunder, thus evoking the history of the Japanese colonization of Korea. The second line on the left interpolates by noting the "*w*" sound absent in *Hangul*, while foregrounding the word "when" in the preceding line on the right and its implication of time, to which the third line on the left—"From the first months of one year"—responds by alluding to a historical time when Japan violated "many solemn treaties" made with Korea "since 1636," referred to in the following lines on the right.

By the same method, these lines allude to how the Japanese invasion in and colonization of Korea were justified by categorizing the Koreans as an inferior other. Responding to the references to Korean history, the closing lines on the right, "The Four Thousand Two Hundred / and Fifty Second Year of the / Kingdom of Korea, Third Month," have multiple resonances. They counter Japanese colonialists "who treat our people / and civilization as / a nation of savages" by evoking the long history of Korean civilization through the Korean lunar calendar, which begins in 2333 BCE, the year that marks the founding of the Kingdom of Korea by King Dangun. The year 4252 CE of the "Kingdom of Korea, Third Month," then, is March 1919, the year and month that marks the beginning of the Korean mass movement for independence from Japan. A Korean national heroine, Guan Soon, at age sixteen, traveled "on foot to 40 towns, organizing the nation's mass demonstration to be held on March 1, 1919" (Cha *Dictée* 30). Kim's use of the traditional Korean calendar and Korean way of telling time also articulates an alterity that cannot be assimilated by a universal time or a hegemonic language like English. At the same time, her evocations of Korean history introduce an otherness that intervenes in Eurocentric and American-centric productions of historical knowledge.

By situating language in transcultural narratives and between national borders, Kim's poetics of fragmentation enables her to achieve a greater capacity for her lyric to engage with ethical, social, historical, and political issues. Although resolutely unique in her experimental poetics, Kim's articulation of alterity, like that of other contemporary Asian American poets, addresses socially constructed otherness as well. With the freedom and capacity she achieves by resisting syntactic enclosure, interrupting narrative, and breaking down chronological time, Kim is able to deal with, in a single section of her poem, complex otherness in vastly different geopolitical situations separated by time and space. Continuing to track Korean history through a traversal between Korean and English consonants, in section "[j]" of "Primer" Kim arranges the lines so as to foreground the power relations embedded in language across national, cultural, and historical boundaries:

[j]

> Considering the ban
> Emperor letter of law
>
> Heads down on desktops
> Pretense of rest
>
> Transom transgression
>
> Never audible
>
> Commit to memory   *ga gya guh gyuh*

mostly translations of
the Scriptures into chinese                                    to learn
which educated Koreans   inculcate its shame   the English
could read                                                             of a midwest
                                                                              town

for many years Hangul
was used by the less               never having been native
privileged and by women

Call and cull

Send to the proofing house
(*Bounty* 23)

Through fragmentation, correspondence, and resonance, Kim brings
into juxtaposition power relations in three languages at three differ-
ent historical moments. Situated in the colonial context of the ban-
ning of Korean by Japan, the inaudible practice of enunciating the
Korean "g" and "j" syllables — "*ga gya guh gyuh*" — becomes a trans-
gression and political act. But in an earlier historical period, *Hangul*
was accepted and practiced as the language of the "inferior" people.
The correlation between hegemonic languages and dominant pow-
ers, suggested in the banning of Korean to Koreans during Japanese
colonial rule, is reiterated in a different context by the lines on the
left, which refer to the hierarchical relation between Chinese and
*Hangul*. Before the invention of *Hangul*, the Korean language was
written in Chinese, which was the language of the privileged and
the ruling class. The mastery of Chinese characters and classical
learning used to be the basic requirements for Korean state officials.[6]
As the official term of *Hangul* — "The Orthophonic Alphabet for
the Instruction of the People" — indicates, King Sejong's creation and
promulgation of *Hangul* were in part intended to address widespread
illiteracy among Koreans (Kim-Cho 2, 17). While *Hangul*, a writing
system which can be learned easily, was intended to enable common
people "to seek justice through proper litigation," it also had the
function of educating and "enlightening" the majority of Koreans,
thus constituting them into law-abiding subjects for "stability in
a time of national unrest" (Kim-Cho 48). Ironically, Sejong and
his ruling class did not use *Hangul*, which the King himself had in-
vented. Kim employs juxtaposition to highlight the "inferior" status
of *Hangul* as a writing system for women and the less privileged,
while alluding to the hegemony of Chinese and colonial and patriar-
chal domination embedded in language. Just as the inaudible enunci-
ation of *Hangul* syllables was an act of resistance to Japanese colo-
nialism, Kim's inscription of "chinese" in contrast to "Hangul"

challenges Chinese hegemony and Korean patriarchy. Her rehearsal of *Hangul* consonants through English, moreover, undermines the purity and authenticity of Korean, just as her enactment of the romanization of Korean consonants suggests proximity, not accuracy.

In juxtaposition to the status of *Hangul* during the Japanese colonization of and Chinese domination over Korea, Kim evokes another form of power relation in language. The parallel lines on the right allude to the privileged status of standard American English, the kind spoken by Midwesterners like Tom Brokaw, the anchor of NBC's "Nightly News." The coercion for Korean immigrants "to learn / the English of a midwest town" evokes the coercion for Koreans to learn Chinese, and the imposition of Japanese on Koreans. It instills the feeling of "shame" about Korean/*Hangul* and what is identified with it. Kim tactfully positions the line "inculcate its shame" below and between the lines above and on the right and left, thus holding the three different historical moments and politics of language in a spatially separated, yet ideologically associated relation. Moreover, the effects of power in inculcating "its [Korean/*Hangul*'s] shame" are undermined in all three cases — by the enunciation of *Hangul* syllables and by the inscription of "Chinese" and "Midwest." Similarly, the rest of the lines in the middle respond and correspond to all three situations of power and language. The fragmentary line "never having been native" is applicable to the situation of a Korean with regard to Japanese, Chinese, and American English. So too are the remaining lines — "Call and cull / Sent to the proofing house" — which suggest authoritative policing of the standard official language.

Through such intricate deployment of lines in the textual space, Kim renders the present moment of identity formation through language uncannily similar to those of the distant past. As one line from the closing section "[h]" indicates, "that of succeeding purport call out to signal caution" (*Bounty* 30), Kim's references to Korean history in her investigation of language caution against the domination of English as a hegemonic language and against authoritative guardianship over its standard usage as a form of inculcating the "shame" of nonstandard English or minority (subjugated peoples') languages, whose inferior status is produced by power relations. Given these contexts and concerns, Kim's use of nonstandard English inflected by Korean and of a Korean unsanctioned by official standard, is a political act, and an ethical response to questions of "transcultural narratives" and "*hybridizations* of human communities," to quote her words again (J. K. Lee 103). Explaining the ending of the title poem, "The Bounty"—"synaptic / unruly enter" (99)—Kim says that these words are "a call to myself to write" (J. K. Lee 101). Writing for Kim entails "the question of how one might enter human discourse under the largest possible terms. . . . according to no rule—without rule—without crowns—without dictation—enter the Imaginary, enter language, enter the human" (J. K. Lee 103). This entrance, for Kim, must usher in "time action matter" ("Pollen Fossil Record" *Commons* 109) to ensure that her participation in interrogating and reinventing the operations of language, and her engagement with discourses, are enacted under "the largest possible terms" for the human. In her third volume, *Dura*, Kim explores further the possibilities for her participation under such terms as a poet who is "attentive to acts of living between and among borders, interstices" of nations and cultures (J. K. Lee 102–103).

### Historical Encounters with the Other

In her third volume, *Dura* (1998), Kim further develops her strategies of fragmentation to achieve much mobility and historical and geographical scale. As a result, she is able to investigate the consequences of encounters between nations and cultures in the contexts of transnational movements of capital and labor in her poetry. In fact, all seven poems in *Dura* could be read as parts of one serial poem and interpreted as Kim's response to the 1992 multiracial riots in Los Angeles following the acquittal of police officers in the beating of an African American, Rodney King. Korean American shopkeepers suffered the heaviest losses during the riots, which reflect the complexity and crisis of race relations in the United States. In response to this crisis, Kim explores "the entire complex of historical, economic, and political confluences that shape an event." She believes that in seeking to understand this crisis, her work "must lead into a negotiation with an entire historical/political continuum" (in J. K. Lee 101). The continuum Kim negotiates in her poems is set in motion in the process and consequences of the meeting between the East and the West in global capitalism, imperialism, and colonialism.

The opening poem of *Dura*, "Cosmography," indicates the transnational scale of the movement of capital, labor, and populations. Kim's poetics of fragmentation here enables the fragmented lines to usher in "time matter action" on the largest possible scale with unlikely heterogeneity. The colons at the top of the poem stress enunciation, while compelling the reader to listen:

:      :

Who even came this way, bellow or saw

Thirty and five books

Paper            script            document

Vowels unwritten

Kinglists        proverbs        praise phrases

They say it is the ocean

Indistinguishable water horizon net of worth

False vocalization of the consonantal text

Rose thorn and reported ocean

The beginnings of things (*Dura* 9)

These "beginnings of things" evoke nations, cultures, travels, discoveries, and encounters of which contamination of the hegemonic language and production of writings — "False vocalization of the consonantal text"— are part of the consequences of human contact across the ocean.

In one of the sections of "Cosmography," which rehearses variations of consonants in English words, Kim evokes power, authority, and subjugation in the encounters between peoples across cultures and nations through fragmentary lines. However, the fragmentation of the lines and the composition of the poem by verbal sound break down this implied hierarchical binary, resisting the construction of any discrete identity of race, culture, or nation, while refusing to tie language to thought, or utterances to a lyric I. This refusal enables Kim to push the boundary of lyric poetry by the enacting of what Deleuze and Guattari call "a relation of multiple deterritorializations with language" (*Kafka* 19). In so doing, Kim also breaks down the hierarchical relations between languages, without erasing differences, including the differences engendered by power. Her use of phonemes or syllables as a principle for structuring the lines high-lights the sound of language, whose materiality, as Charles Bernstein says in his introduction to a critical anthology, *Close Listening: Poetry and the Performed Word*, "can never be completely recuperated as ideas, as contents, as narrative, as extralexical meaning. The tension between sound and logic reflects the physical resistance in the medium of poetry" (Introduction 21). In the context of cross-cultural encounters, the physicality of verbal sound in Kim's poems, as shown in the following section of "Cosmography," brings out those aspects of language which are irreducible to or uncontainable by any totality:

:         :

Prime of it tender tendril

Another copier scribe to sound

Affectionate taking and undertaking

Swift the rusher, thrushes

Bora                    barium          buffer

If the cucumber surpasses its ideal growth overnight

If thrown off the house or horse

And the.        You must designate the article

Lop off the top where the milliner's wooden box doesn't reach
  (*Dura* 12)

Here Kim creates a unique prosody which breaks away from conven-tional regulated prosodic structures of the poem, but produces an equally prominent musicality in the sounding of the language. This central dimension of verbal sound unbounded by argument or logic is similar to the practice of Language poems grounded in apparently nonsensical sound patterns. Speaking of sound as a "nonlogical fea-ture of language," Bernstein expounds a poetics of "verbal perform-ance" that tests the limits of consciousness: "In sounding language, we sound the width and breadth and depth of human consciousness — we find our bottom and our top, we find the scope of our ken. In sounding language we ground ourselves as sentient, material beings, obtruding into the world with the same obdurate things as rocks or soil or flesh. We sing the body of language, relishing the vowels and consonants in every possible sequence. We stutter tunes with no melodies, only words" (Introduction 21). Kim's lines, such as "Affectionate taking and undertaking / Swift the rushes, thrushes / Bora barium buffer," indeed accomplish those functions of verbal performance through the sounding of language that Bernstein celebrates. But the world into which Kim's sounding language obtrudes is a social world, as well as a world of nature.

In engaging the social world through verbal sound, Kim avoids the pitfall of a socially disengaged poetics of verbal performance, which Bruce Andrews has warned against. In his essay "*Praxis*: A Political Economy of Noise and Informalism," Andrews cautions against the loss of "social charge" in poetry which foregrounds the sound dimension of language. "The challenge for Noise and Informalism in writing is to simultaneously cut the ties that bind sound to traditions of lyric harmony and speech or autonomous, inward-absorbing form *and*, through drastic and emancipated construction, to highlight what we call its 'social tone' or its 'semantic music'—*in praxis*" (73–74). In Kim's poem, the fragmentary line about the grammatical rule for using the definitive article "the" evokes colonial power and its hegemonic language. It also alludes to immigrants' experience of learning English, the official language of their host country, thus transcribing into the language both power and vulnerability. Cross-cultural encounters hinted at here are accentuated in the next section with new elements of language and culture.

Continuing to highlight the sound dimension of language situated in a world of differences, this section enriches the resonances of verbal sound and develops the complexity of transcultural encounters. The consonantal alliteration of the first half of this section is disrupted and replaced by vowel alliteration with the incorporation of Korean:

|  | : | : |  |
| --- | --- | --- | --- |
| Pilferage | | orphanage | raise |

Progress in learning

The cow and her calf

First flute cut from bamboo

First fabric dye from snails

Five tone and seven tone scales

시조 ──────── — a short lyric poem
                         or, the founder of a family

신 보 ──────── — an ancestral tablet

신세계 ──────── — a new world

시래기 ──────── — dried radish leaves (*Dura* 13)

Rather than advancing the development of argument or thought, like the prosody in conventional modes of lyric, Kim's prosody resists syntactic or rhetorical enclosure. However, its intonations and sound patterns help generate the movement of the lines, and bring isolated words and fragmentary references separated by time and space into juxtaposition and a relation evocative of history. For instance, the repetition and variation of consonantal words in the first line — "Pilferage   orphanage   raise"— create a sense of succession and change which enhance the meanings of these words and their implications associated with colonial plunder, war, and their aftermaths such as poverty, orphanages, and the raising of thousands of Korean orphans through adoption. Proceeding by repetition of the consonant $p$, the second line echoes the experience of learning English alluded to in the previous section, and anticipates the consequences resulting from cross-cultural encounters enacted in the second part of this section through translation of Korean into English. This moment of encounter is ushered in by the $f$-consonantal alliteration, followed by a shift from consonantal to vowel alliteration which corresponds to change taking place with the presence of Korean in English. While giving the reader the pleasure of "relishing the vowels and consonants in every possible sequence," as Bernstein says of the verbal performance of Language poems (Introduction 12), the three $f$-consonantal lines move speedily from the separate beginnings of Korean ("First flute cut from bamboo") and Western ("First fabric dye from snails") civilizations to their encounters suggested by the third line — "Five tone and seven tone scales"— which alludes to the meeting between East/Korean and Western/American cultures, for the Pentatonic scale is often used as the basis for East Asian music and the seven-tone scale is used in Western music. The meeting of these different scales of tones is further performed in subsequent lines in the poem excerpt, which translate Korean phrases into English.

The English translation of the lexical meanings of the Korean words brings into the poem another dimension of language and cross-cultural encounter. The sight of unromanized Korean words retains the untranslatability of Korean, resisting assimilation by the hegemonic language. This method is strategically similar to the "foreignizing translation" proposed by translator and translation theorist Lawrence Venuti, who is critical of "transparent" translations that domesticate foreign texts. The domesticating translation model, Venuti notes, aims to "bring back a cultural other as the same, the recognizable, even the familiar; and this aim always risks a wholesale domestication of the foreign text," which serves the domestic agendas of the target-language country. Thus "Whatever difference the translation conveys is now imprinted by the target-language culture, assimilated to its positions of intelligibility, its canons and taboos, its codes and ideologies" (18). Countering such assimilating models, Venuti argues that "Foreignizing translation in English can be a form of resistance against ethnocentrism and racism, cultural narcissism and imperialism, in the interests of democratic geopolitical relations" (20). Kim's inscription of Korean words in *Hangul*, like her references to Korean history and culture, and like her exploration of the contamination of English by Korean, achieves such effects of intervention. But she attempts something further.

Kim seeks to develop a poetics that engages with urgent questions such as those raised in her poem "Pollen Fossil Record": "How can the diction(s), register(s), inflection(s) as well as varying affective stances that have and will continue to filter into 'English' be taken into account? What are the implications of writing at this moment, in precisely this 'America'?" (*Commons* 110). In *Dura*, Kim integrates her interrogation of those questions with her negotiation with "an entire historical/political continuum" that shaped the 1992 L.A. riots. Corresponding to the references to history, travel, and cross-cultural encounters in "Cosmography," the second poem or rather the second part, "Measure," begins with two epigrams which are citations from texts of the same historical period, one from *The Travels of Marco Polo*, the other from a fourteenth-century Korean poem:

> "All desirous of knowing the diversities of the races of mankind as well as the diversities of kingdoms, provinces, and regions of all parts of the East, read this book."
> — *The Travels of Marco Polo*

> "All of you whose boats are leaky
>     heed the warning and take care"
> — *14th century Korean sijo* (*Dura* 21)

These citations evoke trade between East and West followed by colonization and wars, which are to be echoed through various historical references, leading toward global mass migration.

As is characteristic of Kim's poetics of fragmentation and strategies of a network of evocations, resonances, and references, "Measure" proceeds by enacting the implicit themes through reoccurring evocative words and images. Moreover, situated in a new context, these recurrent words and images develop the central themes they evoke or assert. At the same time, Kim continues to explore various possibilities of collage juxtaposition for her negotiation with the history of global capitalism and colonialism, not by narrative, but by fragmentary images and utterances. She arranges the lines in such a way that their groupings suggest different time and space, while their juxtaposition produces a relationship among these separate times, places, and actions:

Motion on the seas

Larded ships

    :  Gather soil and water

    :  Morning risen evening fallen mushroom

So writ the purpose
Voyage lay bare (*Dura* 23)

Positioned between the first and last two lines, the lines in the middle suggest a different geographical location, while alluding to activities on land with its daily living rhythms in human life and in nature. This time-space and its activities contrast with those embedded in the lines above and below. Although the first two lines evoke activities on the sea, they do not quite correspond to those suggested by the last two lines, whose official involvement and purposefulness foreshadow officially sanctioned voyages of conquest, colonization, and slave trade. The space in-between these four lines, and the middle lines intersecting them, helps produce a sense of distance between different historical periods and geographical locations.

As the top and middle lines continue to allude to activities in human societies and in nature, the bottom two lines suggest the meeting between East and West in most sections of "Measure." For example, the first two lines of the following sections refer to ingenious human productivity such as "Extract salt from brine / Dig black stone from veins," "Irrigation channels blasted from rock / Mulberry's inner bark beaten and matted" (*Dura* 24–25). And the middle lines show nature's rhythms and riches: "One flower when first my eyes wake / One blossom first eyes open"; "Reed stems, red dates / Grown fat and sleek" (*Dura* 25–26). In juxtaposition to such human ingenuity and nature's cycle of time, the last lines of these sections reveal the consequences of voyages over the seas with decreed purposes: "No fewer than a thousand carriages loaded with silk"; "Paper follows the trade route west"; and "Ships of trade accompanied by ships of war" (*Dura* 24, 25, 26). Beginning with section 5, Kim breaks down the structure of the two-line units to visually reflect the violence brought by war to human societies and nature. Corresponding to the arrival of "ships of war," human activities of invention and productivity have disappeared. So have the delightful sights of nature:

A way is open(ed), a hole is made

:

| | | |
|---|---|---|
| Introduce | single horse | turnback |
| Introduction | ride alone | |
| (Capital) | (fight alone) | make a turn (*Dura* 27) |

Ships of war following ships of trade from the West have brought not only destruction, but also profound social changes, including the rise of capitalism and individualism.

In addition, the transportation of goods and accumulation of capital ensured by military might, Kim suggests in the last section, lead to the circulation of a particular kind of product that "Transported as goods travel to gladdened hands"—travel writings, Orientalist discourses, the production of knowledge of the other, and even slaves and coolies. The first and last lines of the closing section resonate with the citation from *The Travels of Marco Polo* and its implications: "To speak of another region and its goods"; "Signets to authenticity and foremost authority" (*Dura* 28). But questions concerning the production of colonial discourses about the other are not as central in *Dura* as they are in Kim's most recent book, *Commons*. The poems following "Measure" shift to the discovery and colonization of North America — "Be added to the discovery to constitute / A valid title to territory in the New World" (*Dura* 32)—and to the importation of slave labor from Africa and indentured labor from Asia to the New World. The consequences of colonial expansion "With foremost authority assume" (*Dura* 31), and the movement of labor and capital eventually converge in the 1992 L.A. riots, dealt with in the fifth poem or part, "Thirty and Five Books."

The openness and expansiveness of the serial form together with her poetics of fragmentation enable Kim to incorporate multiple voices into a historical continuum. In "Thirty and Five Books," for instance, Kim juxtaposes the voice of slaves, coolies, or indentured laborers: "When we stayed all together working the fields and / went home at dusk and ate together. Many birds / sing ornate songs" (*Dura* 59); the voice of the displaced and exiled: "In so locating a time of geography before the compass. / Do not ask again where are we" (*Dura* 63); and the poet's comments and challenging voice: "Population gathered to population. More uninhabited / space in America than elsewhere. Is that accurate" (*Dura* 63). While raising questions about the interpretation and representation of history, Kim also incorporates the voice of the mother of Edward Lee, who was killed during the L.A. riots. She weaves the mother's words about her son's dead body depicted in the newspapers, with allusion to the fire that burnt down Korean Americans' stores and African Americans' and Latinos' fire of rage that erupted — "Body moving in circle be fire / If fire be the body carried round" (*Dura* 65). Apart from situating the riots in the historical continuum of global circulations of capital and labor Kim refuses to simplify the conflict between African Americans and Korean Americans by contextualizing their social statuses in the world history of colonialism and the American history of racism and imperialism, as well as referring to the impact of economic and political inequity on them. As these lines from "Thirty and Five Books" indicate:

Natural motion of fire to move in a straight line.

_____arrived in America. Bare to trouble and
foresworn. Aliens aboard three ships off the coast.
_____ and _____ clash. Police move in.

What is nearest is destroyed. (*Dura* 67)

Interpolated between the descriptions of destruction during the L.A. riots, the middle lines evoke the history of slavery and coolie labor by mentioning the ships off the coast with aliens aboard. Moreover, by leaving blank the spaces for the denominated agents of action, Kim forces the reader to rethink the identities of those who arrived in America on ships as "aliens" in the past.

Following those lines, Kim warns against hasty, oversimplified judgments about the causes of the riots — apparently class-based conflict or tensions deriving from "cultural difference." As these lines indicate: "Error gathering. Listen with your eyes because here / you cannot decipher what is said out of the effort / of mouths" (*Dura* 68). Kim calls the reader's attention to the social, economic, political, and historical conditions which gave rise to the L.A. riots through employment of fragmentary lines to allude to the social injustice of the cultural, political, and economic exclusion of people of color, while critiquing the politics of the manipulative racial divisions which shaped the L.A. riots (*Dura* 68–69). Given the complexity of social and historical forces that led to the riots, Kim raises questions about translation, not simply as a matter of translating language, literature, or culture, but also as an interpretation of and negotiation with history and social conflict, and as a matter of reproduction and circulation of knowledge.

Torch and fire. Translate: 38th parallel. Translate:
the first shipload of African slaves was landed at Jamestown.
(*Dura* 68)

By juxtaposing the burning of Korean stores during the L.A. riot with these two historical moments, Kim suggests that the L.A. riots must be understood in the context of the consequences of U.S. military and political interventions in Korea, marked by the division of North and South Korea along the 38th parallel, as well as the context of the history of slavery and its legacy in the United States. Through her strategy of collage juxtapositions, resonances, and allusions, these historical forces are "[r]eleased into our moment, shaped as it is by geographical and cultural displacements, an exponentially hybrid state of nations, cultures, and voicings" (*Commons* 108).

Moreover, Kim's use of the imperative, "Translate," foregrounds the challenges entailed in translation, or rather writing as translation, which examines the entanglement of history and memory, and of the past and the present. This insistence on locating what appears to be a racial or cultural conflict in the intricate relations among capitalism and imperialism, colonialism and racism, disrupts essentializing discursive knowledge of the racial and cultural other, which justifies social inequity. The implications of *translation* as a mode of writing that engages with social, historical, and cultural issues undermine the accuracy, authenticity, and authority assumed in "realistic" reports, narratives, or observations.

Translation, then, for Kim, proposes an alternative mode of language and writing which acknowledges the approximation of inscription or articulation. Writing as translation and negotiation, as proposition and transformation, can activate a form of contestation and intervention. Translation in cultural and postcolonial studies, as well as in translation theories, has become a site of critical investigation in part because of what Lawrence Venuti calls "violence" residing in the "purpose and activity of translation," which reconstitutes what is foreign according to the beliefs and values of the target-language culture (18). This potential violence of translation is associated with economic and political power. Venuti contends that "translation wields enormous power in the construction of national identities for foreign cultures, and hence it potentially figures in ethnic discrimination, geopolitical confrontations, colonialism, terrorism, war" (19). However, translation can also become a form of resistance and intervention through pluralizing and destabilizing, as well as foreignizing, strategies, which Kim explores in her poems.

## Writing as Constant Translation

A Levinasian ethics of alterity resides in Kim's proposition and practice of writing as "constant translation" (*Dura* 78). This mode of writing entails using language whose "Letter, syllable, and word model plurality" (*Dura* 105). Kim's practice of plurality in language entails a critical investigation of the relations between power and knowledge, between authority and text. Kim poses the question in the last poem of *Dura*, "Hummingbird": "Who wrote the word on the page that is the word on the page" (*Dura* 98)? In her poems, Kim reveals the ways in which power produces the knowledge of the abject other, including the female other, through writing that assumes the authority of scientific accuracy. One of the strategies she employs is to demonstrate that the meaning of culture, history, race, and gender is constructed and emergent, always unstable, and always in process.

"Hummingbird" is a salient example of Kim's enactment of writing as constant translation. It begins with a sample of a translation exercise for learning a foreign language. But the values and beliefs of a particular culture embedded in the language of each of the twelve sentences listed for the translation exercise indicate that translation can only be an approximation. What is translated, then, is never completely captured or contained in the translation. By extension, the alterity of the other cannot be enclosed or assimilated; it forever eludes words that attempt to fix it or absorb it into the same. However, acknowledgment of absolute alterity and the fact that meaning is emergent can be a generative and liberating force for writing. Scattered through the poem, the variations on Kim's translations of the hummingbird illustrate both the elusiveness of the hummingbird and the various expressions it elicits:

Hummingbird brown to match the pinecone it circles (*Dura* 99)

. . . . . . . . . . . . . . . . . . . . . . . .

Hummingbird   No word for its size (*Dura* 100)

. . . . . . . . . . . . . . . . . . .

Hummingbird, there is no speed to match yours (*Dura* 101)

. . . . . . . . . . . . . . . . . . . .

O hummingbird, swift thrill (*Dura* 102)

. . . . . . . . . . . . . .

Hummingbird happens as a sound first (*Dura* 106)

. . . . . . . . . . . . . . .

Hummingbird on lavender (*Dura* 107)

Corresponding to these varied translations of the hummingbird, the closing lines perform a series of translations, which suggest that the meaning or definition of a single entity is always multiple, provisional, and contingent upon the conditions under which it is produced.

Kim takes those implications for her writing even further in *Commons*. While continuing to use language in such a way so as to "model plurality," and to enact writing as constant translation, Kim employs intertextual juxtaposition in "Lamenta" to expose and counter the assumptions of stable, transparent meanings residing in the other to be completely grasped and possessed as knowledge. "Lamenta" consists of a series of poems with numbers as subheads, beginning with 229 and ending with 722. Arranged sequentially, the numbers of the poems show that some numbers/poems are missing. In fact, Kim's choice of using numbers beginning at 229, rather than 1, and ending at 722, indicates the incompleteness and infinite possibilities of extension for "Lamenta." The opening statement of "229" suggests a philosophical and aesthetic turn manifest in Kim's poetics of fragmentation:

229

The transition from the stability and absoluteness of the world's contents to their dissolution into motions and relations.

P: Of what use are the senses to us — tell me that

E: To indicate, to make known, to testify in part

Burning eye seen

Of that

One eye seen

*bo-bo-bo*      *k-k-k-*

Jack-in-the-pulpit    petaling

To a body of infinite size there can be ascribed neither center nor
  boundary

say   .   siphon

Sign scarcity, the greeting — *have you eaten today?*

Signal of peonies       singing given to bullfrogs

Give ear to the quarrels of the marketplace (*Commons* 13–14)

Corresponding to the opening statement, the rest of the poem pro-
ceeds with heterogeneous fragments. The principle underlying Kim's
collage composition is in part implied in the statement, "To a body of
infinite size there can be ascribed neither center nor boundary." Even
though the collage fragments in this poem resist coherence or formal
structure, they constitute a dialogic relation of propositions and con-
testations with regard to seeing and hearing, which resonate through-
out "Lamenta." The question and response between "P" and "E" ad-
dress a major concern of Kim's poetics, which challenges the centrality
of the lyric I/eye, whose vision or observation serves as the ground of
knowledge, the process of discovery, leading to a moment of epiphany.
The plurality of senses and the partiality of their functions of indicat-
ing, making known, and testifying, acknowledged in the exchanges
between "P" and "E," are enacted by the following fragments in which
sight and sound performances at once expose and supplement each
other's limitations. With the I/eye decentered, the vocalization of
"*bo-bo-bo   k-k-k*" claims an equal status as that of what is seen. So do
"signal of peonies" and "singing given to bullfrogs." Similarly, the
everyday speech of greetings, quarrels of the marketplace, and philo-
sophical statements are given equal attention and space in the poem.

In undermining the privilege of the I/eye and its vision, and by
highlighting and giving space to sound and the speech of the other(s),
Kim subverts the authority of the visible, while refusing to reduce the
world or the other(s) to knowledge. The significance of this subver-
sion becomes more explicit later in "Lamenta" with the incorporation
of prose texts that were written during the age of discovery and whose
influence led to the rise of colonialism. Between "322" and "324," Kim
inserts a fragment from an anatomy text describing a female body,

and uses "Vocalise" as its subtitle and imperative. By demanding that this written text be vocalized, Kim foregrounds the politics of articulation, calling the readers' attention to questions such as Who is speaking? In what capacity? And who is silenced?

> "the woman I had anatomized in the past year, or A.D. 1315, in the month of March had a uterus

> "twice as large as one whom I anatomized in the month of January in the same year . . . And because

> "the uterus of a pig which I anatomized in A.D. 1306 was a hundred times larger than it can ever

> "be seen in a human being, there may be another cause, i.e., because it was pregnant and had

> "in the uterus 13 little pigs. In this I showed the anatomy of the fetus or of pregnancy. (*Commons* 24)

Under such clinical observation, the female body becomes the object of scientific knowledge, completely visible, knowable, and containable in the text by the intentional "I" who is in complete mastery of himself and the object of his observation. The detailed description of what is seen assumes the authority of authenticity on which the knowledge of the female body is produced.

Levinas has critiqued the idealization of knowledge grounded in the "presence" of what is seen and at hand, which promises something "graspable, solid." He notes that "this prototypical trait of the knowledge of things is the necessary forerunner of the abstractions of understanding's idealized knowledge" (*EN* 160). Thus "Seeing or knowing, and taking in hand, are linked in the structure of intentionality, which remains the intrigue of a kind of thought that recognizes itself in consciousness." But he adds, "once that step is taken, intelligibility and intelligence — being situated in thought understood as vision and knowledge, and being interpreted on the basis of intentionality — consist in privileging, in the temporality of thought itself, the present in relation to the past and the future" (*EN* 160–61). Similarly, to comprehend alterity as visible, solid, and knowable facts "received, and synchronized in the presence within the *I think*" is to reduce otherness to sameness (*EN* 161). Hence, "The other becomes the *I*'s very own in knowledge, which secures the marvel of

immanence. Intentionality, in the aiming at and thematizing of be-
ing — that is, in presence — is a return to self as much as an issuing
forth from self" (*EN* 161). It is precisely such self-affirming knowledge
of the other or the world that Kim calls into question. In an interview,
she mentions her interest in the historical contexts of the emergence
of anatomy and the expansion of Europe. "I've been thinking also
about the way anatomy emerges as a science around the time of voy-
ages to the 'New World.' The idea of looking at the body . . . to incul-
cate a culture of dissection (discovering/owning/naming)" (J. K. Lee
99). The descriptive, narrative, and authoritative language in the text
quoted above reflects such functions of observation leading to dis-
covery, to naming, and to possession.

Resisting such a mode of language and mastery of the self over what
is seen, Kim insists on using fragmentary images, sounding language,
and disrupting sentences to indicate the uncontainable, irreducible al-
terity of the other and the world. In response to the quotations on the
female body, and in juxtaposition to other quotations from *De Fabrica
Humani Corporis* by Vesalius, published in 1543, that describes the
vivisection of a dog for observation of "the recurrent nerves" (*Com-
mons* 31), Kim employs multiple, heterogeneous fragments in "404" to
call into question knowledge grasped on the basis of what is visible:

404

Her name and her mother's name
Her name and her sister's name

Carcass of coyote and deer separated by a stream linked by bones

*sk-sk*

Meaning the spectator part of the theatre but also, stall,
    birdcage, beehive

*sahl-rlim-sah-ri*        house
                           chores (*Commons* 30)

In contrast to Vesalius's concise, minute, sequential description of the
vivisection of the dog on the operation table, Kim's fragmentary ref-
erence to the coyote carcass is located in a nexus of complex relation-
ships with things in the world. Just as "her name" is related to her

mother's and her sister's names, just as "the spectator," like "stall, bird-cage, and beehive," is part of the theatre, and just as "house" and "chores" are inseparable in Korean, the coyote carcass or the sound of "*sk - sk*" has to be perceived as part of and in relation to other things in their environments. As the last line of "312" in "Lamenta" indicates: "The thing seen is the thing seen together with the whole space" (*Commons* 16). Kim insists on situating individual events, utterances, and phenomena in specific environments and complex historical forces.

Apart from her strategy of juxtaposition as exposure and contestation, Kim further undermines through her method of resonance the subject's mastery of the visible as complete knowledge to be possessed. For instance, the confidence in possessing complete knowledge of the visible in the statement from *The Notebooks* of Leonardo da Vinci about dissecting "more than ten human bodies" as a way of "render[ing] my knowledge complete" resonates with Vesalius's complete faith in his mastery of anatomy. But transparent meaning of the visible as the ground for complete knowledge of the seen is challenged by contending statements and countering facts through juxtapositions and resonances such as these lines from "312": "All that we see could also be otherwise / All that we can describe could also be otherwise" (*Commons* 16). These statements are echoed and substantiated by another citation from yet another medical record written on August 6, 1945, which Kim incorporates into "Lamenta" and also entitles "Vocalise." This citation describes a girl who had no visible burn or injury on her body, though she "complained of being thirsty." The author found her dead the next day, but didn't understand why. "I can only surmise that her inside had imploded. / Acute internal injuries and not one mark on her body. No one ever knew who she was" (*Commons* 50). The date of the medical record suggests that the girl died at the end of World War II, possibly from exposure to nuclear explosion. Given the historical period and geographical location of the girl's death, its unknowable cause concealed by her body seems to indicate that the doctor, like the girl, was not aware of the effects of atomic bombs. While historicizing scientific knowledge, Kim undermines the equation of seeing with knowing, of vision with knowledge. At the same time, in vocalizing the written texts, Kim exposes what is reduced to and possessed as the objects of the observing, thinking, and knowing subject's knowledge. In locating scientific discourses in history and geography,

Kim enacts what she calls "a translation between world and language" (J. K. Lee 98).

In another serial poem entitled "Works," Kim explores other possibilities of translation. She incorporates texts in Korean into her poem through pluralizing and "foreignizing" translations which retain the alterity of the source language and texts. In the translation subtitled "Siege Document," Kim transcribes five lines of *Hangul* and transliterates them into two romanized phonetic variations.[8] These variations of transcription and transliteration of Korean challenge the dominance of English, while illustrating the plurality and contingency of meaning, and enacting resistance of Korean to assimilation by translation. Venuti calls such foreignizing translation "a dissident cultural practice, maintaining a refusal of the dominant by developing affiliations with marginal linguistic and literary values at home, including foreign cultures that have been excluded because of their own resistance to dominant values." In addition, Venuti adds, a translator can also break away "from the prevailing hierarchy of domestic discourses . . . by choosing to translate a text that challenges the contemporary canon of foreign literature in the target language" (148).

Translation for Kim is in part "a dissident cultural practice" which seeks intervention through difference and resistance. Departing from the canon formation of classical poetry from Asia through translation, Kim's choice to translate and transcribe into her poem the speech by a Korean woman, Olga Kim, who is "speaking about her forty years of living in Siberia" (*Commons* 110), is an act of resistance to both hierarchy and the hegemony of language. Except for the beginning three lines, Kim transcribes the rest of the speech/poem in *Hangul*.

Sometimes they dug holes and ordered us to get into them

If you don't work
You don't eat

.  .  .  .  .

[The following eleven lines, including Olga Kim's signature, that
    I have omitted here are written in Korean, *Hangul*.]
                                        The Elder Olga Kim
                                            Siberia, 1992 (*Commons* 83)

While the location, Siberia, written in English indicates that Olga's experience is part of the global migration of labor, the translation in

English maintains the prosaic, commonplace language of Olga Kim. Moreover, Kim's transcription of Olga's words in *Hangul* maintains the otherness of both the language and its speaker. The presence of *Hangul* asserts its irreducible foreignness in the dominance of English, and its illegibility for non-Korean speakers makes it impossible to formulate any essence that defines its otherness.

This foreignizing translation differs fundamentally from Orientalist stereotyping of the racial or cultural other, whose difference is at once inscrutable yet completely knowable. The sight of mute Korean words that cannot be pronounced inscribes a cultural otherness that articulates resistance to assimilation by the hegemonic language or dominant discourse. As Levinas contends: "The formal structure of language thereby announces the ethical inviolability of the Other" (*TI* 195). By refusing to translate the complete speech by Olga Kim, Kim establishes through language an ethical relationship with the other, which renders it impossible for the I/subject to possess the other or the world as knowledge. "The relationship with the Other," says Levinas, " is not produced outside of the world, but puts in question the world possessed" (*TI* 173). Kim's partial translation and transcription of Olga Kim's speech are characteristic of what Levinas calls a language event that is "not a manifestation or a knowledge," but "a contact," "the ethical event of communication" ("Language and Proximity" *CPP* 125). Olga Kim remains the subject of her enunciation, maintaining her irreducible otherness.

For Levinas, language as manifestation of and response to the other breaks the totality of knowledge and the autonomy of the Cartesian subject. He contends that "The calling in question of the I, coextensive with the manifestation of the Other in the face, we call language" (*TI* 171). Levinas emphasizes in particular the importance of speech in articulating difference. "Speech proceeds from absolute difference. . . . Absolute difference, inconceivable in terms of formal logic, is established only by language" (*TI* 194–95). These concepts and functions of language are embedded in Kim's language-centered poetics of fragmentation and heterogeneity, which, among other things, seeks to "Counter the potential totalizing power of language that serves the prevailing systems and demands of coherence" (*Commons* 110). Moreover, the ethical language that counters "the potential totalizing power of language," and calls into question the self as the intentional I who seeks to master the other and the world, is also a creatively liberating language in Kim's poetry. As one of Kim's mottos for her poetics indicates: "Enter language as it factors in, layers in, and crosses fields of meaning, elaborating and extending the possibilities for sense making" (*Commons* 110).

Although the lyric I is absent from Kim's language-centered poems, the agency of the speaking subject is not erased, but is rather enacted through multiple speakers and different, even contending, voices and utterances. Even though Kim's poems differ radically from those of the other poets discussed in the preceding chapters, her innovative poetics is no less subversive or provocative in confronting the ethics and politics of alterity. Kim brands otherness in the materiality of language and the form of her poetry as she reinvents the lyric with new possibilities opened up by an altered relationship among self, other, and language.

# Conclusion

The relationship between self and other entails both ethics and politics, as shown in the work of seven contemporary Asian American poets. In their investigations of the ethical and political questions of otherness, these poets demonstrate an intricate relationship among aesthetics, poetics, and politics, which is embedded in a Levinasian ethics. "Levinasian politics is the enactment of plurality, of multiplicity," states Simon Critchley in arguing for "a Levinasian politics of ethical difference" (225). By enacting a political plurality and multiplicity through an ethics and poetics of alterity, contemporary Asian American poets confront the relationship between American poetry and American democracy. Whitman passionately asserted this relationship in *Leaves of Grass* in the midnineteenth century. At the beginning of the twenty-first century, Robert Pinsky reemphasizes the same in his book *Democracy, Culture and the Voice of Poetry* (2002). Refusing to regard the lyrical and the social as mutually exclusive, Pinsky contends: "Lyric poetry has been defined by the unity and concentration of a solitary voice. . . . But the vocality of poetry, involving the mind's energy as it moves toward speech, and toward incantation, also involves the creation of something like — indeed, precisely *like* — a social presence. The solitude of lyric, almost by the nature of human solitude and the human voice, invokes a social presence" (18). While emphasizing the presence of the other(s) in terms of the lyric speaker's audience, Pinsky adds something new to the conventional definition of lyric poetry: "Poetry, then, has roots in the moment when a voice makes us alert to the presence of another or others. It has affinities with all the ways a solitary voice, actual or virtual, imitates the presence of others. Yet as a form of art it is deeply embedded in the single human voice, in the solitary state that hears the other and sometimes recreates that other" (39).

In developing a poetics of alterity that insists on confronting social injustice against the other and exploring the ethics and aesthetics of otherness, Asian American poets demonstrate that their transformation and displacement of the lyric I engage with broader issues than merely the poetic. Their poetry and poetics call critical attention to the philosophical foundation of binarized concepts of self and other, which underlie racism, sexism, colonialism, and Orientalism. At the same time, by locating questions of otherness in language, discourse, popular culture, and our everyday experience of encounters with the other(s), Asian American poets help advance critical studies in race, gender, and culture, as well as in poetry.

In discourses of feminism, cultural studies, and postcolonial studies, the term *otherness* has been used, more often than not, in a negative sense, while *difference* has taken on a positive connotation, even though otherness and difference are also used alternately. Barbara Christian critiques forcefully the positioning of people of color as the "'historical' other" of the West (337). Luce Irigaray in *An Ethics of Sexual Difference* points out that, "the *Other* often stands in our tradition for *product of a hatred* for the other. Not intended to be open to interpretation" (112). Keenly aware of the fact that women have been defined as the lesser other of men, the East has been represented as the inferior other of the West, and people of color have been positioned as the subordinate other of whites, feminists of color and scholars of cultural studies and postcolonial studies propose alternative ways for rearticulating otherness in terms of difference outside binary schemes. Audre Lorde cautions against the erasure of differences among women's experience of oppression, and argues for a new concept of differences as "forces for change" and as sources of women's strength and creativity, rather than as "causes for separation and suspicion" (99). On a similar note, Gloria Anzaldúa offers an alternative concept of difference which rejects binarism and embraces hybridity, ambivalence, and contradictions of "a new *mestiza* consciousness, una conciencia de mujer," which is "a consciousness of Borderlands" (*Borderlands* 77). This new "borderlands" consciousness, Anzaldúa contends, seeks to "break down the subject-object duality that keeps her a prisoner" (80). Like Lorde and Anzaldúa, Trinh T. Minh-ha points out the dangers of erasing differences: "Hegemony works at leveling out differences. . . . Uncovering this leveling of differences is, therefore, resisting that very notion of difference which defined in the master's terms often resorts to the simplicity of essence." Hence Trinh asserts the necessity for a reconceptualization of difference. "Many of us still hold on to the concept of difference not as a tool of creativity to question multiple forms of repression and dominance, but as a tool of segregation, to exert power on the basis of racial and sexual essences. The apartheid type of difference" ("Not You/Like You" 372). Addressing difference from the critical perspectives of cultural studies, Rey Chow also points out the persistence of binarism in maintaining a racialized power structure and hierarchy of culture. In her book, *Ethics After Idealism: Theory — Culture — Ethnicity — Reading*, Chow emphasizes the absolute necessity for cultural difference to "retain its critical and political impetus in the current intellectual climate" of multiculturalism which "is intent on promoting a liberalist politics of recognition," one that "is still largely a one-way street — in the form, for instance, of *white culture recognizing non-white cultures only*" (13, 11). To break down binaries as such and to dissolve their familiar coordinates, Homi Bhabha contends that the transformation of the objectified other into a subject must entail a conceptual shift from cultural diversity as "an epistemological object" to cultural difference as "a process of signification." This shift, Bhabha adds, "opens up possibilities for other 'times' of cultural meaning . . . and other narrative spaces" so that "objectified others may be turned into subjects of their history and experience." With this shift, the objectified others can also escape the fixity of binarism and occupy the ambivalent "Third Space of enunciations," which Bhabha considers the "precondition for the articulation of cultural difference" (34, 178, 38).

Asian American poets mobilize more than the critical impetus of cultural difference or the difference of race, gender, class, and sexuality. By transforming the lyric I and the lyric voice, by challenging representation, and denaturalizing language through a poetics of alterity, these poets compel a rethinking of the politics and ethics of otherness, while turning difference into a source of creativity and a form of resistance and critical intervention. Apart from the particular differences of experience, identity, ideology, and aesthetics, Asian American poets insist on addressing the Levinasian ethics of otherness or alterity in relation to subjectivity, language, knowledge, and representation. Hence their poems radically reconceptualize not only the other, but also the self outside binarized hierarchies of identities, and beyond Western metaphysics.

In addition, Asian American poets' insistence on confronting the difference of race, gender, class, ethnicity, and sexuality in their critical and creative engagement with feminist and poststructuralist theories poses the kind of "significant threat" to the literary establishment which Chow speaks of with regard to cultural studies:

> Cultural studies, by its dogged turns toward the other not only within language and text but also outside language and text, in effect forces poststructuralist theory to confront the significance of race — and with it the histories of racial discrimination and racial exploitation — that is repressed in poststructuralist theory's claim to subversiveness and radicalism. By so doing, *cultural studies challenges poststructuralist theory's own position as the "other" of Europe, as the "other" within the European tradition.* And this, I think, is cultural studies' most significant threat to the once avant-garde theorists who, like [Harold] Bloom, must literally junk it. (5)

By refusing to elide social power relations in language and poetics, Asian American poets disrupt the circular knowledge of the other, break the silence of the other, and force literary criticism to confront the tendency of socially detached postmodern poetics and poststructuralist discourses to continue the repression of the other by replacing the autonomy of the Cartesian subject with the autonomy of the text.

Most importantly, in reconceptualizing the lyric I and rearticulating the other and its relation to the self, Asian American poets pose a challenge to the disembodied and self-sufficient lyric I — a challenge that shakes the autonomous subject to its roots. Conceived in terms of the Western metaphysical tradition, Levinas contends, the self cannot allow the otherness of the other to challenge its sameness. Traditional Western philosophy is characterized by "the thought of being" — "the thought of that which is meaningful, affirming itself against impression." This mode of a self-affirming being, Levinas contends, is self-centered and self-enclosed: "One affirms the fact of remaining in oneself, returning to oneself, positing oneself as a oneself, as the sense of the world, as the sense of life, as spirit. As if the meaningful or the reasonable always came back to the event of the perseverance in existence, which finds its full expression in the apparition of an 'I' understood at the same time as an 'in-itself' and a 'for-itself'" ("Vocation of the Other" *IIRTB* 105). Embedded in this primacy of being and concept of the self resides a potential "threat," or animosity, with regard to the other. Levinas asks: "But within this priority of being, this insistence on the oneself, isn't there something like a threat against all others, a war inherent in this affirmation of oneself? An atom which is closed unto itself and which, after fission, physicists call 'confinement': hardness, cruelty, materiality in the physical sense of the term — shock and pure pressure in the guise of an exteriorization which would be the negation and misrecognition of all alterity?" (*IIRTB* 105). In contrast to this ontology of being-for-itself, Levinas proposes to posit "the priority of an irreducible alterity" as the first principle of philosophical reflections on humanity. For him, "the question of the other seemed . . . to be anterior to the problem of ontology" (*IIRTB* 106). In seeking to situate the question of the other "at least on the same level as the famous question of being," and insisting on "the primordial intellectual role of alterity" (*IIRTB* 105) in the constitution of the self as subject and in the production of knowledge, culture, and literature, Levinas also indirectly poses the question of the other in the formation of communities, nations, and empires.

Most important and most provocatively, Levinas relates the philosophical, aesthetic, and ethical questions of the other to questions of social justice, and to the horror of the Holocaust. In his dedication of one of his major works, *Otherwise Than Being: Or Beyond Essence*, Levinas writes in both English and Hebrew: "To the memory of those who were closest among the six million assassinated by the National Socialists, and of the millions on millions of all confessions and all nations, victims of the same hatred of the other man, the same anti-semitism." While confronting the genocide of Jews, Levinas's ethics of alterity enables us to think in terms broader than the historical contexts of Hitler's regime by directing our attention to the social and cultural environment that made the Holocaust possible.

The significance of Asian American poets' development of an ethics and poetics of alterity concerns much more than the celebrated enrichment and wider creative possibilities of difference. Insisting on speaking as the other, allowing the voices of the other and others to be heard, and taking into account the alterity of the other in their poems, Asian American poets such as Li-Young Lee, Marilyn Chin, David Mura, Kimiko Hahn, Timothy Liu, John Yau, and Myung Mi Kim, among others, re-frame the question of otherness raised by feminists, poststructuralists, and theorists of cultural studies and postcolonial studies, with its historical weight and current exigency. Their exploration of otherness is not unrelated to Jewish writers' investigation of

Jews as the other in Western culture. Edmond Jabès's statements about what it means to insist on being the other will further illuminate the significant ramifications of the ethics and poetics of alterity in Asian American poetry:

> To want to be — even at the risk of one's life — *the other*, isn't that, à priori, an unreasonable provocation? All the more so since this "other" could hardly be integrated, or accepted as such directly.
>
> However, if the Jew persists in wanting to be recognized in his difference — that is to say as the *other* — he does so first because he sees it as fundamental progress — and not only for himself — as a victory over the self's total intolerance.
>
> . . . It is a question of getting "the other" accepted in his strangeness, in the sovereignty of his difference. (62–63)

For Asian American poets, then, to accept the other's alterity as irreducible, and to insist on being recognized as the other even at the risk of alienation, exclusion, or marginalization, is an ethical and political act in poetry. As Jabès says of the necessity and responsibility of poetry for humanity: "To Adorno's statement that 'after Auschwitz one can no longer write poetry,' inviting a global questioning of our culture, I'm tempted to answer: yes, one can. And, furthermore, one has to. One has to write out of that break, out of that unceasingly revived wound" (62). Poetry written "out of that unceasingly revived wound" has to take into account what Levinas calls "the ethical inviolability of the Other" (*TI* 195). It is by practicing the poetic as the ethical and political, without equating the poetic with the ethical or the political, that Asian American poets enact their social responsibility and explore their artistic creativity. Their work suggests that insisting on practicing an ethics and poetics of alterity is in some ways an effort to work toward what Jabès has called a "fundamental progress" for humanity.

# Notes

INTRODUCTION

1. For historical documents on the debates which led to the laws that barred Chinese and other Asian immigrants from U.S. citizenship, see Hyung-Chan Kim, ed., *Asian Americans and Congress: A Documentary History* (Westport: Greenwood Press, 1996), 22–25.

2. I use the term *minority* in this study to refer to the difference of social status and political position of people of color from that of whites in the United States.

3. The use of *Other* (with an uppercase *O*) and *other* (with a lowercase *o*) is inconsistent among writers of various disciplines. Some use both alternately, employing Other to refer to otherness in general such as the socially, politically, and culturally constructed collective identity of women, the outsider, or people of color; and other to refer to the other person, the particularized others. Others use either Other or other for both the generalized and the particular other. Similarly, translators of Emmanuel Levinas do not follow a single uniform rule for capitalizing other. Alphonso Lingis, a major translator of Levinas's works, always translates the French word *autrui* as the 'Other,' and *autre* as 'other,' regardless of the occasional capitalization of *autre* in Levinas's texts. Richard A. Cohen, another major translator of Levinas, follows the convention Lingis has established. In this book, I use the lowercase other consistently while keeping the uppercase and lowercase variations intact in all my citations.

4. Some critics challenge a homogenous definition of Romantic lyric poetry. See for example, Sarah Zimmerman, *Romanticism, Lyricism, and History* (Albany: State University of New York Press, 1999) and Linda A. Kinnahan, *Lyric Interventions: Feminism, Experimental Poetry, and Contemporary Discourse* (Iowa City: University of Iowa Press, 2004).

5. See for instance, Charles Altieri's discussion of the self and subjectivity in his two books, *Self and Sensibility in Contemporary American Poetry* and *Subjective Agency: A Theory of First-Person Expressivity and Its Social Implications*.

6. It should be noted that Shelley Wong raises those questions in a note to her essay. The limited space of a note does not allow her to further explore the questions.

7. Scholars, especially feminists, who engage with Emmanuel Levinas's views on ethics have made significant contributions to the debates on subjectivity and otherness. See for instance, Luce Irigaray, Elizabeth Grosz, Jill Robbins, Simon Critchley, Tina Chanter, and Ewa Płonowska Ziarek.

8. See for instance, Emmanuel Levinas's discussion of art in *Existence and Existents*, trans. Alphonso Lingis (The Hague: Martinus Nijhoff, 1978), particularly chapters 3 and 4. In her book, *Altered Reading: Levinas and Literature* (Chicago: University of Chicago Press, 1999), Jill Robbins offers a thorough, insightful analysis of the apparent contradictions in Levinas's charges of the aesthetic pertaining to the ethical, particularly in chapters 3–7.

CHAPTER ONE

1. For detailed and well-documented discussion on racialization of the body and American identity, see David Palumbo-Liu, *Asian/American: Historical Crossings of a Racial Frontier* (Stanford, CA: Stanford UP, 1999), chapters 3 and 4.

2. Helen Vendler, for example, defines lyric poetry in terms of the lyric moment when the disembodied self "is alone with itself" and gives voice to the "soul." See Vendler, *Soul Says: On Recent Poetry* (Cambridge: The Belknap Press of Harvard UP, 1999), 6–7.

3. For a thoughtful, close reading of "The Cleaving" from a different perspective from mine, see Jeffrey F. L. Partridge, "The Politics of Ethnic Authorship: Li-Young Lee, Emerson, and Whitman at the Banquet Table," in *SLI: Studies in the Literary Imagination*, a special issue on "Cross Wire: Asian American Literary Criticism," 37.1 (Spring 2004): 101–24. My reading of Lee focuses on his difference from Emerson and Whitman, whereas Partridge emphasizes his similarity with them.

4. According to Li-Young Lee, in a brief conversation with the author in 1995, he read Emerson's remarks about the Chinese features in his journals. For more information about and analysis of that particular entry of Emerson's journal, see Partridge, 115–118.

CHAPTER TWO

1. See Sucheng Chan, ed., *Entry Denied: Exclusion and the Chinese Community in America, 1882–1943* (Philadelphia: Temple UP, 1994); Ronald Takaki, *Iron Cages: Race and Culture in 19th-Century America* (New York: Oxford UP, 1990); and Maxine Hong Kingston, "The Laws," in *China Men* (New York: Alfred A. Knopf, 1980), 152–59.

2. Chin's words in a telephone conversation with the author, May 12, 1998.

3. Ch'an is a school of Buddhism influenced by Daoism, practiced in China and Japan where it is known as Zen.

4. See *The Essential Cavafy*, intro. Edmund Keeley, trans. Edmund Keeley and Philip Sherrard (Hopewell, N.J.: Ecco, 1995, 20–21).

5. See Loni Ding, dir. *Ancestors in the Americas: Coolies, Sailors, Settlers*. San Francisco: Center for Educational Telecommunication, 2001.

6. I borrow the phrase "white voice" from Timothy Yu. In his provocative article, "Form and Identity in Language Poetry and Asian American Poetry," Yu contends that Asian American poets expose "the mainstream voice as a white voice" through "injection of explicitly Asian American themes and voices into poetry" (425).

7. See Dorothy Joan Wang, "Necessary Figures: Metaphor, Irony and Parody in the Poetry of Li-Young Lee, Marilyn Chin, and John Yau," Diss. University of California, Berkeley, 1998.

8. See eds. Mark Lai Him, Genny Lim, and Judy Yung, *Island: Poetry and History of Chinese Immigrants on Angel Island, 1910–1940* (San Francisco: San Francisco Study Center, 1980). For more information about Angel Island and about "paperson," see Ronald Takaki, *Strangers from A Different Shore: A History of Asian Americans* (New York: Penguin, 1989), chapter 6.

CHAPTER THREE

1. See Harold Bloom, "They Have the Numbers; We, the Heights," *Boston Review* 23.2 (April/May 1998): 24–29. This essay appears as the introduction to *The Best of the Best American Poetry, 1988–1997* (New York: Scribner, 1998).

2. See James Baldwin, "The Last Interview," in *James Baldwin: The Legacy*, ed. Quincy Troupe, 186–212 (New York: A Touchstone Book, published by Simon and Schuster, 1989), 240.

3. These questions are from Commission on Wartime Relocation and Internment of Civilians, *Personal Justice Denied: Report of the Commission on Wartime Relocation and Internment of Civilians* (Washington, D.C., 1982): GPO 191–92, quoted in Ronald Takaki, *Strangers from a Different Shore: A History of Asian Americans* (New York: Penguin, 1989), 397. For a more detailed account of the Japanese American internment, see pp. 379–405.

4. Mura, letter to the author, 18 December 1998.

5. *Shoyu* is soy sauce, and *Hana*, a Japanese card game.

6. For discussions of Mura's poems collected in his first book, *After We Lost Our Way* (1989), see George Uba, "Versions of Identity in Post-Activist Asian American Poetry," 33–48 in Shirley Geok-lin Lim and Amy Ling eds., *Reading the Literatures of Asian America* (Philadelphia: Temple University Press, 1992).

7. See Frantz Fanon, *Black Skin, White Masks*, trans. Charles Lam Markmann (New York: Grove Press, 1967) 150–65.

8. See David L. Eng, *Racial Castration: Managing Masculinity in Asian America* (Durham: Duke UP, 2001).

# CHAPTER FOUR

1. For an in-depth discussion of Levinas's influence on Luce Irigaray, see Elizabeth Grosz, *Sexual Subversions: Three French Feminists*, (St. Leonards, Australia: Allen and Unwin, 1989), chapter 5.

2. Japanese women's literature gained prominence during the Heian period (794–1192) largely due to historical circumstances, especially the development of the Japanese language. Japan had no writing system before *kanji* (Chinese characters) were introduced from China around the fifth century. From the ninth to the eleventh centuries, certain *kanji* were modified, or rather simplified, to form phonetic symbols. Eventually a Japanese syllabary called *kana* was developed and replaced *kanji* as phonetic symbols. *Kana* consists of two types—*hiragana* and *katakana*—each consisting of 47 symbols representing the same phonemes in Japanese. *Katakana* were formed from parts of Chinese characters, and *hiragana* were developed by abbreviating and modifying whole characters. While *katakana* is used for foreign words, *hiragana*, also known as "woman's hand," was the system which Japanese women used to write. *Kanji* was the language of men and the privileged. Today Japanese is usually written with a combination of *kanji* and *hiragana*, with an admixture of *katakana*. While *kanji* represents blocks of meaning, *hiragana* indicates the grammatical relationships among them.

3. For a sensitive reading of this and Hahn's other poems from a feminist perspective, see Traise Yamamoto, *Masking Selves, Making Subjects: Japanese American Women, Identity, and the Body* (Berkeley: University of California Press, 1999), 236–61.

4. A shorter and slightly different version of my reading of "The Hemisphere: Kuchuk Hanem" appears in my essay, "Two Hat Softeners 'in the Trade Confession': John Yau and Kimiko Hahn," included in *Form and Transformation in Asian American Literature*, ed. Zhou Xiaojing and Samina Najmi, 168–89 (Seattle: University of Washington Press, 2005).

5. For a provocative psychoanalytical reading of "The Hemisphere: Kuchuk Hanem," see Juliana Chang, "'I Cannot Find Her': The Oriental Feminine, Racial Melancholia, and Kimiko Hahn's *The Unbearable Heart*," 239–60 in *Meridians: feminism, race, transnationalism* 4.2 (2004). Chang critically examines "the oriental feminine" as "the site not only of imaginary and symbolic fantasy, but also the site of the traumatic real" (241). The otherness of this oriental feminine that is constructed as "modernity's 'other,'" and "remains outside of modern history and modern subjectivity"

(Chang 240) is fundamentally different from the irreducible feminine alterity which Hahn seeks to articulate in her poems.

6. Hahn began to explore the politics and aesthetics of femininity outside of patriarchy and Orientalism by incorporating and reinventing non-European women's cultural and literary traditions in her first volume, *Air Pocket* (1989). She continues to do so in her subsequent volumes.

7. For more information about and samples of *nu shu*, see Gong Zhebing, ed. and intro. *Nu Shu* by Gao Yinxian and Yinian Hua (Taibei: The Association of Women's Renaissance Foundation, 1991).

8. In several of her poems, Hahn explores Genji's never-ending longing for his mother, and the social conditions which give rise to women's jealousy of and rivalry against one another over Genji's love. Traise Yamamoto offers an insightful reading of Hahn's intertextual engagement with *The Tale of Genji*. See Yamamoto, 238–49.

9. For more information about Hahn's reference to the Seven Immortal Sisters of Daoism, see *The Immortal Sisters: Secrets of Taoist Women*, ed. and trans. Thomas Clearly (Boston: Shambhala Publications, 1989).

CHAPTER FIVE

1. In an interview with Eileen Tabios, Timothy Liu says that even though he thinks "a lot about being Asian American in my life," issues of his racial identity are not "available" to him as poetry mostly because "in some ways, we don't really choose our subjects. We just write about what's bothering us." See Eileen Tabios, "Towards Redemption," interview with Timothy Liu, in *Black Lightning: Poetry-in-Progress*, 69–107 (New York: The Asian American Writers Workshop, 1998), 72.

2. For a provocative comparative reading of Timothy Liu with Essex Hemphill and Walt Whitman, see Richard Serrano, "Beyond the Length of an Average Penis: Reading Across Traditions in the Poetry of Timothy Liu," in *Asian American Literature: Form and Transformation in Asian American Literature*, ed. Zhou Xiaojing and Samina Najmi, 190–95, 200–207 (Seattle: University of Washington Press, 2005).

3. I am indebted to Floyd Cheung for calling my attention to the relations between phallocentric masculinity and racism in Theodore Roosevelt's justification of American imperialism.

4. Although Liu does not privilege masculinity in his homoerotic poems as Whitman does, he pays tribute to Whitman's homoerotic poems. See Liu's poem, "Reading Whitman in a Toilet Stall," in his second volume, *Burnt Offerings*. For a close reading of this poem, see Serrano, 201–207.

5. See Verse 11, Chapter 26 of "St. Matthew" in the New Testament.

6. For a comparative reading of this poem with an ancient Chinese poem, see Serrano, 195–200.

Small portions of this chapter have appeared in two different pieces: "Postmodernism and Subversive Parody: John Yau's 'Genghis Chan: Private Eye' Series," *College Literature* 31.1 (Winter 2004): 73–102, and "Two Hat Softeners 'in the Trade Confession': John Yau and Kimiko Hahn," 179–203 in *Asian American Literature: Form and Transformation*, ed. Zhou Xiaojing and Samina Najmi (Seattle: University of Washington Press, 2005).

1. John Yau's essay, "Between the Forest and Its Trees," originally appeared in the *New England Review* in 15.3 (Summer 1993): 185–88. A slightly different version of this essay was published about a year later in *Amerasia Journal*. See 20.3 (1994), 41.

2. Charles Bernstein does not seem to share Bruce Andrews's belief in the death of the author. For Bernstein, "the individual is the most salient concept with which to describe the site for this resistance." See Bernstein, *Content's Dream: Essays 1975–1984*, (Los Angeles: Sun and Moon, 1986), 409.

3. Yau, e-mail letter to the author, May 12, 2002.

4. Hollywood produced forty-eight Charlie Chan films between 1926 and 1947, which were adapted from five novels by Earl Derr Biggers, first published from 1925 to 1932. Hollywood also produced a number of Fu Manchu films between 1920 and 1940, which were adapted from Sax Rohmer's thirteen novels published between 1913 and 1941. In one of the films, *The Mask of Fu Manchu* (1932), Fu Manchu tries to obtain the mask and sword of Genghis Khan so as to unite all people of color to exterminate the white race and rule the world.

5. Yau, e-mail to the author, September 16, 1999.

6. For an extended discussion of Charlie Chan as an embodiment of the assimilated model minority, see Sandra Hawley, "The Importance of Being Charlie Chan," in *America Views China: American Images of China Then and Now*, ed. Jonathan Goldsmith, Jerry Israel, and Hilary Conroy, 132–47 (London: Associated UP, 1991).

7. See for instance, Sucheng Chan, *Asian Americans: An Interpretive History* (New York: Twayne, 1991).

8. Yau, e-mail to the author, August 13, 1999.

9. For a provocative and substantial analysis of the complexity of John Yau's poetry, see Dorothy Joan Wang, "Undercover Asian: John Yau and the Politics of Ethnic Self-Identification," in *Asian American Literature in the International Context: Readings on Fiction, Poetry, and Performance*, ed. Rocío G. Davis and Sämi Ludwig, 135–55 (Hamburg, Germany: LIT Verlag, 2002).

10. Although this collection of songs is known to be in print during the nineteenth century, its publication date is unknown. See Robert G. Lee, *Ori-*

*entals: Asian Americans in Popular Culture* (Philadelphia: Temple UP, 1999), 230, n54.

CHAPTER SEVEN

1. Myung Mi Kim immigrated to the United States at age nine. She made the reference to her Korean competency level at a reading she gave on November 2, 2001, at the State University of New York, Buffalo.

2. The citation in Kim here is from Hélène Cixous's *Stigmata: Escaping Texts* (New York: Routledge, 1998).

3. I am grateful to Professor Tomas Rey for his help in translating this line from a Korean poem into English.

4. See Jacques Derrida, *Positions*, trans. Alan Bass (Chicago: University of Chicago Press, 1981), 20.

5. The Korean orthophonic alphabet *Hangul* was developed in 1443 and promulgated in 1446 by the Korean monarch Sejong (1397–1450). Before the invention of *Hangul*, the writing system of Korea was borrowed from Chinese. According to Sek Yen Kim-Cho, King Sejong's Korean language reform "was motivated by his desire to make Korea culturally independent from China." See Kim-Cho, *The Korean Alphabet of 1446* (Amherst, NY: Humanity Books, 2002), 47.

6. See Kim-Cho, 17, and Kenneth Scott Latourette, *A Short History of the Far East*, 4th ed. (New York: Macmillan, 1964), 267.

7. For a detailed discussion of the "Siege Document" in Kim's poem, see Joseph Jonghyun Jeon, "Speaking in Tongues: Myung Mi Kim's Stylized Mouths, 127–48 in SLI: *Studies in the Literary Imagination*, special issue on "Cross Wire: Asian American Literary Criticism" 37 (Spring 2004), 138–40.

# Bibliography

PRIMARY SOURCES

Chin, Marilyn. *Dwarf Bamboo*. Greenfield, NY: The Greenfield Review Press, 1987.

———. "Introduction." In *Dissident Song: A Contemporary Asian American Anthology*. Eds. Marilyn Chin, David Wong Louie, and Ken Weisner, 3–4. Santa Cruz, CA: Quarry West, 1991.

———. *The Phoenix Gone, The Terrace Empty*. Minneapolis: Milkweed Edition, 1994.

———. *Rhapsody in Plain Yellow*. New York: Norton, 2002.

———. "Translating Self: Stealing from Wang Wei, Kowtowing to Hughes, Hooking Up with Keats, Undone by Donne." In *After Confession: Poetry as Autobiography*. Eds. David Graham and Kate Sontag, 305–16. Saint Paul, MN: Graywolf Press, 2001.

———. "Writing the Other: A Conversation with Maxine Hong Kingston." *Poetry Flash* 198 (September 1989): 1, 4, 17–18.

Hahn, Kimiko. *Air Pocket*. Brooklyn, NY: Hanging Loose Press, 1989.

———. *Earshot*. Brooklyn, NY: Hanging Loose Press, 1992.

———. "Memory, Language and Desire." In *Asian Americans: Collages of Identities*, 63–69. Ithaca, NY: Asian American Studies Program, Cornell University, 1992.

———. *Mosquito and Ant*. New York: Norton, 1999.

———. *The Unbearable Heart*. New York: Kaya Production, 1995.

———, Gale Jackson, and Susan Sherman. "Three Voices Together: A Collage." In *We Stand Our Ground: Three Women, Their Vision, Their Poems*, 9–29. New York: Ikon, 1988.

Kim, Myung Mi. "Anacrusis." Talk at the Page Mothers Conference, University of California at San Diego, March 1999. Online posting at Kim's Web site, http://www.scc.rutgers.edu/v1_2_1999/current/readings/kim.htm (17 pars. 1999).

———. *The Bounty*. Minneapolis: Chax Press, 1996.

———. *Commons*. Berkeley: University of California Press, 2002.

———. *Dura*. Los Angeles: Sun & Moon Press, 1998.

———. *Under Flag*. Berkeley: Kelsey, 1991.

Lee, Li-Young. *The City In Which I Love You*. Brockport, NY: BOA Editions, 1990.

———. *Rose*. Brockport, NY: BOA Editions, 1986.

———. *The Winged Seed: A Remembrance*. New York: Simon and Schuster, 1995.

Liu, Timothy. "Afterword." In *Take Out: Queer Writing from Asian Pacific America*, Eds. Quang Bad and Hanya Yanaginara with Timothy Liu, 506–507. New York: The Asian American Writers' Workshop, 2000.

———. *Burnt Offerings*. Port Townsend, WA: Copper Canyon Press, 1995.

———. *Hard Evidence*. Port Townsend, WA: Copper Canyon Press, 2001.

———. *Say Goodnight*. Port Townsend, WA: Copper Canyon Press, 1998.

———. *Vox Angelica*. Cambridge, MA: Alice James Books, 1992.

Mura, David. *After We Lost Our Way*. New York: Dutton, 1989.

———. *Angels for the Burning*. Rochester, NY: BOA, 2004.

———. *The Colors of Desire*. New York: Anchor, 1995.

———. "Dim Sum Poetics." In *Song for Uncle Tom, Tonto, and Mr. Moto: Poetry and Identity*, 97–101. Ann Arbor: The University of Michigan Press, 2002.

———. "How America Unsexes the Asian Male." *The New York Times* August 22, 1996: C9.

———. "The Margins at the Center, the Center at the Margins: Acknowledging the Diversity of Asian American Poetry." In *Reviewing Asian America: Locating Diversity*, 171–83. Pullman: Washington State UP, 1995.

———. "Mirrors of the Self: Autobiography and the Japanese-American Writer." *Asian Americans: Contemporary and Global Perspectives*. Eds. Shirley Hune, Hyungchan Kim, Stephen S. Fugita, and Amy Ling, 249–63. Pullman: Washington State University Press, 1991.

———. "No-No Boys: Re-X-Amining Japanese Americans." *New England Review* 15.3 (Summer 1993): 143–65.

———. "A Note from Caliban." *Boston Review* 23.3–4 (Summer 1998): 27–28.

———. "A Short Intellectual Biography of a Japanese American Sansei Writer, or How I Learned Not to Write Like James Michener or John O'Hara." *Kyoto Review* (Spring 1987): 34–47.

———. *Turning Japanese: Memoirs of a Sansei*. New York: Atlantic Monthly/Anchor, 1991.

Yau, John. "Between the Forest and Its Trees." *New England Review* 15.3 (Summer 1993): 185–88.

———. "Between the Forest and Its Trees." *Amerasia Journal* 20.3 (1994): 37–43.

———. *Borrowed Love Poems*. New York: Penguin, 2002.

———. *Edificio Sayonara*. Santa Rosa, CA: Black Sparrow Press, 1992.

———. E-mail letters to Zhou Xiaojing. 13 August and 16 September 1999; 15 May 2002.

———. *Forbidden Entries.* Santa Rosa, CA: Black Sparrow Press, 1996.

———. *Radiant Silhouette: New and Selected Work, 1974–1988.* Santa Rosa, CA: Black Sparrow Press, 1989.

SECONDARY SOURCES

*Abstracts of Reports of the Immigration Commission.* 2 vols. Washington, DC: Government Printing Office, 1911.

Altieri, Charles. "Images of Form vs. Images of Content in Contemporary Asian-American Poetry." *Qui Parle* 9.1 (Fall/Winter 1995): 71–91.

———. *Self and Sensibility in Contemporary American Poetry.* New York: Cambridge UP, 1984.

———. *Subjective Agency: A Theory of First-Person Expressivity and Its Social Implications.* London: Blackwell, 1994.

Andrews, Bruce. "Code Words." See Andrews and Bernstein, 54–56.

———. "*Praxis*: A Political Economy of Noise and Informalism." See Bernstein, *Close Listening,* 73–85.

———. "Writing Social Work & Political Practice." See Andrews and Bernstein, 133–35.

Andrews, Bruce, and Charles Bernstein, eds. *The L=A=N=G=U=A=G=E Book.* Carbondale: Southern Illinois UP, 1984.

Anzaldúa, Gloria. *Borderlands/La Frontera: The New Mestiza.* San Francisco: Aunt Lute Books, 1987.

———, ed. *Making Face, Making Soul/Haciendo Caras: Creative and Critical Perspectives by Feminists of Color.* San Francisco: Aunt Lute Books, 1990.

Baldwin, James. "The Last Interview." In *James Baldwin: The Legacy.* Ed. Quincy Troupe, 186–212. New York: A Touchstone Book, published by Simon and Schuster, 1989.

Bataille, Georges. *Erotism: Death and Sensuality.* Trans. Mary Dalwood. San Francisco: City Lights Books, 1986.

Benveniste, Emile. "Subjectivity in Language." In *Critical Theory Since 1965.* Eds. Hazard Adams and Leroy Searle, 728–32. Tallahassee: Florida State UP, 1989.

Bergman, David. *Gaiety Transfigured: Gay Self-Representation in American Literature.* Madison: The University of Wisconsin Press, 1991.

Bernstein, Charles. *Content's Dream: Essays 1975–1984.* Los Angeles: Sun and Moon, 1986.

———. "Introduction." In *Close Listening: Poetry and the Performed Word,* 3–26. New York: Oxford UP, 1998.

———. "Semblance." See Andrews and Bernstein, 15–18.

———. "Writing and Method." In *In the American Tree*. Ed. Ron Silliman, 583–98. Orono, ME: The National Poetry Foundation/University of Maine at Orono, 1988.

Bhabha, Homi K. *The Location of Culture*. London: Routledge, 1994.

Biggers, Earl Derr. *Behind that Curtain*. New York: Paperback Library, 1964.

Bloom, Harold. *Agon: Towards a Theory of Revisionism*. Oxford: Oxford UP, 1983.

———, ed. *The Best of the Best American Poetry, 1988–1997*. New York: Scribner, 1998.

———. "They Have the Numbers; We, the Heights." *Boston Review* 23.2 (April/May 1998): 24–29.

Bow, Leslie. *Betrayal and Other Acts of Subversion: Feminism, Sexual Politics, Asian American Women's Literature*. Princeton, NJ: Princeton UP, 2001.

Buell, Lawrence. *Writing for an Endangered World: Literature, Culture, and Environment in the U.S. and Beyond*. Cambridge: The Belknap Press of Harvard UP, 2001.

Butler, Judith. *Bodies that Matter: On the Discursive Limits of "Sex."* New York: Routledge, 1993.

———. *Gender Trouble: Feminism and the Subversion of Identity*. New York: Routledge, 1990.

Chan, Sucheng, ed. *Entry Denied: Exclusion and the Chinese Community in America, 1882–1943*. Philadelphia: Temple UP, 1994.

Chang, Gordon H., ed. *Morning Glory, Evening Shadow: Yamato Ichihashi and His Internment Writings, 1942–1945*. Stanford, CA: Stanford UP, 1997.

Chang, Juliana. "'I Cannot Find Her': The Oriental Feminine, Racial Melancholia, and Kimiko Hahn's *The Unbearable Heart.*" *Meridians: feminism, race, transnationalism* 4.2 (2004): 239–60.

Chanter, Tina. *Time, Death, and the Feminine: Levinas with Heidegger*. Stanford, CA: Stanford UP, 2001.

Cheung, King-Kok. "Of Men and Men: Reconstructing Chinese American Masculinity." In *Other Sisterhoods: Literary Theory and U.S. Women of Color*. Ed. Sandra Kumamoto Stanley, 173–99. Urbana: University of Illinois Press, 1998.

———. ed. *Words Matter: Conversations with Asian American Writers*. Honolulu: University of Hawai'i Press, 2000.

Chin, Frank, et al., eds. *Aiiieeeee! An Anthology of Asian American Writers*. New York: Mentor, 1991.

Chow, Rey. *Ethics After Idealism: Theory — Culture — Ethnicity — Reading*. Bloomington: Indiana UP, 1998.

Christian, Barbara. "The Race for Theory." In *Making Face, Making Soul /*

*Haciendo Caras: Creative and Critical Perspectives by Feminists of Color*. Ed. Gloria Anzaldúa, 335–45. San Francisco: Aunt Lute Books, 1990.

Chuh, Kandice. *Imagine Otherwise: On Asian Americanist Critique*. Durham, NC: Duke UP, 2003.

Cixous, Hélène. *Stigmata: Escaping Texts*. New York: Routledge, 1998.

Cixous, Hélène, and Catherine Clément. *The Newly Born Woman*. Trans. Betsy Wing. Intro. Sandra M. Gilbert. Minneapolis: University of Minnesota Press, 1986.

Clearly, Thomas, ed. and trans. *The Immortal Sisters: Secrets of Taoist Women*. Boston: Shambhala Publications, 1989.

Cohen, Richard A., ed. *Face to Face with Levinas*. Albany: State University of New York Press, 1986.

———. "Introduction." In *Face to Face with Levinas*. Ed. Richard Cohen, Albany: State University of New York Press, 1986, 1–10.

———. "Translator's Introduction." Emmanuel Levinas. *Ethics and Infinity: Conversations with Philippe Nemo*. Trans. Richard A. Cohen. 1985. Pittsburgh: Duquesne UP, 1999. 1–15.

Commission on Wartime Relocation and Internment of Civilians. *Personal Justice Denied: Report of the Commission on Wartime Relocation and Internment of Civilians*. Washington, DC: GPO 1982.

Critchley, Simon. *The Ethics of Deconstruction: Derrida and Levinas*. West Lafayette, IN: Purdue UP, 1999.

Davis, Colin. *Levinas: An Introduction*. Notre Dame, IN: University of Notre Dame Press, 1996.

Davis, Rocío G., and Sämi Ludwig, eds. *Asian American Literature in the International Context: Readings on Fiction, Poetry, and Performance*. Hamburg: LIT Verlag, 2002.

Deleuze, Gilles. *Difference and Repetition*. Trans. Paul Patton. New York: Columbia UP, 1994.

———, and Félix Guattari. *Kafka: Toward a Minor Literature*. Trans. Dana Polan. Minneapolis: University of Minnesota Press, 1986.

———, and Claire Parnet. *Dialogues*. Trans. Hugh Tomlinson and Barbara Habberjam. London: The Athlone Press, 1987.

Derrida, Jacques. *Positions*. Trans. Alan Bass. Chicago: University of Chicago Press, 1981.

Ding, Loni, dir. *Ancestors in the Americas: Coolies, Sailors, Settlers*. San Francisco: Center for Educational Telecommunication, 2001.

Dorn, Edward. "An Interview with Barry Alpert." In *Interviews*. Ed. Donald Allen, 7–35. Bolinas, CA: Four Season Foundation, 1980.

Duncan, Patti. *Tell This Silence: Asian American Women Writers and the Politics of Speech*. Iowa City: University of Iowa Press, 2004.

Duras, Marguerite. *The Lover*. Trans. Barbara Bray. New York: Harper-Perennial, 1986.

Emerson, Ralph Waldo. "Nature." In *The American Tradition in Literature, Volume One*. Ed. George Perkins et al. 6th ed., 790–817. New York: Random House, 1985.

———. "The Over-Soul." In *The American Tradition in Literature, Volume One*. Ed. George Perkins et al. 6th ed., 870–81. New York: Random House, 1985.

———. "The Poet." In *The Selected Writings of Ralph Waldo Emerson*. Ed. and Intro. Brooks Atkinson, 319–41. New York: The Modern Library, 1968.

Eng, David L. *Racial Castration: Managing Masculinity in Asian America*. Durham, NC: Duke UP, 2001.

*The Essential Cavafy*. Intro. Edmund Keeley, trans. Edmund Keeley and Philip Sherrard. Hopewell, NJ: Ecco, 1995.

Fanon, Frantz. *Black Skin, White Masks*. Trans. Charles Lam Markmann. New York: Grove Press, 1967.

Finkelstein, Norman. "The Problem of the Self in Recent American Poetry." *Poetics* 9 (1991): 3–10.

Flaubert, Gustave. *Flaubert in Egypt: A Sensibility on Tour*. Trans. and ed. Francis Steegmuller. Chicago: Academy Chicago Publishers, 1979. New York: Penguin Books, 1996.

Fone, Byrne R. S. *Masculine Landscapes: Walt Whitman and the Homoerotic Text*. Carbondale: Southern Illinois UP, 1992.

Foster, Edward. "An Interview [with John Yau]" *Talisman* 5 (Fall 1990): 31–50.

Foucault, Michel. *The History of Sexuality, Volume 1*. Trans. Robert Hurley. New York: Vintage Books, 1990.

Fung, Richard. "Looking for My Penis: The Eroticized Asian in Gay Video Porn." In *How Do I Look?: Queer Film and Video*. Ed. Bad Object-Choices, 145–68. Seattle: Bay Press, 1991.

Gao, Zhebing, ed. and intro. *Nu Shu*. By Gao Yinxian and Yi Nianhua. Taibei: The Association of Women's Renaissance Foundation, 1991. (In Chinese)

Gery, John. "'Mocking My Own Ripeness': Authenticity, Heritage, and Self-Erasure in the Poetry of Marilyn Chin." *LIT* 12 (2002): 25–45.

Grewal, Inderpal. "Autobiographic Subjects and Diasporic Locations: *Meatless Days* and *Borderlands*." In *Scattered Hegemonies: Postmodernity and Transnational Feminist Practices*. Ed. Inderpal Grewal and Caren Kaplan. Minneapolis: University of Minnesota Press, 1994.

Grosz, Elizabeth. *Sexual Subversions: Three French Feminists*. St. Leonards, Australia: Allen and Unwin, 1989.

————. *Volatile Bodies: Toward A Corporeal Feminism*. Bloomington: Indiana UP, 1994.

Hall, Stuart. "The Spectacle of the 'Other'." In *Representation: Cultural Representations and Signifying Practices*. Ed. Stuart Hall, 223–79. London: Sage, 1997.

Hawley, Sandra M. "The Importance of Being Charlie Chan." In *America Views China: American Images of China Then and Now*. Eds. Jonathan Goldsmith, Jerry Israel, and Hilary Conroy, 132–47. London: Associated UP, 1991.

Heaney, Seamus. *The Redress of Poetry*. New York: Farrar, Straus and Giroux, 1995.

Hesford, Walter A. "*The City In Which I Love You*: Li-Young Lee's Excellent Song." *Christianity and Literature* 46.1 (Autumn 1996): 37–60.

Howard, Richard. "Foreword." In *Vox Angelica* by Timothy Liu, ix–xi. Cambridge, MA: Alice James Books, 1992.

Huang, Yunte. *Transpacific Displacement: Ethnography, Translation, and Intertextual Travel in Twentieth-Century American Literature*. Berkeley: University of California Press, 2002.

Hummer, T. R. "An Introduction of Questions of Identity: Ethnicity, Apprenticeship, and the New American Writers." *New England Review* 15.3 (Summer 1993): 5–6.

Irigaray, Luce. *An Ethics of Sexual Difference*. Trans. Carolyn Burke and Gillian C. Gill. Ithaca, NY: Cornell UP, 1993.

————. *Je, Tu, Nous: Toward a Culture of Difference*. Trans. Alison Martin. New York: Routledge, 1990.

————. *Sexes and Genealogies*. Trans. Gillian C. Gill. New York: Columbia UP, 1993.

Jabès, Edmond. *From the Desert to the Book: Dialogues with Marcel Cohen*. Trans. Pierre Joris. Barrytown, NY: Station Hill Press, 1990.

Jagose, Annamarie. *Queer Theory: An Introduction*. New York: New York UP, 1996.

Jameson, Frederic. *Postmodernism or, The Cultural Logic of Late Capitalism*. Durham, NC: Duke UP, 1991/1992.

Jeon, Joseph Jonghyun. "Speaking in Tongues: Myung Mi Kim's Stylized Mouths." *SLI: Studies in the Literary Imagination*, special issue on "Cross Wire: Asian American Literary Criticism." 37.1 (Spring 2004): 127–48.

Kang, Laura Hyun Yi. *Compositional Subjects: Enfiguring Asian/American Women*. Durham, NC: Duke UP, 2002.

Kim, Elaine H. *Asian American Literature: An Introduction to the Writings and Their Social Context*. Philadelphia: Temple UP, 1982.

Kim, Hyung-Chan, ed. *Asian Americans and Congress: A Documentary History.* Westport, CT: Greenwood Press, 1996.

Kim-Cho, Sek Yen. *The Korean Alphabet of 1446.* Amherst, NY: Humanity Books, 2001.

Kingston, Maxine Hong. "The Laws." In *China Men.* By Maxine Hong Kingston, 152–59. New York: Alfred A. Knopf, 1980.

Kinnahan, Linda A. *Lyric Interventions: Feminism, Experimental Poetry, and Contemporary Discourse.* Iowa City: University of Iowa Press, 2004.

Komunyakaa, Yusef. "The Autobiographical 'I': An Archives of Metaphor, Imagery, and Innuendo." In *After Confession: Poetry as Autobiography.* Ed. Kate Sontag and David Graham, 144–48. Saint Paul, MN: Graywolf Press, 2001.

Laclau, Ernesto. "Universalism, Particularism, and the Question of Identity." *October* 61 (Summer 1992): 83–90.

Lai, Him Mark, Genny Lim, and Judy Yung, eds. *Island: Poetry and History of Chinese Immigrants on Angel Island, 1910–1940.* San Francisco: San Francisco Study Center, 1980.

Latourette, Kenneth Scott. *A Short History of the Far East.* 4th ed. New York: Macmillan, 1964.

Lee, James Kyung-Jin. "Li-Young Lee." Interview. In *Words Matter: Conversations with Asian American Writers.* Ed. King-Kok Cheung, 270–80. Honolulu: University of Hawai'i Press, 2000.

———. "Myung Mi Kim." Interview. In *Words Matter: Conversations with Asian American Writers.* Ed. King-Kok Cheung, 92–104. Honolulu: University of Hawai'i Press, 2000.

Lee, Robert G. *Orientals: Asian Americans in Popular Culture.* Philadelphia: Temple UP, 1999.

Levinas, Emmanuel. *Alterity and Transcendence.* Trans. Michael B. Smith. New York: Columbia UP, 1999.

———. "Apropos of Buber: Some Notes." See Levinas, *Outside the Subject,* 40–48.

———. *Collected Philosophical Papers.* Trans. Alphonso Lingis. Dordrecht: Martinus Nijhoff, 1987.

———. "Diachrony and Representation." See Levinas, *Entre Nous,* 159–77.

———. "Dialogue with Emmanuel Levinas." Interview by Richard Kearney. See Cohen, *Face to Face,* 13–40.

———. *Difficult Freedom.* Trans. Seán Hand. Baltimore: John Hopkins UP, 1990.

———. *En découvrant l'existence avec Husserl et Heidegger.* Paris: Vrin, 1974.

———. *Entre Nous: On Thinking-of-the-Other.* Trans. Michael B. Smith and Barbara Harshav. New York: Columbia UP, 1998.

———. *Ethics and Infinity: Conversations with Philippe Nemo.* Intro. and Trans. Richard Cohen. Pittsburgh: Duquesne UP, 1985.

———. "Everyday Language and Rhetoric without Eloquence." See Levinas, *Outside the Subject,* 135–43.

———. *Existence and Existents.* Trans. Alphonso Lingis. The Hague: Martinus Nijhoff, 1978.

———. "Hermeneutics and the Beyond." See Levinas, *Entre Nous,* 65–75.

———. *Is It Righteous to Be? Interviews with Emmanuel Levinas.* Ed. Jill Robbins. Stanford, CA: Stanford UP, 2001.

———. "Kierkegaard: Existence and Ethics." See Levinas, *Proper Names,* 66–79.

———. "Language and Proximity." See Levinas, *Collected Philosophical Papers,* 109–26.

———. "Martin Buber and the Theory of Knowledge." See Levinas, *Proper Names,* 17–35.

———. "Martin Buber, Gabriel Marcel and Philosophy." See Levinas, *Outside the Subject,* 20–39.

———. "Meaning and Sense." See Levinas, *Collected Philosophical Papers,* 75–107.

———. "A New Rationality: On Gabriel Marcel." See Levinas, *Entre Nous,* 61–63.

———. "The Other in Proust." See Levinas, *Proper Names,* 99–105.

———. *Otherwise Than Being: Or, Beyond Essence.* Trans. Alphonso Lingis. Boston: Kluwer, 1991.

———. *Outside the Subject.* Trans. Michael B. Smith. Stanford, CA: Stanford UP, 1994.

———. *Proper Names.* Trans. Michael B. Smith. Stanford, CA: Stanford UP, 1996.

———. "The Proximity of the Other." See Levinas, *Alterity and Transcendence,* 97–109.

———. "Reality and Its Shadow." See Levinas, *Collected Philosophical Papers,* 1–13.

———. *Time and the Other.* Trans. Richard A. Cohen. 1987. Pittsburgh: Duquesne UP, 1997.

———. *Totality and Infinity: An Essay on Exteriority.* Trans. Alphonso Lingis. Pittsburgh: Duquesne UP, 1969.

———. "The Trace of the Other." In *Deconstruction in Context: Literature and Philosophy.* Ed. Mark C. Taylor, 345–59. Chicago: The University of Chicago Press, 1986.

———. "Vocation of the Other." Interview with Emmanuel Hirsch. Trans. Jill Robbins. See Levinas, *Is It Righteous to Be?,* 105–13.

Li, David Leiwei. *Imagining the Nation: Asian American Literature and Cultural Consent*. Stanford, CA: Stanford UP, 1998.

Lim, Shirley Geok-lin, and Amy Ling, eds. *Reading the Literatures of Asian America*. Philadelphia: Temple University Press, 1992.

Ling, Amy. "David Mura." Interview in *Yellow Light: The Flowering of Asian American Arts*. Ed. Amy Ling, 112–20. Philadelphia: Temple UP, 1999.

Lingis, Alphonso. "Translator's Introduction." In *Otherwise Than Being: Or, Beyond Essence*. Emmanuel Levinas, xi–xlii. Boston: Kluwer, 1991.

Liu, Lydia H. "Introduction." In *Tokens of Exchange: The Problem of Translation in Global Circulations*. Ed. Lydia H. Liu, 1–41. Durham, NC: Duke UP, 1999.

Lorde, Audre. "The Master's Tools Will Never Dismantle the Master's House." In *This Bridge Called My Back: Writings by Radical Women of Color*. Eds. Cherrie Moraga and Gloria Anzaldúa. 2nd. ed., 98–99. Brooklyn, NY: Kitchen Table Women of Color Press, 1983.

Lorenz, Johnny. "The Way a Calendar Dissolves: A Refugee's Sense of Time in the Work of Li-Young Lee." See Davis and Ludwig, 157–69.

Martin, Robert K. *The Homosexual Tradition in American Poetry*. Iowa City: University of Iowa Press, 1998.

McCormick, Adrienne. "'Being Without': Marilyn Chin's Poems as Feminist Acts of Theorizing." *Hitting Critical Mass: A Journal of Asian American Cultural Criticism* 6.2 (Spring 2000): 37–58.

Morrison, Toni. *Playing in the Dark: Whiteness and the Literary Imagination*. New York: Vintage, 1993.

Morrison, Yedda. "Generosity as Method: Excerpts from a Conversation with Myung Mi Kim." Interview. *Tripwire: A Journal of Poetics* 1 (Fall 2000): 75–85.

Mosse, George L. *Nationalism and Sexuality: Respectability and Abnormal Sexuality in Modern Europe*. New York: Fertig, 1985.

Moyers, Bill. "Li-Young Lee." Interview. In *The Language of Life: A Festival of Poets*. Ed. James Haba, 257–69. New York: Doubleday, 1995.

———. "Marilyn Chin." Interview. In *The Language of Life: A Festival of Poets*. Ed. James Haba, 67–79. New York: Doubleday, 1995.

Nguyen, Viet Thanh. *Race and Resistance: Literature and Politics in Asian America*. Oxford: Oxford UP, 2002.

Niranjana, Tejaswini. *Siting Translation: History, Post-Structuralism, and the Colonial Context*. Berkeley: University of California Press, 1992.

Okihiro, Gary Y. *Margins and Mainstreams: Asians in American History and Culture*. Seattle: University of Washington Press, 1994.

Okimoto, Daniel. *American in Disguise*. New York: Walker / Weatherhill, 1971.

Palumbo-Liu, David. *Asian/American: Historical Crossings of a Racial Frontier.* Stanford, CA: Stanford UP, 1999.

———. "Universalisms and Minority Culture." *Differences: A Journal of Feminist Cultural Studies* 7.1 (Spring 1995): 188–208.

Partridge, Jeffrey F. L. "The Politics of Ethnic Authorship: Li-Young Lee, Emerson, and Whitman at the Banquet Table." *SLI: Studies in the Literary Imagination,* special issue on "Cross Wire: Asian American Literary Criticism" 37.1 (Spring 2004): 101–24.

Pérez-Torres, Rafael. *Movements in Chicano Poetry: Against Myths, Against Margins.* New York: Cambridge UP, 1995.

Perloff, Marjorie. *The Dance of the Intellect: Studies in the Poetry of the Pound Tradition.* New York: Cambridge UP, 1985.

———. *Poetic License: Essays on Modernist and Postmodernist Lyric.* Evanston, IL: Northwestern UP, 1990.

———. Review of *Forbidden Entries* by John Yau. *Boston Review* 22:3–4 (Summer 1997): 39–41.

Pinsky, Robert. *Democracy, Culture, and the Voice of Poetry.* Princeton: Princeton UP, 2002.

Place, Janey. "Women in Film Noir." In *Women in Film Noir.* Ed. Alan Kaplan, 35–67. London: British Film Institute, 1978.

Rich, Adrienne. *Of Woman Born: Motherhood as Experience and Institution.* New York: Norton, 1995.

Robbins, Jill. *Altered Reading: Levinas and Literature.* Chicago: University of Chicago Press, 1999.

———. *Prodigal Son/Elder Brother: Interpretation and Alterity in Augustine, Petrarch, Kafka, Levinas.* Chicago: The University of Chicago Press, 1991.

Roof, Judith. *Come As You Are: Sexuality and Narrative.* New York: Columbia UP, 1996.

Roosevelt, Theodore. *The Works of Theodore Roosevelt.* 20 vols. New York: Scribner, 1926.

Rossi, Lee. "David Mura." Interview. *ONTHEBUS* 2.2 (Summer/Fall 1990): 263–73.

Said, Edward W. *Orientalism.* New York: Vintage Books, 1979.

Schatz, Thomas. *Hollywood Genres: Formulas, Filmmaking and the Studio System.* New York: Random House, 1981.

Serrano, Richard. "Beyond the Length of an Average Penis: Reading across Traditions in the Poetry of Timothy Liu." In *Form and Transformation in Asian American Literature.* Eds. Zhou Xiaojing and Samina Najmi. 190–208. Seattle: University of Washington Press, 2005.

Shakespeare, William. *The Tempest.* In *The Complete Works of Shakespeare.* 3rd ed. Ed. David Bevington, 1497–1525. Dallas: Scott, Foresman, 1980.

Swann, Brian. "Introduction: Only the Beginning." In *Native American*

*Poetry*. Ed. Duave Niatum. xvii–xxxii. San Francisco: Harper San Franciso, 1988.

Tabios, Eileen, ed. *Black Lightning: Poetry-In-Progress*. New York: The Asian American Writers Workshop, 1998.

———, "Marilyn Chin's Feminist Muse Addresses Women, 'The Grand Victims of History'." *Black Lightning*, 280–312.

———. "Towards Redemption." Interview with Timothy Liu. *Black Lightning*, 69–107.

Takaki, Ronald. *Iron Cages: Race and Culture in 19th-Century America*. New York: Oxford UP, 1990.

———. *Strangers from a Different Shore: A History of Asian Americans*. New York: Penguin, 1989.

Tran, Truong. *Placing the Accents*. Berkeley: Apogee Press, 1999.

Trinh, T. Minh-ha. "Not You/Like You: Post-Colonial Women and the Interlocking Questions of Identity and Difference." See Anzaldúa, *Making Face*, 371–75.

———. *Woman, Native, Other: Writing Postcoloniality and Feminism*. Bloomington: Indiana UP, 1989.

Turner, Bryan S. *The Body and Society: Explorations in Social Theory*. 2nd ed. London: Sage, 1996.

Ty, Eleanor. *The Politics of the Visible in Asian North American Narratives*. Toronto: University of Toronto Press, 2004.

Uba, George. "Versions of Identity in Post-Activist Asian American Poetry." In *Reading the Literatures of Asian America*. Eds. Shirley Geok-lin Lim and Amy Ling, 33–48. Philadelphia: Temple UP, 1992.

Vendler, Helen. *Soul Says: On Recent Poetry*. Cambridge: The Belknap Press of Harvard UP, 1995.

Venuti, Lawrence. *The Translator's Invisibility: A History of Translation*. London: Routledge, 1995.

Walcott, Derek. "A Far Cry from Africa." In *Collected Poems, 1948–1984*. New York: Farrar, Straus, and Giroux, 1986. 17–18.

Waley, Arthur. *Three Ways of Thought in Ancient China*. Stanford, CA: Stanford UP, 1995.

Wang, Dorothy Joan. "Necessary Figures: Metaphor, Irony and Parody in the Poetry of Li-Young Lee, Marilyn Chin, and John Yau." Ph.D. diss., University of California, Berkeley, 1998.

———. "Undercover Asian: John Yau and the Politics of Ethnic Self-Identification." See Davis and Ludwig, 135–55.

Whitman, Walt. *Complete Poetry and Collected Prose*. New York: The Library of America, 1982.

Wong, Sau-ling Cynthia. *Reading Asian American Literature: From Necessity to Extravagance*. Princeton, NJ: Princeton UP, 1993.

Wong, Shawn. *Homebase*. New York: Plume, 1979.

Wong, Shelley Sunn. "Unnaming the Same: Theresa Hak Kyung Cha's *Dictée*." In *Writing Self, Writing Nation*. Eds. Elaine H. Kim and Norman Alarcón, 103–42. Berkeley: Third Woman Press, 1994.

Yamamoto, Traise. *Masking Selves, Making Subjects: Japanese American Women, Identity, and the Body*. Berkeley: University of California Press, 1999.

Yu, Timothy. "Form and Identity in Language Poetry and Asian American Poetry." *Contemporary Literature* 41.3 (Fall 2000): 422–51.

Yue, Gang. *The Mouth That Begs: Hunger, Cannibalism, and the Politics of Eating in Modern China*. Durham, NC: Duke UP, 1999.

Yung, Judy. "Appendix: A Chronology of Asian American History." In *Making Waves: An Anthology of Writings By and About Asian American Women*. Ed. Asian Women United of California, 423–31. Boston: Beacon Press, 1989.

Zhou, Xiaojing. "Two Hat Softeners 'in the Trade Confession': John Yau and Kimiko Hahn." In *Form and Transformation in Asian American Literature*. Eds. Zhou Xiaojing and Samina Najmi. 168–89. Seattle: University of Washington Press, 2005.

Ziarek, Ewa Płonowska. *An Ethics of Dissensus: Postmodernity, Feminism, and the Politics of Radical Democracy*. Stanford, CA: Stanford UP, 2001.

Zimmerman, Sarah. *Romanticism, Lyricism, and History*. Albany: State University of New York Press, 1999.

# Index

Adorno, Theodor W., 280
aesthetics, 21; of alterity, 134; corporeal, 25, 28, 30. *See also* Emmanuel Levinas
AIDS, 22, 168, 182, 183, 187
*Aiiieeeee!* (Chan et al.), 170, 178
alterity: in Asian American poetry, 19–20; and cultural transformation, 135, 166; of culturally marginalized other, 70; of diasporic subjects, 234; ethics of, 5, 13, 16, 19, 21, 23, 52, 103, 134, 151, 162, 201, 275, 277; of female other, 134; as form of resistance and intervention, 19; irreducible, 4, 19, 30, 32, 67, 82, 89–90, 112, 113, 114, 118, 125, 128, 195, 206, 245, 270, 273, 280; loss of, 18; poetics of, 16, 20, 30, 52, 84, 91, 101, 275, 277; violation of, 50. *See also* Emmanuel Levinas, other, otherness, self-other relationship
Altieri, Charles, 37, 91–92
Andrews, Bruce, 199, 258
Anzaldúa, Gloria, 12, 276
*Ariel* (Plath), 168
Asian American: critics, 8–9; feminist literary theory, 13; history, 86–87; poetics, 13, 19; poetry, 5, 9, 17, 37, 91, 104; poets, 2, 3, 4, 7, 10, 13, 17–18, 275–76, 277–78, 280; subject, 9; women writers, 72
Asian Americans: and assimilation, 1, 89; essentialized differences, 238; invisibility of, 3; lack of individuality of, 4; lack of subjectivity of, 4; otherness of, 1, 2, 10; as perpetual foreigners, 2; political struggles of, 10. *See also* stereotypes
assimilation, 39, 72, 77, 78, 86, 88, 118; resistance to, 69, 71

Balcazo, Dan, 169
Baldwin, James, 104, 121
Baraka, Amiri, 74
Bataille, Georges, 179, 183, 187–88, 189
Beckett, Samuel, 238
Benveniste, Emile, 200
Bergman, David, 170–71
Bernstein, Charles, 198–99, 219, 257–58, 259
Berryman, John, 120
Bhabha, Homi, 127, 131, 277
Biggers, Earl Derr, 209, 213
Bloom, Harold, 6, 30, 101, 102, 278
Boas, Franz, 35
body, 25–26, 35–36, 37, 38–39, 55, 63, 93; American politic, 10; Asian American, 26, 27; of Asian men, 126–27, 169; of Asian women, 71; Chinese, 60; as contested site, 62, 63; as cultural text, 35; female, 135, 138, 139, 144, 269; immigrant, 56; raced and gendered, 4, 25, 26, 40–41, 56, 148; racialized, 38, 60, 65, 121, 123, 144, 153, 169, 204, 214;

MacAffee, Norman, 111
Manchu, Fu, 209
Marcel, Gabriel, 69, 77
Martin, Robert, 176
McCormick, Adrienne, 13
Merwin, W. S., 8
Mishima, Yukio, 119
model minority, 1, 19, 88–89, 90, 92
modernist poetry, 3, 4, 6
Morrison, Toni, 131
mortality, 22, 43, 53, 55, 186, 189, 192.
   See also death
Mosse, George, 177
Mura, David, 3, 21, 27, 102–32, 133,
   135, 153, 170, 178, 279; and Asian
   male body, 125, 126–28; and Japa-
   nese American identity, 103; and
   lyric I, 103–104, 114–15, 131; and
   otherness of self, 104; and sexual-
   ity, 119, 121–25, 129–31
Mura, David (Works): "The Affair:
   II—Her Version," 130; After We
   Lost Our Way, 103, 104, 111, 118,
   131; Angels for the Burning, 105;
   "An Argument: On 1942," 104;
   "The Blueness of the Day," 125;
   "The Colors of Desire," 121–23;
   The Colors of Desire, 103–105, 118,
   131; "Intellectual Biography,"
   120–21; "Intermission (1991),"
   126; "Internment Epistles," 105;
   "Letters from Tule Lake Intern-
   ment Camp (1942–45)," 104–108;
   "Lovers and Sons," 125, 128; "Mar-
   guerite (Pigalle, the Mediter-
   ranean, 1947)," 126; "Mirrors of
   the Self: Autobiography and the
   Japanese-American Writer," 118,
   120, 124; "A Nisei Picnic: From an
   Album," 102; "No-no boys: Re-
   X-Amining Japanese Americans,"
   105; "A Note from Caliban," 102;

"Pasolini," 111–18; "Sentences by
   M. Duras (dates unknown)," 126;
   "Song for Uncle Tom, Tonto, and
   Mr. Moto," 108–11; "To the Sub-
   ject, No Address," 112–13; "Tri-
   als," 115–18; Turning Japanese:
   Memoirs of a Sansei, 103; "A Vio-
   lent Life," 114

"Naked" (Liu), 189–90
Native American poets, 6
Nguyen, Viet Thanh, 10, 26, 169
Niranjana, Tejaswini, 243–44
nu shu, 155, 156, 158, 160, 165

O'Hara, Frank, 196
Okihiro, Gary Y., 209
Okimoto, Daniel, 123
Orientalism, 19, 128, 149, 150–54,
   169, 177, 187, 221, 234, 239, 244,
   273, 275, 276
other: abject, 1, 53, 73, 82, 86, 102,
   127, 132, 148, 170, 208, 263, 266; as
   absence and mystery, 18; alterity
   of, 5, 13, 14, 18, 20, 44, 67, 70, 89,
   90, 102, 103, 104, 110, 116, 118,
   130, 152, 154, 170, 184, 191, 219,
   223, 226, 244, 266; Asian Ameri-
   can poets as, 3; Caliban as, 102–
   103, 109–11; desire for, 21, 44, 138,
   162, 180; erotic love for, 45–47;
   ethical relationship with, 4, 18,
   49, 58, 69, 84, 90, 92, 99, 128, 132,
   142, 164, 201, 207, 273; ethical re-
   sponse to, 53, 112; excluded, con-
   demned, and exiled, 21; fear and
   hatred of, 106, 108; female, 86;
   God as, 191; horror of, 18; and il-
   legibility, 244; interiority of, 27;
   invocation of, 206, 207; language
   response to, 15; love for, 230;
   mastery of, 13, 18; presence of, 14;